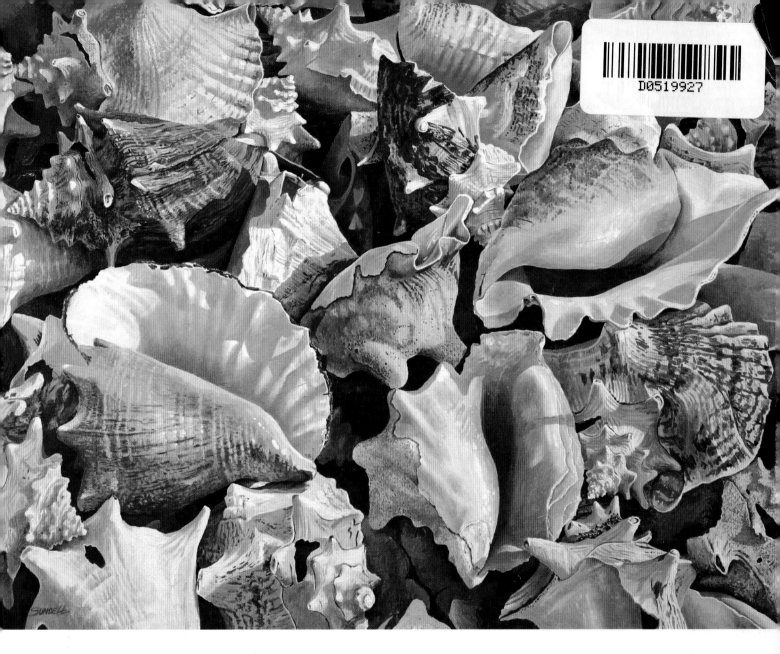

Creating
Exceptional Color
with Acrylics

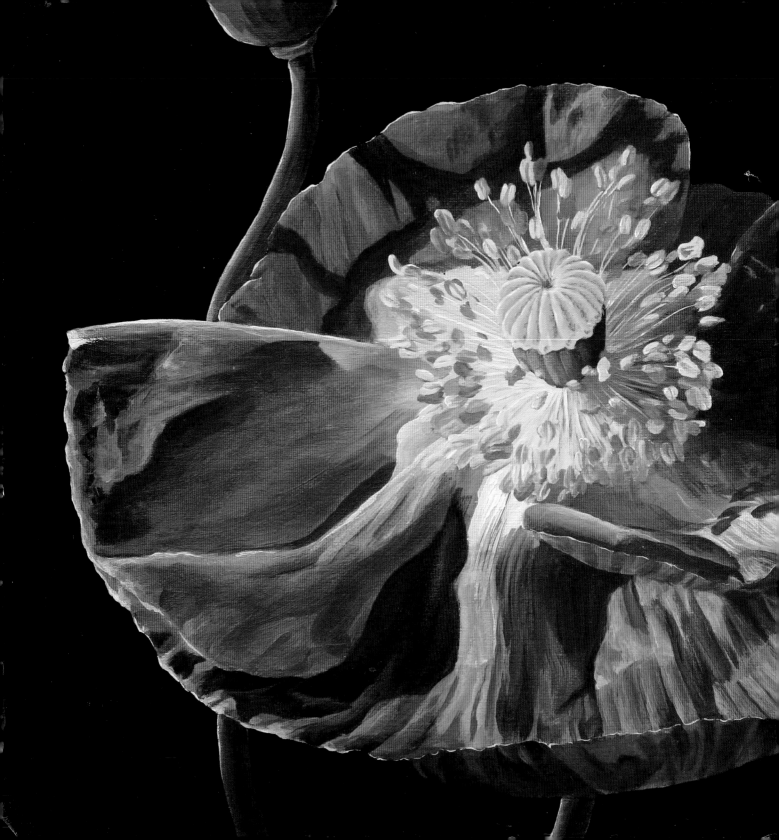

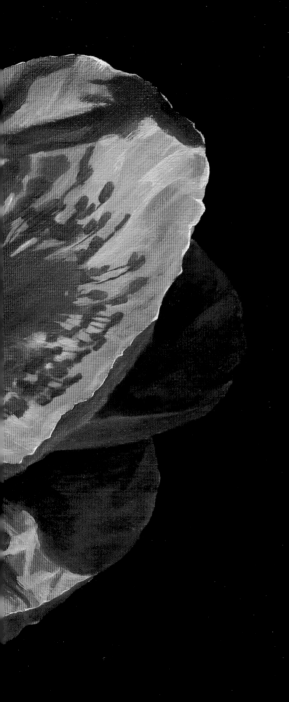

Creating
Exceptional Color
with Acrylics

Lexi Sundell

BARRON'S

A QUARTO BOOK

First edition for North America published in
2012 by Barron's Educational Series, Inc.

Copyright © 2012 Quarto Inc.

All inquiries should be addressed to:
Barron's Educational Series, Inc.
250 Wireless Boulevard
Hauppauge, New York 11788
www.barronseduc.com

Library of Congress Control No.: 2011935408

ISBN 13: 978-1-4380-0096-1

QUAR.CPCA

Conceived, designed, and produced by
Quarto Publishing plc
The Old Brewery
6 Blundell Street
London N7 9BH

Senior Editor: Ruth Patrick
Designer: Karin Skånberg
Design Assistant: Kate Bramley
Picture Researcher: Sarah Bell
Copyeditor: Ruth Patrick
Proofreader: Liz Jones
Indexer: Helen Snaith
Art Director: Caroline Guest

Creative Director: Moira Clinch
Publisher: Paul Carslake

Color separation by Pica Digital Pte Ltd,
Singapore

Printed in China by 1010 Printing
International Ltd

10 9 8 7 6 5 4 3 2 1

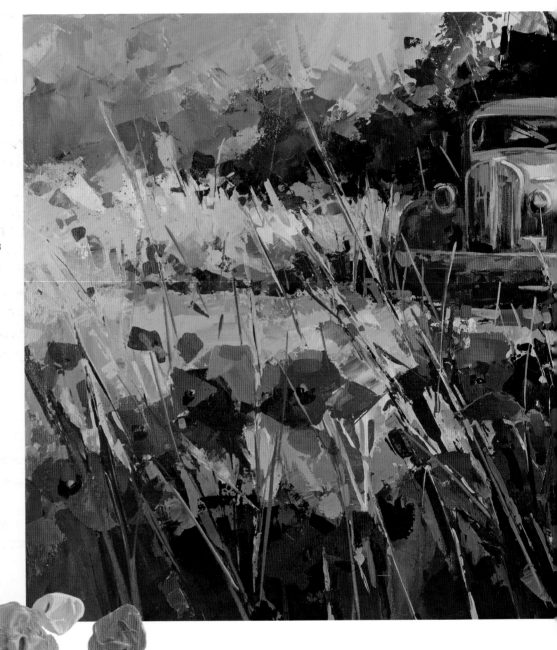

contents

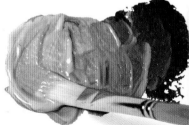

Hibiscus
Acrylic paints include brilliant, semitransparent pigments that can be used to create luminous, glowing flowers that evoke early dawn light. Opaque pigments further extend the range of acrylic paint effects. The rich subtleties of this hibiscus painting come from the qualities of modern acrylic paints.

Subtle treatment
This beautifully understated work, Butterfly Chair by Joseph Krawczyk, is not what many expect to see in an acrylic painting. Early acrylic paints left a lingering impression in the public perception with harsh and garish colors. Although modern acrylic paints range from quiet neutrals to brilliant explosions of color, the degree of subtlety possible in acrylics often surprises people.

introduction

Acrylic paints tease your senses; the high, singing notes of quinacridones accent the deep rumble of Raw Umber and other earth tones. The colors of the rainbow shimmer and dance on the palette, waiting for the touch of the artist to bring a vision to vibrant life on the canvas. Ah, but how do you move from the vision to the completed painting? How do you unleash the amazing color potential of acrylics in your paintings?

Acrylics are the new kid on the block, having been in existence only since the early 1950s, unlike oils and watercolors, which have been around for hundreds of years and complacently bask in their established positions in the arts. So what are acrylics? Are they simply an annoyingly fast-drying substitute for oils or an awkward alternative for watercolors?

In skilled hands, acrylics can indeed be painted to mimic the effects of oils. Acrylics can also be painted with a wide range of watercolor effects. Either approach simply takes old processes and techniques and superimposes them on something new and different. However, to merely mimic oils or watercolors is to miss the true potential of acrylic itself.

Through the centuries, painters have been on a constant quest for the best pigments, the most permanent colors, and the most readily usable paints

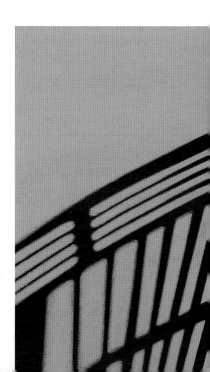

available. A set of acrylic paints we can easily buy today would have seemed like a sacred object to so many of those artists who came before us.

Approaching acrylics with the beginner's mind, and allowing old ways of working with paint to become secondary to discover how acrylics themselves work best opens the door to sheer delight. Once I accepted them for what they really were, they became my favorite paints instead of my most despised.

I love their fast-drying qualities, which allow me to keep painting instead of waiting impatiently for that perfect stage of drying. I love the vivid colors possible, as well as the subtle understated colors I can create with them. Contrasts make art come alive, and acrylics offer a huge range of contrasts.

The permanence of the dried paint is another great virtue of acrylics. I can paint over any color with an opaque white and then paint a fine transparent color over the white with no problems of bleed-through from the former color. This allows me to apply color freely and alter it at will. Such experimentation leads to new color discoveries rather than disaster.

And, oh, the colors! The range of pigments available is enough to make me swoon. Major manufacturers have developed high-quality paints with pigments used for centuries as well as freshly invented synthetic pigments that bring delicious new possibilities to the palette.

Out of this array of beautiful color, you are free to paint anything you can envision. Once the painting is completed, the likelihood is that it will outlast the same painting created with oils because of the unique polymer properties of acrylics. How wonderful is that?

Lexi Sundell

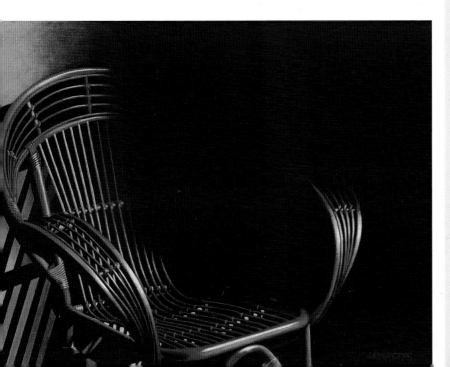

ABOUT THIS BOOK

SPECIAL FEATURE **Fold-out flap** PAGE 127
The Sundell Color Wheel and the list of substitute paints for each position on the wheel are referenced throughout this book, and reproduced here on a fold-out flap for ease of access.

Refer to the color wheel easily when using other parts of the book

SECTION 1 **Pigment properties** PAGE 18
Explains the different types of acrylic paints and mediums available and the physical effects they create.

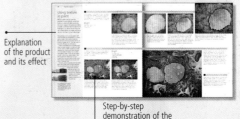

Explanation of the product and its effect

Throughout the book, Titanium White is used for making tints of colors

Step-by-step demonstration of the product in action

SECTION 2 **Pigment aesthetics** PAGE 38
Explains color theory, as well as the visual and aesthetic ways different pigments combine when mixed or painted.

Color wheels showing color positions of paints used

Explanation of color scheme

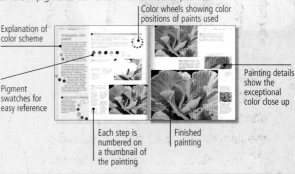

Painting details show the exceptional color close up

Pigment swatches for easy reference

Each step is numbered on a thumbnail of the painting

Finished painting

SECTION 3 **Choosing pigments for painting** PAGE 76
Demonstrating the theory from sections 1 and 2, the author and other artists choose exceptional color for specific subjects.

Color swatches of chosen pigments

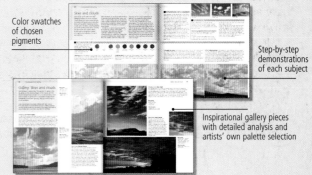

Step-by-step demonstrations of each subject

Inspirational gallery pieces with detailed analysis and artists' own palette selection

Color and vision

We commonly look at color as something external in the world that we see with our eyes. Scientific research has proven that this is incorrect. Color arises in the mind from the way the brain processes and transforms signals from the eyes.

While it may be shocking to realize that color only exists as a useful illusion created in our minds, it opens the door to greater effectiveness as artists. After learning some of the ways the brain interprets visual information, we can deliberately use the right cues in our color handling to trigger recognition of the illusion we are trying to create in paint.

What is color?
Visible light is composed of a fairly narrow section of the electromagnetic spectrum, and the human eye is only able to respond to those particular wavelengths. Visible light is not, however, what we call color—only the

signals from the eyes are translated by the brain into what we call color.

Color can be understood as a combination of value, hue, and chroma because the rods and cones in the eye react to light and send information in those categories to the brain. Rods register only variations of light and dark, the range of values we can illustrate with a grayscale, and they work in dim light. On a moonlit night, a red bike lying in the driveway will be a clearly visible shape defined by light and dark shadows, but it will not look bright red the way it did at noon. That perception of bright red comes from the cones, which work fine at noon but not so well in dim moonlight. The three kinds of cones respond to partially

overlapping ranges of wavelengths that translate into hue and chroma.

The brain's job is to take the mass of signals from the rods and cones and form a useful picture of our environment. One of the techniques it uses is to seek out edges in order to define objects. After identifying edges, the brain is likely to exaggerate them by increasing value contrasts because of the importance of recognizing objects.

The brain also adjusts for changing light conditions so we retain a fairly constant perception of our surroundings—we are aware that the red bike is a red bike at noon, twilight, and midnight under the moon despite changing light conditions.

MIND TRICKS WITH VALUE

The brain's effort to adjust for different light conditions can be surprisingly drastic in affecting how we perceive values. Observe what happens when we combine two different visual examples of value, a gradient, and a grid of circles, illustrating the Bartleson-Brenneman effect.

A simple gradient

Grid of circles

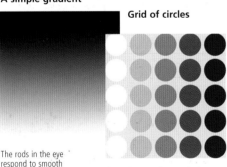

The rods in the eye respond to smooth graduations of value from black to white.

The circles in each vertical column are the exact same value. The circles in each horizontal row are one of each value used.

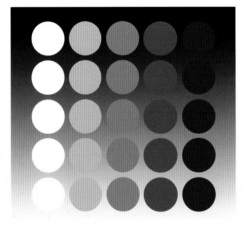

Overlay the circles on the gradient
The mind interprets the circle values as lighter against the dark background and darker against the light background.

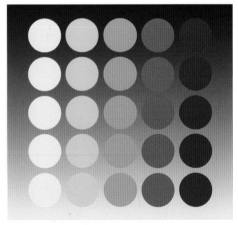

Value affects how we perceive color
The same handling of values in cyan changes how our mind interprets color in the circles. Observe how the horizontal rows of colored circles look different from each other even though the rows are identical.

HUE AND CHROMA

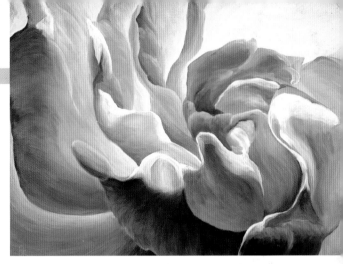

High chroma means the hue is bright and saturated, as shown in this yellow hue.

Low chroma means the hue appears dull in color like this grayed yellow hue.

Value contrasts provide a strong visual structure for color, while hue and chroma add more dimensions to our experience of color. While moonlight is lovely, who wants to see the world in that subdued manner all the time? Hue and chroma bring us the glories of a sunset, the glowing color of a flower, and the richly translucent depths of water.

Chroma often changes in unison with value, although rods respond to value changes and cones

respond to chroma changes. The reason is that cones lose the ability to identify chroma as available light diminishes, so less chroma is perceived when the light dims. The rods perceive the dimmed light as reduced value in the grayscale, so changes in chroma and value can be related but are fundamentally different. Chroma refers to the saturation of hue present and value refers only to light and dark, regardless of hue.

Ways of reducing chroma

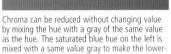

A frequently used method of reducing chroma is by tinting with Titanium White. Applying a thin wash of paint can also reduce chroma.

Chroma can be reduced without changing value by mixing the hue with a gray of the same value as the hue. The saturated blue hue on the left is mixed with a same value gray to make the lower-chroma blue on the right.

Another way of reducing chroma is by desaturating the hue by mixing it with its complementary opposite. Complements are described on pages 56–57. In this example, green and red hues blend into a low-chroma neutral in the middle.

Creation

The practical application of value, hue, and chroma can be seen in this painting. Strong value contrasts provide a dramatic structure while assorted hues vary widely in chroma to create a radiant effect in this flower. Contrasts within all three of these components of color can be used for strong impact in your painting.

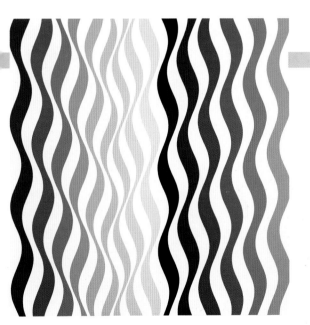

Bridget Riley—mind tricks in action

Op artist Bridget Riley excels at creating paintings that explore the ways our brains interpret and alter values. In Arrest 2, she uses distinctly defined edges and a wide range of values to compose a compelling image. Notice how the individual wavy lines combine into larger patterns because of the way she used values. We see two main groupings of those lines due to the graduated application of values.

ADDITIVE AND SUBTRACTIVE COLOR

We perceive color according to the principles of additive color, but our paints work according to the principles of subtractive color. As artists we must create illusions of light with materials that combine colors altogether differently than the way light combines them.

Additive color

Light works with additive color. If you add blue light to red light, you get magenta light, but a magenta that is radiantly brighter than either the blue light or the red light alone.

The more colors of light you add, the greater the radiance. When you add enough colors it gets so bright all you can see is white. This is called additive color mixing.

Subtractive color

Pigments are not light. They reflect light, but not all of it. A black rock absorbs sunlight while reflecting very little. That is both why it gets hot and why it looks black. Black is the absence of color, the result of a lack of reflected light.

A blue pigment looks blue because it reflects blue light into our eyes. The blue pigment absorbs the other colors in light, sucks them out of sight like a vacuum cleaner. Likewise, a red pigment absorbs everything but red light.

Red and blue pigments mix into a purple, but a duller purple than either the blue or red. When two pigments absorbing light are combined, they reflect even less light than they did separately.

After adding more pigment colors, the mixture turns black as most of the incoming light is absorbed and removed from our sight. Therefore this is called subtractive color mixing.

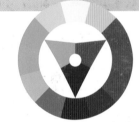

Additive color wheels use red, green, and blue (RGB) as their primaries. Mixing these primaries creates the yellows, magentas, and cyans that we see as the brightest, most radiant colors.

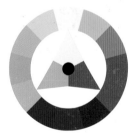

Pigment color wheels use the brightest hues of cyan, magenta, and yellow (CMYK, with "K" referring to black) as the primaries, since they mix to make the other, duller colors.

Paints and pigments

Different manufacturers offer a dazzling array of paints. Just looking at all of them is enough to make your head spin. How do you choose wisely from so many options? What is best: Carbazole Violet or Dioxazine Purple? Or are they the same thing with different names? How do you know without buying every single tube of paint on the market? Paint manufacturers sometimes seem to choose paint names the same way fashion designers often do—romantically without much practical utility. Fortunately there are ways to cut through the confusion and discover what you need to know. On the following four pages paints and pigments are demystified, and color groups are explored. In the equipment guide on page 122 you will find out how to decode the information on the label of a tube of paint.

PIGMENTS AND PAINTS

What is the difference between pigment and paint? Pigment provides the color, and a binder is the vehicle to carry that color. Paint is a mixture of the two.

In acrylic paint, the binder is an acrylic emulsion. In most acrylic paints this is a whitish substance that dries to a clear film if no pigment is added. The fact that the emulsion is white before drying means it slightly obscures the full color of the pigment until it dries, which is why acrylics darken as they dry. Winsor & Newton is the only manufacturer offering an acrylic emulsion that is already clear before drying so the usual darkening does not occur.

Some paints—known as fugitive paints—are not lightfast and tend to fade or discolor over time. Paints with "hue" at the end of their name, such as Alizarin Crimson Hue, usually refer to formulations resembling a paint that is either fugitive or toxic, meaning that the color can be achieved without the negative side effects. Alizarin Crimson Hue is a lightfast paint that resembles the fugitive Alizarin Crimson.

Avoid cheap "student grade" paints as they may lack good pigment strength, may be loaded with useless fillers, and may not meet proper standards of lightfastness. Quality paint—by companies such as Winsor & Newton ("Artists' Acrylic" range), Golden Artist Colors, and Daniel Smith—is worth the small additional cost.

ORGANIC AND INORGANIC PIGMENTS

Organic pigments not only refer to pigments obtained from living plants, but to all pigments that contain carbon. Most pigments in acrylic paints are manufactured in laboratories. Many wonderful synthetic pigments are organic, such as the quinacridones, phthalos, and azos. For vibrant, clear color, these pigments are unsurpassed. Their tinting power is also excellent and many are semitransparent.

Inorganic pigments are primarily minerals and obviously do not contain carbon. Inorganics have inherent color that often comes from iron oxide in various forms as well as hydroxides of copper, chromium, and aluminum. These may be intermixed naturally with clays, which can include talc and silica. While these pigments can be opaque, some are semitransparent.

Synthetic inorganic pigments are more finely ground than natural inorganics, making the color more evenly distributed in the paint. Synthetic inorganic pigments include materials such as manganese and zinc as well as the cobalts and cadmiums.

Organic pigments

Quinacridone Red

Phthalo Green

Inorganic pigments

Cobalt Blue

Raw Umber

COLOR GROUPS

Color evokes powerful emotions, which sometimes vary culturally. For example, some cultures use black as the color of mourning, while others use white. The important point is we all use color to express emotion.

The major color groups and important paints in each group are shown on the following pages. The paints have been selected for their mixing qualities and overall usefulness. Remember to double-check the index number for the pigment you want, since the common names can vary wildly (see page 122). In this book, only permanent pigments are discussed because a great selection of modern permanent pigments have replaced fugitive pigments painters had to use in the past (see above).

All paints shown in color groups except Primary Magenta, Quinacridone Crimson, Cobalt Violet Hue, and Permanent Violet Dark are single-pigment paints.

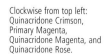

Clockwise from top left:
Quinacridone Crimson,
Primary Magenta,
Quinacridone Magenta, and
Quinacridone Rose.

The magentas
Magenta is the beautiful red-violet (or cool red) between red and purple. Magenta adds rich subtlety and a sense of graciousness to a painting. Soft blends of magenta can be utterly delicious.

As a subtractive primary (see page 9), it is bright and lively when used for high-chroma color. The recent development of quinacridone pigments resulted in gorgeous magentas for the acrylic palette.

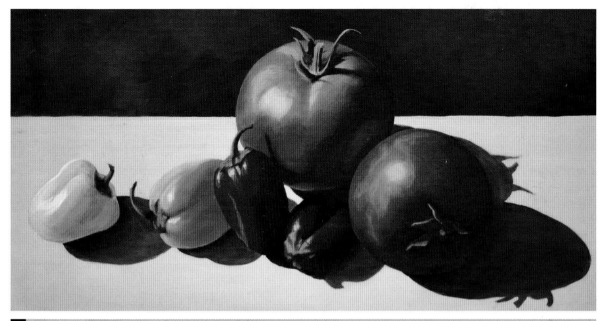

Yellows

 Hansa Yellow Light

Hansa Yellow Medium

Hansa Yellow Deep

Reds

 Cadmium Red

 Cadmium Red Medium

 Cadmium Red Dark

Cadmium Red Deep

Naphthol Red Light

Naphthol Red Medium

Anthraquinone Red

Earth tones and neutrals

Raw Umber

Yellow Ocher

Buff Titanium

Titanium White

Oranges

Cadmium Orange Medium

Pyrrole Orange

RED AND ORANGE COLOR STUDY

Exploring different reds, oranges, and yellows from the color groups below (and the yellows on page 12) allows you to discover the most effective uses of the wide variety of paints available in this color range.

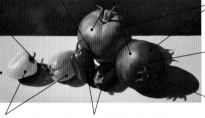

Cadmium Red Deep makes excellent shadows.

Tints of Cadmium Orange Medium form the highlights and surrounding area in both tomatoes.

Background and shadows on table painted in mixtures of Buff Titanium, Raw Umber, and Yellow Ocher.

Buff Titanium and a small amount of Raw Umber are used in the table top.

Full range of Cadmium Reds blended into each other for both tomatoes.

Cadmium Red Medium makes a rich body color.

All stems are painted in tints of Chromium Oxide Green and Raw Umber.

Hansa Yellows with a small amount of Pyrrole Orange for the shadows in the two left peppers.

Naphthol Reds with shadows in Anthraquinone Red and highlights in tints of Naphthol Red Light in the two red peppers.

Clockwise from top left: Anthraquinone Red, Cadmium Red Medium, Naphthol Red Medium, and Quinacridone Red.

The reds

Red is vibrant, hot, and sexy, sometimes spilling over into outright violence. Red is the color of blood and passion, yet some cultures regard it as a divine color of spirituality.

Many fine reds are available in acrylic paints and as you become familiar with them, you will learn to choose the best ones for different purposes. Some are opaque and some are semitransparent, and they vary from cool to warm.

Clockwise from top left: Cadmium Orange Deep, Cadmium Orange Medium, Pyrrole Orange, and Quinacridone Gold.

The oranges

Orange is the color of vitality and strength. Balanced between red and yellow, orange carries the passion of red made gentle by the sunny joy of yellow. Orange adds a sense of lively action.

The cadmium pigments make fantastic orange paints, but other choices are also available. Cadmiums are opaque, so pyrroles and quinacridones are needed for transparent effects. They can also be mixed from warm reds and yellows.

GREEN COLOR STUDIES

A good exercise to learn how to control greens for the desired effect is to paint the same subject repeatedly in different greens to see how they handle. Adjusting single-pigment green paints to appropriate chroma levels often defeats artists. Creating a harmonious, natural range of greens can also be difficult because of mixing problems, particularly with the brilliant phthalos. In this example the geranium leaf is painted, and then two sections of the leaf are painted in alternate colors for further exploration.

 Chromium Oxide Green

 Quinacridone Burnt Orange

 Quinacridone Nickel Azo Gold

 Yellow Ocher

Cadmium Yellow Light

Raw Umber

Quinacridone Coral

Chromium Oxide Green is a low-chroma green that adjusts well with small amounts of Yellow Ocher and Raw Umber to make natural-looking foliage. Tints of this mixture are used for the green areas of the leaf and stem.

More Raw Umber is used in the Chromium Oxide Green tints for the darker shadows.

A thin glaze of Quinacridone Coral is applied over the dried tint of Yellow Ocher.

A thin layer of Quinacridone Burnt Orange is brushed over the lighter tint of Yellow Ocher.

A tint of Yellow Ocher is used for the lighter areas in the decaying leaf edge.

Mixtures of Quinacridone Burnt Orange and Quinacridone Nickel Azo Gold are used in the outer decaying leaf edge.

A tint of Cadmium Yellow Light is used for the veins of the leaf.

Quinacridone Coral is lightly painted over the dried Quinacridone Burnt Orange outer leaf edge.

A little Quinacridone Burnt Orange is scumbled over the darker green leaf areas.

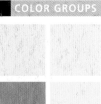

 Phthalo Green

Alizarin Crimson Hue

Anthraquinone Red

Quinacridone Gold

Neutralizing the Phthalo Green/Quinacridone Gold tint with Anthraquinone Red gives a suitable green for the leaf.

Even when using Phthalo Green mixed with Quinacridone Gold instead of a yellow, this tint is far too bright and high-chroma for a subdued geranium leaf green.

Tints of Quinacridone Gold are used, keeping the color integrated with the green.

Anthraquinone Red is used for the decaying edge of the leaf.

Anthraquinone Red is scumbled over this darker area of the leaf.

The deepest shadows in the decaying edges are rendered in Alizarin Crimson Hue.

Cobalt Green is a low-chroma green so a tint of Cobalt Green and Cadmium Yellow Deep makes a satisfactory geranium-leaf green.

A tint of Cadmium Red Deep is applied over the tint of Yellow Iron Oxide.

The darkest shadows in the decaying edge are painted with Cadmium Red Deep.

Cadmium Red Deep is scumbled over the darker area of the green leaf.

The decaying leaf edge is rendered in tints of Cadmium Red Deep with a little Quinacridone Crimson.

A tint of Yellow Iron Oxide works for this lighter area.

Cobalt Green

Cadmium Red Deep

Quinacridone Crimson

Yellow Iron Oxide

Cadmium Yellow Deep

COLOR GROUPS (CONTINUED)

The yellows

Yellow is the essence of sunshine and is a joyful color. Yellow is both light and bright, usually much more so than other hues, so it works well for luminous accents in a painting. The inspired light in religious paintings is often painted in yellow.

The arylides, cadmiums, and bismuth make fine high-chroma yellows. Iron oxide produces lower-chroma yellows.

Clockwise from top left: Cadmium Yellow Medium, Hansa Yellow Medium, Lemon Yellow, and Yellow Ocher.

The greens

Green is the metaphorical color of envy but also the color of burgeoning life in spring. Greens challenge the beginning artist perhaps more than any other color (see above).

Starting with single-pigment greens is preferable to using convenience mixtures, because adding additional paints to the mixture may create an unexpectedly muddy appearance. Chromium Oxide Green and the phthalo and perylene greens each mix beautifully with Bismuth Yellow or Hansa Yellow to make a wide range of greens. Chromium Oxide Green can be further adjusted with Yellow Ocher and/or Raw Umber for natural-looking foliage greens. Greens can also be mixed from blues and yellows.

Clockwise from top left: Chromium Oxide Green, Perylene Green, Phthalo Green (Blue Shade), and Phthalo Green (Yellow Shade).

BLUE AND PURPLE COLOR STUDY

A variety of blues and purples can work well together. In this example several blues are used with two different purples. You can try a similar exercise that includes Phthalo Blue and Cerulean Blue, which were not used here.

The background is painted in tints of Cobalt Blue and Cadmium Orange Hue, which combine to make a lovely soft neutral.

A bright Cobalt Teal is used for the main body color of this stoneware vase, which has a richly colorful barium glaze.

Highlights are rendered in pure Titanium White because of the shiny surface of the vase.

Tints of Ultramarine Violet are used for a softer, lower-chroma purple.

Ultramarine Blue makes a rich transition from Dioxazine Purple into the Cobalt Teal and Cobalt Blue body color of the vase.

Dioxazine Purple is used to blend into the Indanthrone Blue shadows. Tinted Dioxazine purple blends into a vibrant purple.

A lighter tint of Dioxazine Purple shows reflected light on the underside of the vase.

Tints of Cobalt Blue are painted over the Cobalt Teal for variation in the surface color of the vase.

Indanthrone Blue is used for the darkest shadows on the vase, which are almost black.

The shadow of the vase is painted in a neutralized tint of Indanthrone Blue and Cadmium Orange Medium Hue.

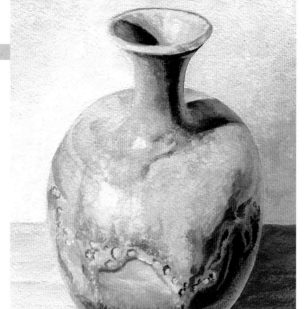
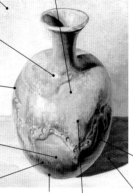

Blues

Cobalt Teal — Cobalt Blue — Ultramarine Blue — Indanthrone Blue

Purples

Ultramarine Violet — Dioxazine Purple

Other

Cadmium Orange Hue — Titanium White

PIGMENT CONSIDERATIONS

• Always read the paint label to see what pigments are in the paint before you buy it. The common name on the front of the tube can be misleading as you may find that you are buying the same pigment with a different name from a different manufacturer.
• Choose single-pigment paints for your mixing palette. Single-pigment paints provide maximum chroma, which always reduces as more pigments are added to a mixture.
• When possible, choose a single-pigment paint that has hue and chroma matching your subject as closely as you can.
• Use multiple-pigment paints as convenience mixtures to save time mixing combinations you use frequently.
• Experiment with different paints to discover which ones work best for your purposes, sometimes by painting the same subject in several different combinations of paints.
• As you become familiar with your paints, you will learn to create paintings with flair and personality!

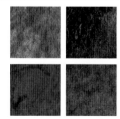

The blues
Blue can be the color of the sky, and open water in the landscape. Blue can be intense and bold or soft and retiring. Blue expresses quiet introspection and sometimes sadness. However, the vibrant feathers of the bluebird are associated with happiness. Blue can convey quite a range of emotions!
    Cerulean Blue is often used for skies, while Indanthrone Blue goes to a dark midnight color. Phthalo Blue and Ultramarine Blue are vibrant and bright, mixing well with other paints to make greens and purples.

Clockwise from top left: Cerulean Blue, Indanthrone Blue, Phthalo Blue (Green Shade), and Ultramarine Blue.

The purples and violets
Purple is the traditional color of royalty because it was legally reserved for royalty due to its expense. Still regal, purple is far more widely available now, delighting painters with its richness. Today purple is often favored as a spiritual color.
    Although now affordable, only a few permanent purple pigments are available for artists. For that reason, two convenience mixtures are included here (see page 17). Cobalt Violet Hue is a mixture created to emulate the extremely toxic cobalt arsenate formerly used by artists. Permanent Violet Dark is the other mixture.

Clockwise from top left: Cobalt Violet Hue, Dioxazine Purple, Permanent Violet Dark, and Ultramarine Violet.

Basic mixing

When you pick up a paintbrush, the first thing you need to know is how to mix paint to create the amazing effects you imagine for your art. In acrylics there are several mixing methods.

You can mix paint directly on the canvas, board, or paper using techniques common to both oil and watercolor painting. You can paint wet-into-wet or use glazes and scumbles. Mixing paints on your palette is also an effective way to create the colors you want.

MIXING FUNDAMENTALS

The wheel at right shows the relationship of the generic colors to each other and displays high-chroma single-pigment paints that mix well together. The Sundell Color Wheel on page 17 provides a good starting point for mixing pigments. The chart of substitutes on the same page allows other paints to be correctly used in the framework of the color wheel.

One paint used almost constantly is not shown on this color wheel or the chart. White, specifically Titanium White, appears in most paintings. By mixing white with other colors, varying tints are created, which is immensely useful. Although "tint" refers to a color mixed with any white, in this book, for convenience, a tint will always refer to a Titanium White mixed with the color unless specified otherwise.

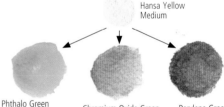

1	Yellow
2	Yellow-orange
3	Red-orange
4	Red
5	Magenta
6	Red-violet
7	Blue-violet
8	Blue
9	Cyan
10	Green
11	Yellow-green
12	Green-yellow

FIVE PRINCIPLES OF MIXING

1 Single-pigment paints mix together with less chroma loss than multiple-pigment paints.

2 The closer together the paints are found on the color wheel, the higher the chroma of their mixture will be.

3 Lower tinting strength paints must be used in larger amounts to balance more powerful tinting strength paints in a mixture.

4 Paints opposite each other on the color wheel mix to a low-chroma neutral.

5 Adding an opposing color can neutralize a high-chroma mixture if it is too bright.

TINTING STRENGTH

Tinting strength refers to the ability of a pigment to affect the color of another pigment. Pigments vary widely in their tinting strength and that affects how they handle in a mixture. Information about the tinting strength of each pigment can be found on the label, in manufacturers' catalogs, or online. Your own experience of mixing will quickly inform you as well.

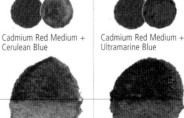

Cadmium Red Medium + Cerulean Blue

Cadmium Red Medium + Ultramarine Blue

Cadmium Red Medium + Indanthrone Blue

Titanium White

Titanium White was painted across the bottom half while wet to bring the color out of the dark mixture.

Cadmium Red Medium mixed with Cerulean Blue does not show much Cerulean Blue as it has weaker tinting strength than Cadmium Red Medium.

The stronger tinting strength of Ultramarine Blue mixes to a nice purple with an equal amount of Cadmium Red Medium.

The powerful tinting strength of Indanthrone Blue overwhelms the same amount of Cadmium Red Medium.

EXPERIMENTAL MIXING TO CHOOSE A SPECIFIC PAINT

The quick method of mixing directly on heavy watercolor paper makes it easy to select from several paints in the studio. In this case, three green paints are tested in mixtures with Hansa Yellow Medium to see which one might match a particular subject best. Try this freely with any paint combinations you would like to see for yourself. Hands-on experience will bring a whole new understanding of your paints.

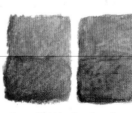

Hansa Yellow Medium

Phthalo Green (Yellow Shade)

Chromium Oxide Green

Perylene Green

MIXING MULTIPLE PIGMENTS

Our exploration of greens expands to multiple-pigment mixtures instead of just combining a single-pigment paint with another single-pigment paint. This requires careful handling to avoid making mud.

Cadmium Red Medium—opposite to the greens on the color wheel—was added to the mixture across the bottom half.

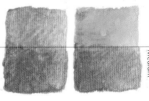

Green Gold + Cobalt Green

Green Gold + Phthalo Green (Blue Shade)

Cadmium Yellow Medium + Cobalt Green

Cadmium Yellow Medium + Phthalo Green (Blue Shade)

Cadmium Red Medium

Green Gold is already a three-pigment mixture in the tube, so adding more pigments creates a dull, muddy look. These swatches each contain five pigments and are dull and muddy. Adding the red makes an even duller mix.

Cadmium Yellow Medium is a single-pigment paint and was used for this example. These mixtures of three single-pigment paints show that you can reduce chroma without making lifeless and uninteresting mixtures.

WAYS TO PRACTICE PAINT MIXING

Paints can be mixed on the palette with either a palette knife or a flat brush. These paints can be completely and evenly mixed or left in an uneven state, depending on what you want to paint and how you want to paint it.

When creating a painting, your paint can be mixed on the paper, canvas, or board directly but this has to be done rather quickly because of the fast drying time of acrylics. If you let the paint dry on the substrate, glazing and scumbling techniques can be used for additional optical mixing.

Apply your curiosity to paint mixing. It is useful to discover for yourself what happens when you try different combinations. After you have become familiar with your paints through simple experimental mixing, you can explore more detailed methods of paint mixing on pages 40 through 45.

AVOID MIXING MUD

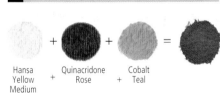

Hansa Yellow Medium + Quinacridone Rose + Cobalt Teal =

A dull muddy color results from mixing the three primary colors, Hansa Yellow Medium, Quinacridone Rose, and Cobalt Teal. Mixing too many pigments widely spaced apart on the wheel is a quick way to create a muddy mess.

MIXING IN STEPS AROUND THE COLOR WHEEL

Mixing color directly on heavy watercolor paper is a great way to quickly explore colors for later use. This example uses Hansa Yellow Medium from the first position on the color wheel and mixes it with each of the next eleven colors in sequential steps to see what happens. Adjacent colors on the color wheel always make the highest-chroma—meaning brightest—mixtures so the mixes with yellow-orange (Cadmium Orange Medium) and green-yellow (Bismuth Yellow) will be the brightest. To see these paints in context on the Sundell Color Wheel, turn to page 17.

1 Mixed with the adjacent color, Cadmium Orange Medium, a lively yellow-orange is created.

2 Pyrrole Orange is two steps away from Hansa Yellow Medium, and this mixture creates a slightly duller color; however it is still fairly bright.

3 The mixture of Hansa Yellow Medium and Cadmium Red Medium makes a color that once again is slightly duller than the previous step. As these are single-pigment paints being combined, the loss of chroma is still fairly mild.

4 When mixed with Quinacridone Rose, an even more subdued red-orange mixture results. This is actually the mixed secondary for the number three red-orange position on the color wheel because Hansa Yellow Medium and Quinacridone Rose are both primaries. This mixture is obviously duller than the single-pigment Pyrrole Orange on the color wheel in the third position.

5 Quinacridone Violet with Hansa Yellow Medium makes a mixture that no longer looks orange. A warm brown appears instead.

6 The opposite color of Ultramarine Violet neutralizes Hansa Yellow Medium.

7 Ultramarine Blue produces a low-chroma green when mixed with Hansa Yellow Medium. This mixture is slightly duller than the Quinacridone Violet mixture, also five steps away from Hansa Yellow Medium on the Sundell Color Wheel.

8 Cobalt Teal mixed with Hansa Yellow Medium offers a brighter chroma than we might expect, since both pigments are high chroma, despite their distance apart on the Sundell Color Wheel.

9 The high chroma of Phthalo Green (Blue Shade) creates a rather lively green when mixed with Hansa Yellow Medium. A lower-chroma substitute for this placement on the wheel would not look as bright as this mixture.

10 Phthalo Green (Yellow Shade) mixed with Hansa Yellow Medium is livelier yet, only two steps away from the Hansa Yellow Medium placement on the color wheel.

11 Bismuth Yellow has low tinting strength (see page 14) and its mixture with Hansa Yellow Medium is extremely bright and yellow.

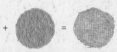

1 Hansa Yellow Medium + Cadmium Orange Medium

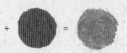

2 Hansa Yellow Medium + Pyrrole Orange

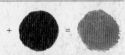

3 Hansa Yellow Medium + Cadmium Red Medium

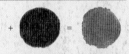

4 Hansa Yellow Medium + Quinacridone Rose

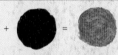

5 Hansa Yellow Medium + Quinacridone Violet

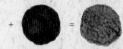

6 Hansa Yellow Medium + Ultramarine Violet

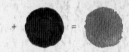

7 Hansa Yellow Medium + Ultramarine Blue

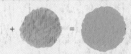

8 Hansa Yellow Medium + Cobalt Teal

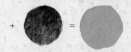

9 Hansa Yellow Med. + Phthalo Green (Blue Shade)

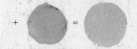

10 Hansa Yellow Med. + Phthalo Green (Yellow Shade)

11 Hansa Yellow Medium + Bismuth Yellow

Color wheels

Color wheels, those rainbow circles of possibility, entice us with their glowing hues. Just looking at a color wheel is enough to inspire a run to the easel and brushes.

Who thought these up in the first place? Mother Nature certainly does not present us with ready-made color wheels. The arc of a rainbow is the closest she comes, and those hues are not arranged at all the way we organize our color wheels.

Of course, it took the genius of Isaac Newton to first imagine connecting the spectrum seen in a slice of rainbow into an unending circle. He was thinking of light when he did so, but artists adopted the idea for paints as well.

The collision between the way light works and the way pigments work still continues today, both in color wheel choices and in the ways we try to understand our paints (see Color and vision, page 8).

THE REALITIES OF PIGMENT OPTIONS

Bruce MacEvoy found the hue, chroma, and value for most of the pigments in use for modern paints and mapped them using Munsell's methods. The three-dimensional model was too awkward for daily use, so he flattened the value scale, resulting in this color wheel, right. Notice the uneven distribution of the available pigments. They do not march neatly around a color wheel like the even distribution of light wavelengths. Instead, some hues are represented by many pigment choices and others by few. These pigments also vary widely in chroma, tinting strength, and values. This brings us face to face with the reality of pigment choices. Our paints can't show everything we can see. For more information, go to www.handprint.com.

MAPPING COLOR

Albert Henry Munsell took the next step in color mapping, after Newton. Color wheels showed a spectrum of hues, but lacked the other two components of color: chroma and value. He created a 3D graph with a vertical value scale running up through the center of the hue circle and a horizontal axis for chroma, to make a model that maps hue, chroma, and value accurately for each color. In this illustration, the hue circle is shown at Value 6 and Chroma 6. We also see two different values of chroma in the red hue increasing outward from the center to Chroma 8, but the chroma scale may actually go much farther. A strong bright red, for example, could be located at Value 5 and Chroma 24.

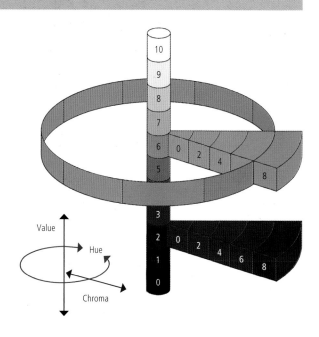

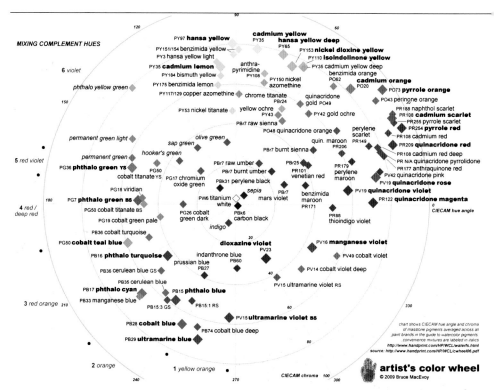

artist's color wheel
© 2009 Bruce MacEvoy

SUNDELL COLOR WHEEL AND SUBSTITUTE PAINT LISTING

Trying to corral our irregular assortment of pigments into a functional color wheel is a little like herding cats. The pigments will behave according to their own unique makeup, but we can still group them according to their shared hues and opposing complements to simplify palette choices.

The author's color wheel is designed to provide a reliable tool for the artist seeking exceptional color in acrylics. Building a palette with single-pigment paints is a good idea because it gives the widest array of color-mixing options. The more pigments are combined, the lower the chroma drops, so starting with single-pigment paints allows higher-chroma choices when desired. Most of the chosen pigments have high tinting strength (see page 14). The mixtures may easily be reduced in chroma if needed for specific paintings.

A chart is included below showing suitable substitutes for each of the 12 color positions on the wheel. This makes exploring alternate paints less daunting, since you know where they fit into an established framework.

The pigment numbers are also given with the paint name in the wheel and the chart. Remember to make a habit of reading the pigment numbers for any paint you buy so you select exactly what you want from any brand of acrylic paint (see page 122).

Paints that are convenience mixtures of multiple pigments are included in some color categories. They are placed at the end of the list after the single-pigment choices. You can readily identify them by the multiple pigment numbers following a paint name.

Neutrals and earth tones may be found on pages 72–75. After you are comfortable with this color wheel, a few neutrals and earth tones are excellent additions to a working palette.

If you are concerned about lightfastness, information can be found on the paint tube, in the manufacturer's catalog, or online. All paints included in the Sundell Color Wheel and substitute paint listing are lightfast when produced by quality manufacturers.

The Sundell Color Wheel and substitute paint listing can also be found on the fold-out flap on page 127.

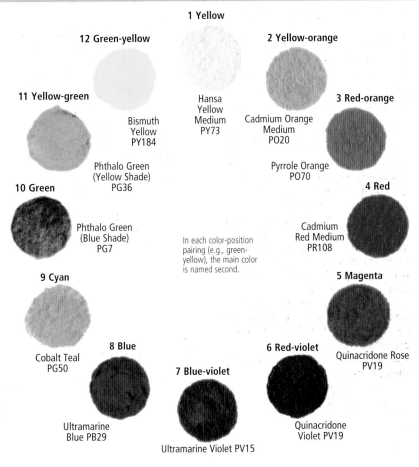

In each color-position pairing (e.g., green-yellow), the main color is named second.

Color wheel positions:
- **1 Yellow** — Hansa Yellow Medium PY73
- **2 Yellow-orange** — Cadmium Orange Medium PO20
- **3 Red-orange** — Pyrrole Orange PO70
- **4 Red** — Cadmium Red Medium PR108
- **5 Magenta** — Quinacridone Rose PV19
- **6 Red-violet** — Quinacridone Violet PV19
- **7 Blue-violet** — Ultramarine Violet PV15
- **8 Blue** — Ultramarine Blue PB29
- **9 Cyan** — Cobalt Teal PG50
- **10 Green** — Phthalo Green (Blue Shade) PG7
- **11 Yellow-green** — Phthalo Green (Yellow Shade) PG36
- **12 Green-yellow** — Bismuth Yellow PY184

1. Yellow	2. Yellow-orange	3. Red-orange	4. Red	5. Magenta	6. Red-violet
Cadmium Yellow Medium PY35	Cadmium Yellow Deep PY35	Cadmium Orange Deep PY35	Cadmium Red Dark PR108	Primary Magenta PV19	Cobalt Violet Hue PV19
Hansa Yellow Deep PY65	New Gamboge PY153	Perinone Orange PO43	Cadmium Red Deep PR108	Permanent Rose PV19	PR122 PW4 PV23
Yellow Iron Oxide PY42	Azo Yellow Deep PY65	Quinacridone Coral PR209	Naphthol Red Light PR112	Anthraquinone Red PR177	Alizarin Crimson Hue PR122
Nickel Azo Yellow PY150	Quinacridone Gold PO49	Quinacridone Burnt Orange PR206	Naphthol Red Medium PR5	Quinacridone Crimson PR206	PR206 PG7
Cadmium Yellow Medium Hue PY74 PY65	Cadmium Yellow Deep Hue PY184 PY74 PY65	Quinacridone Burnt Scarlet PR206	Permanent Red PR170	PR202	
Primary Yellow PY3 PY73 PW6	Cadmium Orange Hue PO73 PY65 PY74	Quinacridone Nickel Azo Gold PO48 PY150	Pyrrole Red PR254	Quinacridone Magenta PR122	
Naples Yellow Hue PW6 PY42 PY83		Quinacridone Sienna PO49 PR209	Pyrrole Red Dark PR264		
			Quinacridone Red PV19		
			Perylene Maroon PR179		

7. Blue-violet	8. Blue	9. Cyan	10. Green	11. Yellow-green	12. Green-yellow
Dioxazine Purple PV23	French Ultramarine Blue PB29	Cerulean Blue P36	Cobalt Green PG26	Chromium Oxide Green PG17	Lemon Yellow PY175
Carbazole Violet PV23	Phthalo Blue (Green Shade) PB15	Cerulean Blue Deep PB36	Cobalt Green Deep PG26	Chromium Oxide Green Dark PG17	Cadmium Yellow Light PY35
Indanthrone Blue PB60	Cobalt Blue PB28	Cerulean Blue Chromium PB36	Permanent Green Light PY3 PG7	Green Gold PY150 PG36 PY3	Hansa Yellow Light PY3
Permanent Violet Dark PB60 PR122	Cobalt Blue Deep PB73	Cobalt Turquoise PB36	Permanent Green PY3 PG7	Rich Green Gold PY129	Cadmium Lemon PY35
Prism Violet PV23 PW6 PR122	Anthraquinone Blue PB60	Primary Cyan PB15 PW6	Cascade Green PBr7 PB15		Cadmium Yellow Light Hue PY184 PY3
	Cobalt Blue Hue PB29 PB15 PW6	Manganese Blue Hue PG15 PG7 PW6			

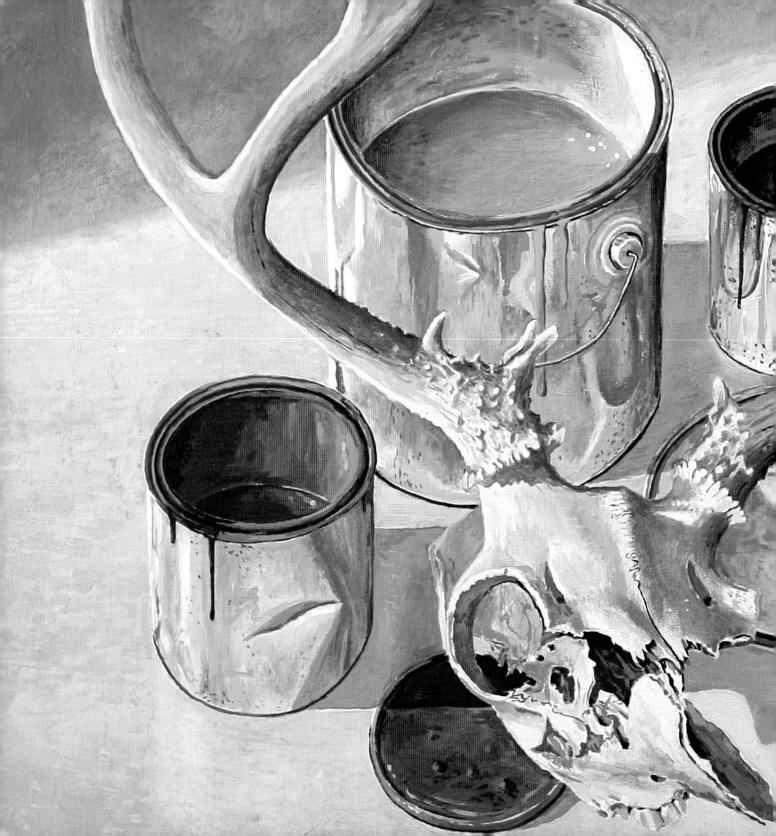

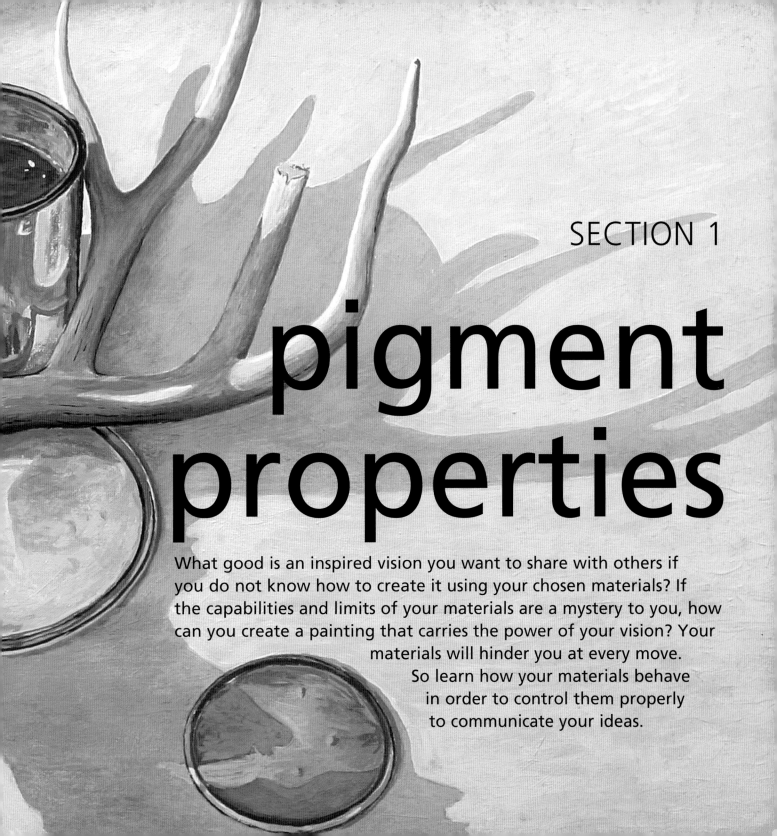

SECTION 1

pigment properties

What good is an inspired vision you want to share with others if you do not know how to create it using your chosen materials? If the capabilities and limits of your materials are a mystery to you, how can you create a painting that carries the power of your vision? Your materials will hinder you at every move. So learn how your materials behave in order to control them properly to communicate your ideas.

Fluid and heavy-body acrylics

After going through the process of pigment selection, you are now confronted with yet another choice—which kind of paint to use? The two main groupings of acrylic paints are fluid and heavy-body paints. How do you choose the best kind of paint for your artwork?

The terms fluid acrylics and heavy-body acrylics are self-explanatory. Here we see a puddle of liquid acrylic and a blob of heavy-body acrylic straight from the tube.

Heavy-body acrylic

Fluid acrylic

FLUID ACRYLICS

Fluid acrylics are the best choice for painting without showing brush strokes. They are also excellent for spattering effects. Fluid acrylics sold in bottles typically have the same pigment density as their thicker counterparts that come in heavy-body acrylic paint tubes. This can be useful for painting glazes but sometimes a thinner pigment density may be desirable for a more delicate glaze.

You can thin a fluid acrylic by mixing it with water or with a glazing medium. Mixing with water dilutes the fluid acrylic, but if it is too diluted and thinly spread on the painting, no acrylic film will develop in drying. The tiny scattered bits of dried paint will be in danger of separating from the painting and can be easily rubbed off the surface. Diluting with a glazing medium is preferable because it allows the density of pigment to be reduced as much as required but also allows the paint to dry to a durable acrylic film.

HEAVY-BODY ACRYLICS

Heavy-body acrylics are usually the main paints chosen by artists because of their versatility. They can be used to create texture and impasto effects but can also be brushed to a smooth surface.

Heavy-body acrylics can be diluted into a fluid, but this will reduce the pigment density accordingly. As with fluid acrylics, mixing with glazing medium is preferable to mixing with water, especially given the amount of dilution needed to make a heavy-body acrylic into a fluid.

Heavy-body acrylics also can be mixed with other mediums, which is discussed on pages 30 and 31.

USING FLUID AND HEAVY-BODY ACRYLICS IN A PAINTING

In this example both heavy-body acrylics and fluid acrylics are used in the same painting for different purposes. Pyrrole Orange opposes Cobalt Teal, and a trio of blue-violet placements—Ultramarine Violet, Dioxazine Purple, and Indanthrone Blue—oppose Cadmium Yellow Medium. Indanthrone Blue is listed for blue-violet because when applied heavily it is dark and almost looks like Dioxazine Purple. Yet, when tinted with Titanium White, the paint shows much less violet in its appearance.

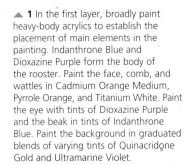

 Indanthrone Blue

 Dioxazine Purple

 Ultramarine Violet

 Cobalt Teal

 Cadmium Yellow Medium

 Cadmium Orange Medium

 Quinacridone Gold

 Pyrrole Orange

 Cadmium Red Medium

 Titanium White

▲ **1** In the first layer, broadly paint heavy-body acrylics to establish the placement of main elements in the painting. Indanthrone Blue and Dioxazine Purple form the body of the rooster. Paint the face, comb, and wattles in Cadmium Orange Medium, Pyrrole Orange, and Titanium White. Paint the eye with tints of Dioxazine Purple and the beak in tints of Indanthrone Blue. Paint the background in graduated blends of varying tints of Quinacridone Gold and Ultramarine Violet.

▼ **2** This closeup shows the dark edge of the eye being painted in Indanthrone Blue. Continuing with the same palette, apply glazes of fluid acrylic paints over the comb, face, and wattles to add more definition.

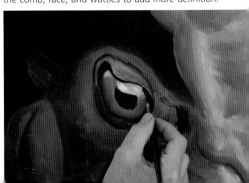

3 Develop the comb, face, and wattles with the fluid acrylic glazes shown in the previous detail. Paint additional heavy-body acrylics into the rooster's feathers. Paint the background in another layer of the previous colors with heavy-body acrylics but add Dioxazine Purple in the darkest areas around the face and side of the bird. The painting is now ready for fluid acrylic spattering.

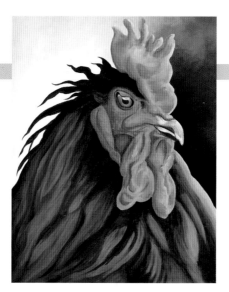

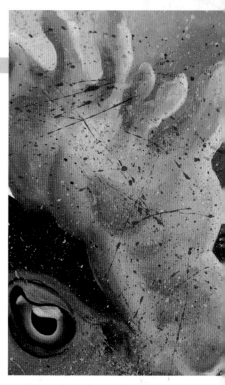

4 As the background is lighter on the left to emphasize the dark feather outlines and darker on the right to emphasize the highlighted comb, beak, and feathers, the spatters work with this imbalance. Add more Cobalt Teal spatters to the dark background to accent the opposition with the red-orange in the comb and wattles. Add orange spatters to the lighted background to contrast with the greater mass of blue feathers there. Apply spatters unevenly to the feathers and face to create more variation. Apply red spatters to the comb, face, and wattles as a lively spark, since red is analogous to the yellows and oranges.

5 Paint a heavy-body mixture of Cadmium Yellow Medium and Cadmium Orange Medium along the leading edge of the comb to emphasize the highlights. Allow some spatters to remain and obscure others for an interesting effect. You will see the lively effect of the Cadmium Red Medium fluid spatters on the comb.

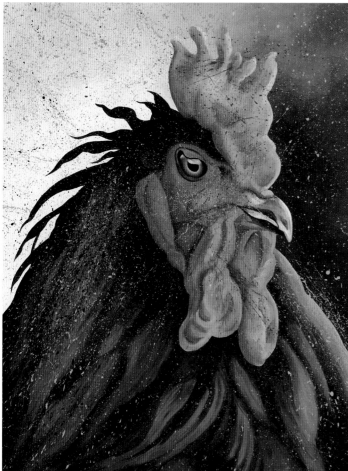

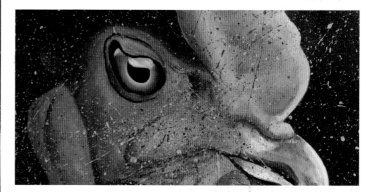

6 Repaint both the eye and the beak with heavy-body acrylics after spattering, again obscuring some spatters and allowing others to remain, otherwise the eye and beak will be excessively obscured by spatters. Notice how the spatter pattern on the face was accented with the fluid Cobalt Teal in particular, a vibrant complement to the Pyrrole Orange in the face.

Pigment permanence

How long will the art you create last? Paintings that crack, fall apart, fade, discolor, and otherwise degenerate are a dreadful outcome for creative inspiration. So what are the important factors you need to know about pigment permanence?

PIGMENT PERMANENCE AND PAINT STABILITY

Not only is it important to use lightfast pigments to avoid fading and discoloring, but the binder used to make the paint is worth considering as well. High-quality paint with a dense pigment load is far more effective for painting than poorer-quality offerings.

The so-called "student grade" paints are not good choices. Fugitive pigments may be used to save

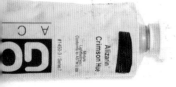
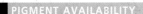

Alizarin Crimson Hue replaces the fugitive Alizarin Crimson, a dye made from the cochineal insect. Quinacridone Burnt Scarlet is a lovely example of a new inorganic pigment that also can be used as an alternative to Alizarin Crimson.

money in manufacturing, and pigment density is reduced to lower the price, so these paints should be avoided.

The acrylic emulsion used in formulating acrylic paints is usually quite reliable. This acrylic emulsion dries into a flexible film, which is the main reason acrylics are not prone to the cracking problems that can plague oil paints.

The clear emulsion is also not subject to the yellowing over time that happens with oil-based paints. Lightfast colors consistently remain true to their original appearance.

The main concern with permanence in acrylics is the fact that the fully dried surface of the paint remains slightly porous and sticky. Dust and other contaminants can embed themselves into the surface. Varnishing helps prevent any difficulties with this issue.

HISTORICAL OVERVIEW

Humans have always created artwork with whatever materials were available at the time. Clays found in the soil were a good early source of earthy colors durable enough for ancient cave paintings to survive to the present. Plants and some insects were used for colorants, all too often with short-term results. Carmine was derived from scale insects. Alizarin Crimson came from madder root and proved to be a fugitive color (see page 10). Indigo was originally made from a plant called woad but is now synthetically made. Still fugitive, indigo is now used in blue jeans.

In their quest for permanent color, artists suffered through the use of extremely toxic materials that provided colors otherwise unavailable. Vermilion was the result of alchemical experiments mixing sulfur with cinnabar, an ore of mercury. Artists loved the color, but mercury is the element formerly used in hat making that caused mercury poisoning, long before anyone understood its toxic qualities.

Lead was another dangerous material used in many paints. Red lead was substituted for the more expensive vermilion, providing an equally toxic alternative. It is possible that lead paints aggravated Van Gogh's mental and physical health problems.

Let us not forget arsenic, which appeared in many different paint formulations. Cobalt Violet contained arsenic, but greens including Scheele's Green and Paris Green were more commonly created with the material. Paris Green was used in wallpapers in homes where cases of arsenic poisoning were reported.

The array of permanent pigments that can be used with reasonable safety in the studio today are truly a treasure for the modern artist. We are far more fortunate with our paint options than our ancestors.

PIGMENT AVAILABILITY

*Lamborghini Spyder **Lou O'Keefe***
Characterized by two pairs of complements, blue with orange and purple with yellow, this painting of a car was made possible by modern manufacturing. The pigments used in

contemporary art materials are developed for other uses first, such as automotive paints. So this painting about a manufactured luxury car is also created with paints related to the manufacture of that car.

You may be surprised to learn that a flashy sports car is directly related to your acrylic paint choices. The main pigment consumers are the automotive and plastics industries, so if an inorganic pigment falls out of fashion for cars, after a few years you probably won't be able to find it as an artist's pigment. For example, Quinacridone Gold (PO49) is a lightfast, transparent, staining, mid-valued, moderately intense earth-yellow pigment. Manufacture of PO49 ceased in 2001 because there was insufficient demand for the pigment from automobile manufacturers, its principal consumers. Most artist's paints made with this pigment were discontinued in 2005. See the listings on www.handprint.com for more information on discontinued pigments.

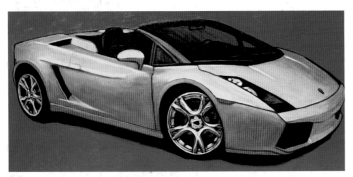

SUBSTRATES

Pigment permanence is related to the binder in the paint and also on the substrate used. You could use the most permanent possible pigment in your paint but if you create your painting on newsprint, the life of that painting will be short.

Newsprint is made from wood fiber and contains cellulose, which causes the paper to decay, become yellow and brittle, and eventually disintegrate. Besides the problems of a substrate made of poor materials, issues may also arise with unwanted chemical reactions between the paint and the substrate.

Acrylics can be painted on a multitude of surfaces but are most commonly painted on canvas, watercolor paper, or board. Of the three, boards can present the most problems with pigment permanence.

Boards are made with a wide range of materials, not all of them archival or permanent. Cradled and sealed birch is the most archival choice as it is less acidic than other woods and the sealing prevents oxidation. Pressed boards are made with non-archival glues that can delaminate over time.

Canvas primed with gesso is an acceptable substrate for acrylics. In addition to the cottons and linens, some new synthetic polyflax or polyflax/cotton blends are available. Although too new for long-term testing results, they look promising.

Heavy watercolor paper is also an excellent substrate for acrylics. High-quality papers will not contain cellulose and should last extremely well with proper care.

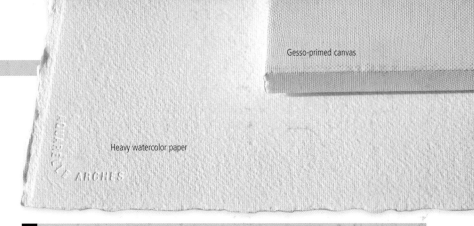

Gesso-primed canvas

Heavy watercolor paper

ENVIRONMENTAL FACTORS

Place a completed painting in an inappropriate environment and the most permanent, most archival materials in the world do not stand a chance. Extreme moisture and temperature fluctuations are deadly for the stability and unblemished appearance of a painting. Air pollution may also cause unwanted chemical reactions in the paint.

Furthermore, you need to keep in mind the standards behind the lightfastness ratings of the paint manufacturers (see page 122). These standards are based on indoor placement of the painting without direct sunlight in a steady humidity that is not too high and a similarly steady temperature that does not go to extremes.

Electric Casey **Jennifer Bowman**
This striking painting features two pair of complements, blue with yellow-orange and cyan with red-orange. Notice the unusual background treatment with the geometric patterns. Using permanent pigments in high-quality paints on an archival substrate and taking proper care of the finished painting will ensure that beauty such as this can be enjoyed long into the future.

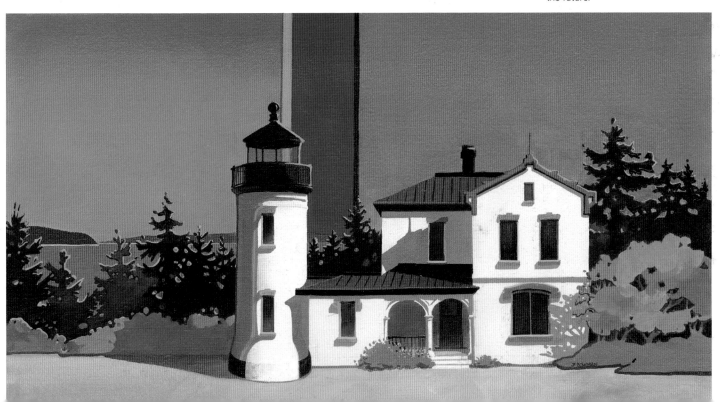

Opaque and semitransparent acrylics

Acrylic paints have some unique properties that can be used to excellent advantage once they are understood. They can be used thickly, like oil paint, and as thin washes, as in watercolor. Pigments vary from opaque to semitransparent.

Do not confuse pigment qualities with the qualities of the acrylic emulsion holding them. Those emulsions may be heavy-body or fluid and that makes no difference to whether or not the pigment they carry is opaque or transparent.

Unlike oils, where a hidden layer may later bleed into a more recent layer, changing the visible color even weeks after drying, a lightfast acrylic color will remain exactly as you see it once it has dried. When using opaque acrylics, this means that any part of a previously painted layer can easily be completely covered so it has no further effect in the painting. This offers a great freedom to experiment in color, especially with the quick-drying time of these paints.

Titanium White is opaque and an excellent choice to cover areas that need to be completely repainted. Many other colors are also opaque. If in doubt about the opacity of a specific acrylic color, you can quickly test a color to see how well it can hide an existing color layer.

Other acrylic paints are semitransparent and lend themselves to other possibilities. Applying thin glazes of these semitransparent paints modifies the colors under them. Allowing a glaze to dry before adding another allows optical color mixing where directly mixing the colors on the palette would create a different and unwanted look. Multiple layers of glazes can be used to create richly varied tapestries of color in your paintings. Commonly used semitransparent acrylics are the quinacridones, synthetic pigments that have only recently become available for painters. The quinacridones add a stunning warm brilliance to the palette. Other semitransparent acrylic paints such as Indanthrone Blue and Carbazole Violet have much stronger tinting ability and must be handled with restraint if fully saturated color is not wanted.

Opaque and semitransparent acrylic paints are most commonly combined in paintings. They can be used to create bold areas of dramatic color or delicately graduated blends as desired.

CHANGING ACRYLIC COLORS

Opaque paints are extremely useful if you make a mistake or change your mind. If a disruptive texture has not been added to the painting, it is easy to completely repaint an annoying compositional element to change or eliminate it. If you want to change it to a combination of opaque paints, you can do so directly. If you want to change it to semitransparent paints, the old color will partially show through them. In that case, paint the area to be replaced with the extremely opaque Titanium White and let it dry. This allows semitransparent paints to be used without distortion by the former colors.

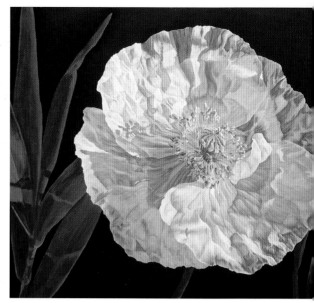

The illusion of transparency

Just because a paint is opaque itself does not mean it cannot be used to create the appearance of transparency. White Gossamer was painted entirely with opaque acrylic paints and shows transparent glowing flower petals. The petals were painted in tints of Ultramarine Blue and Raw Umber with Titanium White in varying mixtures. Since these paints themselves are not transparent, the effect was achieved by careful control of tonal values in the mixes.

Main palette
Titanium White
Carbon Black
Chromium Oxide Green
Raw Umber
Ultramarine Blue
Cadmium Orange Medium
Cadmium Yellow Medium

COMPARING OPAQUE AND SEMITRANSPARENT

Painting opaque and semitransparent acrylics over each other is a good way to see how the paints will affect each other. In these examples, the first circle was allowed to dry before painting the second overlapping circle.

Semitransparent over opaque

The overlap area shows the optical color mix that resulted from the semitransparent Quinacridone Red painted over the dried layer of opaque Cadmium Yellow.

Quinacridone Red is close to a complementary color to the Opaque Chromium Oxide Green, so the overlap area is quite neutralized (see page 74).

Opaque over semitransparent

Opaque Cadmium Yellow covers the semitransparent Quinacridone Red so almost none of the red shows in the overlap.

Opaque Chromium Oxide Green even more thoroughly covers the semitransparent Quinacridone Red in the overlap.

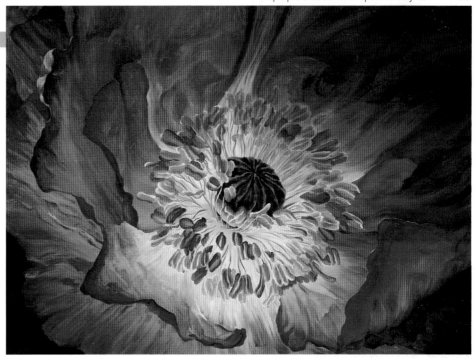

EXPLORING TRANSPARENCY

Semitransparent acrylic paints can readily be used to create the effect of glowing, transparent petals, as shown here in *Cup of Fire*. The petals were painted with the quinacridones on a lightly gessoed canvas. The slightly absorbent surface made it easy to paint soft blends in varying colors. Additional glazes of the quinacridones were used to create the deeper color areas of the petals.

In order to maximize the richly saturated brilliance of these paints, no opaque paints were used in the outer petal colors, but Titanium White was used as a blending color for the gradations painted into the center.

Main palette
Quinacridone Red
Quinacridone Pink
Quinacridone Gold
Quinacridone Magenta

Flower center
Chromium Oxide Green
Raw Umber
Phthalo Green (Yellow Shade)
Cadmium Yellow
Cadmium Orange
Titanium White

OPAQUE AND SEMITRANSPARENT ACRYLICS TOGETHER

In this detail of *Bahama Treasures* by Bern Sundell opaque and semitransparent acrylic paints work well together. In different areas of the painting, Titanium White was mixed with all of the paints except Burnt Sienna. Titanium White combines with Burnt Sienna to make an unpleasant chalky color, a problem not found in the rest of the palette.

The semitransparent quinacridones were painted in glazes over the dried opaque mixes. They were also mixed with Titanium White and other colors to create softer, subtler blends in some of the conch shells. A small amount of Carbon Black accented the deepest shadows.

Main palette
Titanium White
Raw Umber
Burnt Sienna
Yellow Ocher
Cadmium Orange Medium
Cadmium Yellow Medium
Ultramarine Blue
Cerulean Blue
Quinacridone Red
Quinacridone Coral
Carbon Black

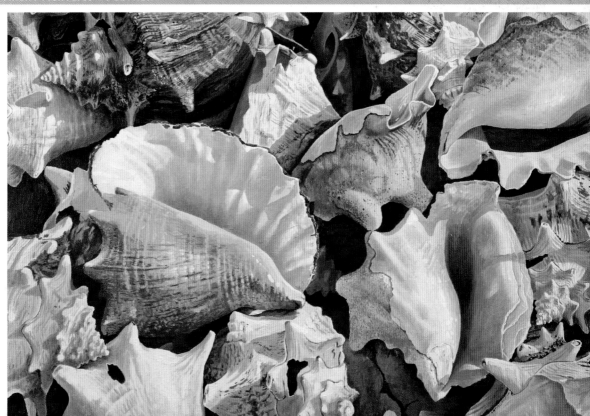

Luminescent acrylics

Luminescent acrylics are a category all of their own in acrylic paints. They sparkle, glitter, and refract light in completely different ways than heavy-body or fluid acrylic paints. But what is the difference between duochrome, interference, pearlescent, and iridescent paints, and how do you use them?

This group of paints—luminescent acrylics—causes inherent difficulties when the artist tries to integrate them into their normal palette. These paints play by different rules in their surprising and unexpected color shifts. They constantly change color with the movement of the viewer. And how do you categorize a paint that is a sparkling light aquamarine on white paper but turns gold when painted across black? The behavior of these paints defies the color wheel.

Luminescent paints form color with mica platelets, titanium dioxide, and metallic oxides. They are quite stable since the metals are already oxidized so they will not change color with further oxidation, and the other materials can be trusted for durability.

Titanium dioxide is familiar to us as the pigment for Titanium White, which is a dense, opaque paint. How can the same pigment be used for these wild rainbow effects? The answer lies in the particle size used. The particles in Titanium White are large compared to the particle size used in luminescent paints.

Coating mica platelets with the paints creates some amazing color shifts. Controlling the process precisely allows the manufacturer to make paints that reflect and refract light in certain hues but not others. Painting them in thin layers and separating those layers with a glossy (not matte) gel or medium may further enhance them.

Luminescent acrylics can be mixed with other acrylics. For example, Iridescent Electric Blue mixed with heavy-body acrylic paints can produce some startling colors. Duochrome acrylics, however, lose their characteristic dual color shifts when mixed with other acrylics. Some of the other luminescent paints can be used to colorful advantage in such mixtures.

PEARLESCENT ACRYLIC PAINTS

Pearlescent acrylics are transparent—except for Black—and look fairly similar to each other on white watercolor paper. The differences between them are much more pronounced when painted across a stripe of black paint.

Pearlescents mix well with other paints, including other iridescent and regular acrylic paints. Do not expect them to look white over an area of your painting that has a layer of bright color. If you need a whiter look there, you will need to paint some Titanium White, let it dry, and then paint the pearlescent paint over it.

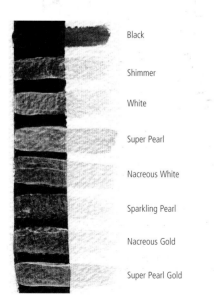

Black

Shimmer

White

Super Pearl

Nacreous White

Sparkling Pearl

Nacreous Gold

Super Pearl Gold

INTERFERENCE ACRYLIC PAINTS

Interference colors have subtle effects and have been compared to oil sheen on water. As you might guess, this does not photograph particularly well, but the swatches offer an idea of the main color changes you can expect from the different colors.

The alternate green shown is simply by another manufacturer. These paints have distinct variations from manufacturer to manufacturer so you may want to explore all your options.

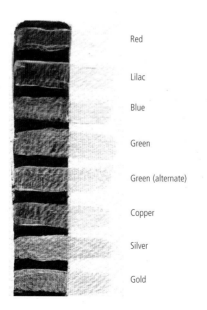

Red

Lilac

Blue

Green

Green (alternate)

Copper

Silver

Gold

SILVER AND GOLD IRIDESCENT PAINTS

The paint swatches in this example show a variety of silver and gold metallic iridescent acrylic paints. The variations between manufacturers can be extreme in this category, as you can see from some of the alternates in the swatches.

Iridescent paints mix well with each other, so obtaining the desired brilliance can be achieved that way if the color straight from the tube is not what you want for a given effect.

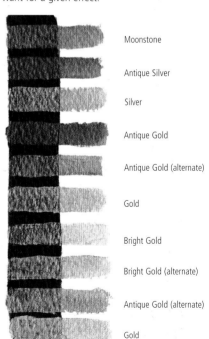

Moonstone

Antique Silver

Silver

Antique Gold

Antique Gold (alternate)

Gold

Bright Gold

Bright Gold (alternate)

Antique Gold (alternate)

Gold

DUOCHROME ACRYLIC PAINTS

Painting duochromes across a stripe of black paint and onto white watercolor paper shows their oddities immediately. Radical color shifts that one would not predict from looking at the often nondescript dab of paint on the palette immediately appear.

What is lost in this still photo of the paint swatches is the way they change with the movement of the viewer. All of the luminescent acrylics are similar to opal in the way we perceive their shifted, refracted colors in movement.

Autumn Mystery

Adobe

Cactus Flower

Hibiscus

Violet Fantasy

Mauve

Blue Silver

Lapis Sunlight

Aquamarine

Arctic Fire

Tropic Sunrise

Oceanic

Saguaro Green

Desert Bronze

IRIDESCENT ACRYLIC PAINTS

As you can see from the painted swatches, iridescent acrylic paints are both more consistent painted over black and white and more opaque as well. For predictable results they are easier to use than duochrome or interference acrylics.

Some of the paints pictured are metallics. A still photograph cannot properly convey how bright they can be in real life.

Iridescent acrylics mix well with regular acrylic paints to offer a wide and sparkling range of colors. Iridescent paints are an excellent choice for experimenting with luminescent acrylics.

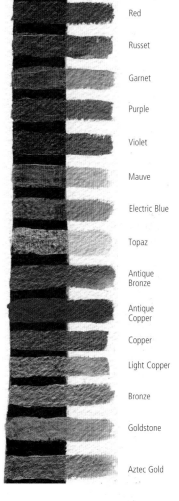

Red

Russet

Garnet

Purple

Violet

Mauve

Electric Blue

Topaz

Antique Bronze

Antique Copper

Copper

Light Copper

Bronze

Goldstone

Aztec Gold

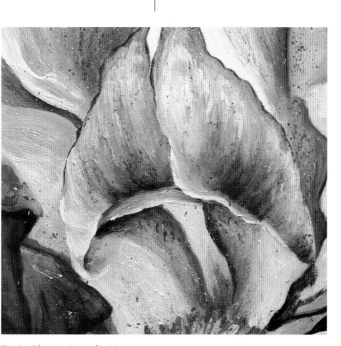

This detail from a painting of an iris is an example of the use of Iridescent Red and Shimmer Pearlescent. Mixing a pearlescent paint with a normal acrylic paint such as Cadmium Yellow Medium can add a striking liveliness, effective for an inner glow of light in this flower.

DISCOVERING DISADVANTAGES OF LUMINESCENT ACRYLICS

One of the biggest disadvantages of luminescent acrylics cannot be seen in these photographs of paint swatches, but becomes immediately obvious in a completed painting. The surface of luminescent acrylics is drastically different than that of regular acrylic paints.

At certain angles depending on the light, luminescent acrylics are obvious patches against the other paints, and that pattern can overwhelm your actual colors and composition in the painting.

Mixing the luminescent paints with all other paints in the painting can eliminate the problem, but it may not be the solution you want. Using small areas of luminescent acrylics is another way to minimize the problem.

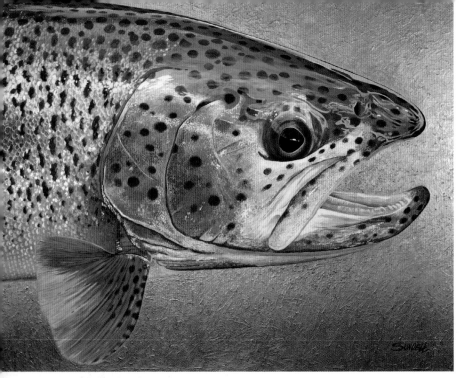

River King **Bern Sundell**

Pearlescent and iridescent acrylics were used along with heavy-body acrylics in this work. The background was painted with metallic gold iridescent paint that was also used in part of the head of the fish to integrate the fish with the background.

Fish scales are a naturally iridescent subject for painting. The following example of a rainbow trout shows them off to good advantage.

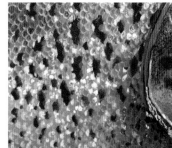

The detail of fish scales from *River King* starts to give some idea of the contrast between the surfaces of luminescent acrylics and regular acrylics. This is more apparent in real life and the artist has since discontinued using luminescent acrylics in his popular series of trout paintings.

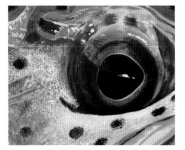

The richness of the iridescent paints intermingled with heavy-body acrylics is shown in this detail from *River King*. The effect is colorful and lively against the contrasting darker colors of the eye and upper part of the head.

Careful selection of subject matter is important in making luminescent paints aesthetically pleasing in your painting. Naturally iridescent subjects make sense for these materials.

New Zealand Paua
Shaugn Briggs
Luminescent acrylics were used in this painting of a paua shell. The artist concentrated them in the areas of the shell that would actually be iridescent and avoided them in the outer coating of the shell that typically is dull and opaque.

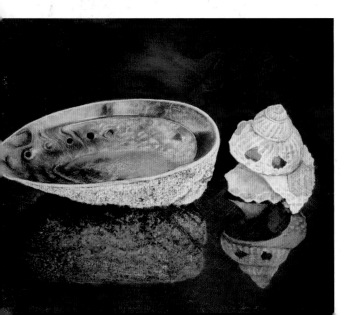

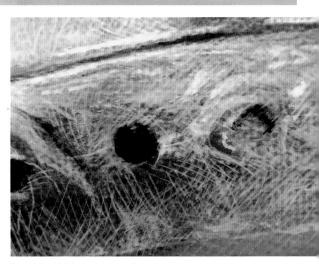

The artist applied the luminescent paints with skill and delicacy over a paint layer that is not luminescent. The varied colors catch the light in a convincing way.

PAINTING WITH LUMINESCENT ACRYLICS

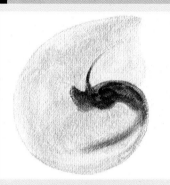

Palette Pearlescent White, Pearlescent Shimmer, Pearlescent Black, Nacreous Gold, and Super Pearl Gold.

1 Pearlescent paints provide the base coat of paint for the shell. Pearlescent paints have a subtle shimmer that can be quite lovely. The colors used in this layer are slightly more varied than the still photograph implies, because of the color shifts seen in movement.

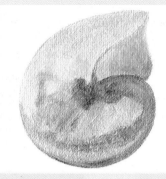

Palette Arctic Fire, Aquamarine, Blue Silver, Lapis Sunlight, Mauve, Violet Fantasy, Hibiscus, Cactus Flower, Autumn Mystery, and Adobe.

2 Duochrome acrylics have been applied over the pearlescent colors. The shell shows more lively color at this stage. The lighter areas have an attractive pink glow that appears with movement but is less apparent in this still photograph.

A nautilus shell provides the subject for a painting that shows the application of different kinds of luminescent acrylics. Small amounts of heavy-body acrylics were also incorporated into the painting.

Normally the author would not paint the different kinds of luminescent acrylics in entirely separate layers as shown in this example, but for demonstration purposes it was useful to better indicate their nature.

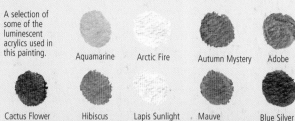

A selection of some of the luminescent acrylics used in this painting.

Aquamarine   Arctic Fire   Autumn Mystery   Adobe

Cactus Flower   Hibiscus   Lapis Sunlight   Mauve   Blue Silver

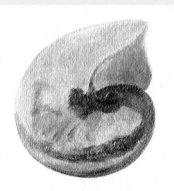

Palette Paints used include Blue, Green, Lilac, Red, Silver, and Gold.

3 Interference acrylics have been painted over the preceding two layers. The photograph shows the more subtle appearance of the shell but does not illustrate the delicate sheen in movement. The dark shadow began shifting to a blue-gray in the shell.

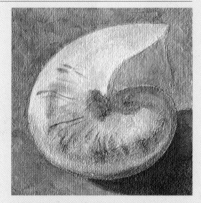

Palette Luminescent paints used were Electric Blue, Aztec Gold, Bronze, Antique Copper, Topaz, Violet, Purple, and Russet. Heavy-body acrylics used were Quinacridone Gold and Yellow Ocher.

4 Iridescent paints were introduced at this stage of the painting. The background shadow was first painted in Electric Blue and the brightly lit background area in a tint of Pearlescent Shimmer and Electric Blue. After drying, a mixture of Quinacridone Gold and Yellow Ocher was thinly applied to allow the layer underneath to still show luminescence.

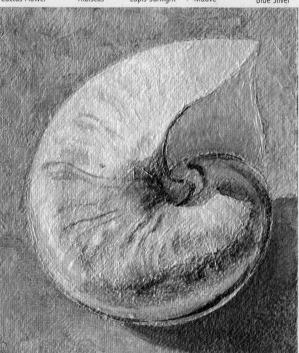

▲ Multiple layers of iridescent and pearlescent paints along with Titanium White and Indanthrone Blue completed the shell. The Titanium White highlights and Indanthrone Blue shadows were allowed to dry and then painted with Pearlescent Shimmer to avoid any variation in surface sheen. Pearlescent Shimmer or other white pearlescent paints work well to tint other luminescent paints to dilute the intensity of their colors when needed.

Gel mediums and grounds

Grounds are used to prepare the substrate—typically canvas or board—to take paint. Gesso, the most commonly used ground, is used to partially soak into the substrate and form a surface that will receive paint without flaking or separating from the substrate. Gel mediums are used to modify acrylic paint in order to create different textures while painting. Gel mediums are not used as grounds, and vice versa. Knowing the characteristics of the grounds and gel mediums available allows you to choose the best options for bringing your own creative vision to life.

Gesso is the standard and most reliable ground for both canvas and board. Many prepared canvases and boards come already primed with gesso. Even if you stretch your own canvas, primed rolls of canvas can be bought.

Yet it can be handy to keep some gesso in the studio even if you use already primed materials. Sometimes the canvas texture may need to be smoother and additional coats of gesso can do the trick.

Gel mediums come in a wild assortment of characteristics to change the way your paint handles. Some are stiff and others soft, and yet others may be stringy or even coarsened with silica. The array of products can be startling, but properly chosen gels can make it easier to accomplish your objectives in painting.

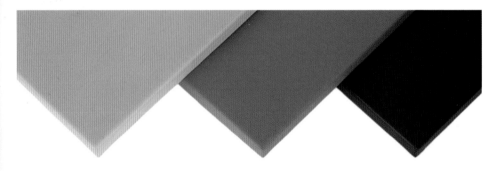

Gesso ground After applying three coats of gesso to the canvas, the sealing of the fibers in the canvas was complete, so nothing more could be absorbed. Dioxazine Purple, Quinacridone Coral, and Cobalt Blue were painted with a flat taklon brush, using the same amount of paint as the example painted on absorbent ground. Notice the brushstrokes are more pronounced and the colors brighter on the gesso ground than on the absorbent ground (right).

Absorbent ground Despite using the same amount of paint and the same brush as the gesso ground example (left), the paint on the absorbent ground has softer blends and is not as bright. Some of the paint was absorbed by the ground, which reduced the brightness of the colors.

EXPLORING GROUNDS

Gesso is the most common type of ground and is usually applied in a minimum of two coats for proper priming of a canvas or board. It is better to buy high-quality gesso. The bargain gesso is not really cheaper since it will require more coats to do the same job. An alternative to gesso is absorbent ground. This will allow some of the paint to soak into it and allow softer effects (see above). The absorbent ground is more delicate and should have a protective coating of soft gel and varnish when completed.

Colored gesso can be purchased for a colored ground. Black is the most commonly available alternative to plain white gesso. If you want to make your own colored gesso you can add heavy-body acrylic paint to white gesso. Initial white coats of gesso on the canvases above were followed by gesso mixed with Raw Sienna, Raw Umber, and Mars Black, from left to right. Because of the white opacity of gesso, the Raw Sienna looks more like Yellow Ocher and the Raw Umber is similarly muted. The black canvas had more paint added. A finished painting on the Raw Umber gesso can be seen on page 37 in Using texture in paint.

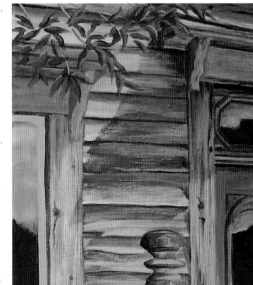

A colored ground gives the advantage of a ready-made undertone, as this detail shows, which can be quite lovely as additional layers of paint are added. Sometimes the undertone is subtle, as in these window reflections with their subdued radiance, or more obvious in the boards where the Raw Sienna/gesso mixture shows more clearly through the paint. The finished painting can be seen on page 95.

DIFFERENT TYPES OF GEL

Heavy Gel is best for strongly textured work, Regular Gel is a good general-purpose gel, and Soft Gel is more subtle in its texture. Soft Gel can be used as a protective barrier before varnishing. Self-leveling Gel is usable in glazing and is not as runny as the liquid mediums. Gels can be chosen that dry in a glossy, satin, or matte surface. Mixing gloss and matte gels produces a satin gel. Gloss gels dry transparently clear, but matte or satin does not. The addition of titanium particles makes a gel satin or matte but reduces its opacity at the same time. This reduces the chroma of the paint mixed with it or lying under it in the painting, so choose according to what you need.

The shadows make it obvious how well each gel medium holds its shape.

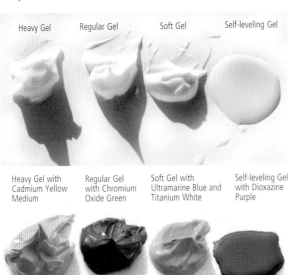

Heavy Gel   Regular Gel   Soft Gel   Self-leveling Gel

Heavy Gel with Cadmium Yellow Medium

Regular Gel with Chromium Oxide Green

Soft Gel with Ultramarine Blue and Titanium White

Self-leveling Gel with Dioxazine Purple

IMPASTO EFFECTS WITH GELS

In the three examples below, three different gels were mixed with heavy-body acrylics to demonstrate how they can be used to paint impasto effects. The same flat, hog-bristle brush was used in all three examples because of its stiff and coarse bristles that leave a pronounced brushstroke.

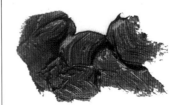

Heavy Gel Medium was mixed with Pyrrole Orange. Powerfully textured and dimensional effects can be created with this gel.

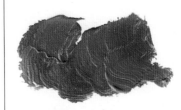

Regular Gel Medium and Cobalt Green do not show the same depth and ability to hold extreme shapes as the Heavy Gel Medium. However, it makes an attractive textured brushstroke nonetheless.

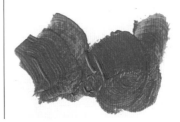

Soft Gel Medium and Manganese Blue Hue were mixed for this example. This gel does not hold as much texture as the others but still provides a good appearance. This gel can also be used to protect fragile layers, such as the Crackle Paste ground.

The detail from a painting at right using Soft Gel Medium with several different paint combinations shows the rich effects possible with multiple layers of gel. Varying tints of Dioxazine Purple, Ultramarine Blue, and Cobalt Turquoise were mixed with Soft Gel Medium and applied with either a flat taklon brush or palette knife. Each layer dried completely before the next was added.

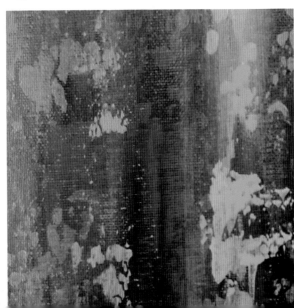

CRACKLE PASTE, A SPECIALTY GROUND

Crackle Paste is an unusual ground that has to be applied heavily and then allowed to cure for three days. As it is fragile, it must be used on a rigid substrate, in this case Masonite. The Crackle Paste was applied with a palette knife, and in the course of drying, these radiating cracks appeared. A finished painting using this ground can be seen on pages 36–37 in Using texture in paint.

Heavily applied Crackle Paste results in a dried pattern of dramatic spider-web cracks, creating a unique painting surface.

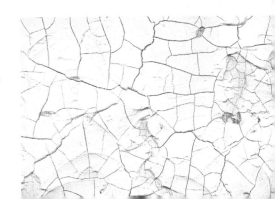

Flow release, varnishes, and drying extenders

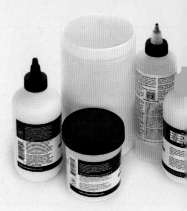

Fortunately for the artist, specialty products have been developed to make some of the standard characteristics of acrylic paints more versatile. Flow release permits delicate flowing lines to be painted easily in acrylics and also changes the way paint can be absorbed. Varnishes help minimize the harmful effects of ultraviolet rays and the tendency of acrylics to remain slightly absorbent after drying. Drying extenders lengthen the working time of the paint to allow easier blending of color on the painting.

FLOW RELEASE EXPLAINED

Flow release is a liquid product that is a surfactant, which means it reduces surface tension. Surface tension is what makes water hold the rounded shape of a dewdrop. Reducing surface tension makes it impossible to hold the normal rounded shape and water immediately flattens and flows.

Mixed with water and acrylic paint, flow release reduces the surface tension of the entire mixture, allowing our paint to flow smoothly and readily penetrate absorbent surfaces like watercolor paper and raw canvas. This creates stronger staining effects than paint alone can do (see right).

The lack of surface tension also allows thin and delicate lines to be painted, a task that can be quite challenging with heavy-body acrylics. Wonderfully fine detailing can be achieved using flow release.

FLOW RELEASE FOR STAINING

In this example, transparent Quinacridone Rose was used to demonstrate staining on heavy watercolor paper.

Without flow release Quinacridone Rose was painted directly on heavy watercolor paper. A fairly smooth blend appears and a ragged edge at the bottom shows the behavior of the paint.

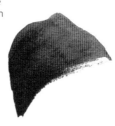

With flow release A similar swatch was painted with a water and flow release mixture added, according to the manufacturer's instructions. Notice the smooth blend and the greater depth of color achieved with the same amount of paint and the same brush on the same piece of paper.

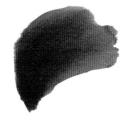

USING VARNISHES

Varnishes protect the completed painting by preventing dust and dirt from becoming embedded in the acrylic paint, which remains very slightly absorbent and sticky, even after drying. Some varnishes may also provide protection from ultraviolet rays.

Applying a layer of Soft Gel Medium mixed with a little water provides an additional protective layer between the paint and the varnish. After the gel has dried, a polymer acrylic varnish or an MSA varnish can be used. Polymer varnishes are the easiest to use but may be more difficult to remove later. For the most archival purposes, MSA varnish with UVLS (ultraviolet light stabilizers) is recommended.

MSA stands for Mineral Spirits Acrylic and has to be thinned in a ventilated area with either mineral spirits or turpentine. Do not even attempt to use it without the necessary ventilation. This varnish dries to a hard protective surface but can be removed with mineral spirits or turpentine if that is required later.

Varnishes can be matte, satin, or glossy, just like gel mediums. They also have the same opacifying effects because titanium dioxide is used to dull the gloss. If your painting has strong darks, a matte or satin varnish will lighten the look of those dark colors.

FLOW RELEASE FOR FINE LINES

Delicate detailing of fine lines, such as in small tree branches against the sky, or in the signature on a painting, can make artists mutter irritably at acrylic paint. Flow release offers a delightful solution to such difficulties.

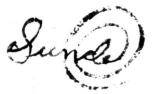

Without flow release No flow release was used in painting the author's name on heavy watercolor paper. Notice the breaks and skips in the lines.

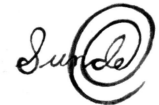

With flow release With a correctly mixed flow release solution, the signature becomes almost effortless to paint.

USING DRYING EXTENDERS

The quick-drying characteristics of acrylic paint can be either a delight or a frustration, depending on what you are trying to do. Use drying extenders if you want to work an area of paint into soft blends before it dries. They also keep the paint in better working condition on an ordinary palette if you have the misfortune to not be using a Sta-Wet palette (see page 123).

Drying extenders are available as an additive to be mixed with acrylic paint. Some paints are specifically formulated to be slower-drying straight from the tube, such as Golden's Open line of paints or the Winsor & Newton paints.

Drying extenders can be an excellent choice for painting skin tones. For this example, drying extender was mixed as an additive into regular heavy-body acrylic paints, but some Golden Open acrylics and Winsor & Newton acrylics were also used. Without drying extenders the soft, smooth glow of this young face would have been far more difficult to achieve.

A modified split-complementary palette was used. Quinacridone Rose opposes Chromium Oxide Green, Phthalo Green (Yellow Shade), and Naples Yellow Hue. Raw Umber was used for shadows and to partially neutralize some of the other colors. Titanium White completed this limited palette.

Quinacridone Rose   Chromium Oxide Green   Phthalo Green (Yellow Shade)

Naples Yellow Hue   Raw Umber   Titanium White

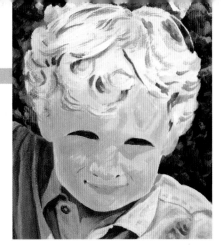

1 Use tints of Quinacridone Rose for the shirt, and tints of Quinacridone Rose and Naples Yellow Hue for the skin tones. Use Chromium Oxide Green with Raw Umber and a little Titanium White for the background hollyhocks. Use Quinacridone Rose and Titanium White for the flowers and Raw Umber for the darker shadows in the painting.

2 Develop the background foliage and flowers further with the same paints used in step 1, as well as a little Phthalo Green (Yellow Shade). Glaze the shirt with varying mixtures of Chromium Oxide Green, Raw Umber, and Titanium White. Allow a slight glow of the underlying Quinacridone Rose to remain visible. Paint tints of Raw Umber mixed with Quinacridone Rose into the hair for the darkest shadow areas.

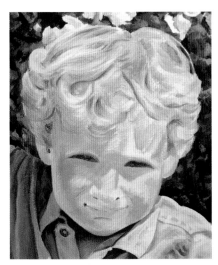

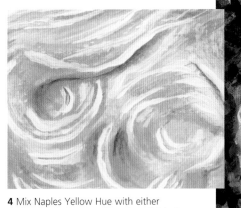

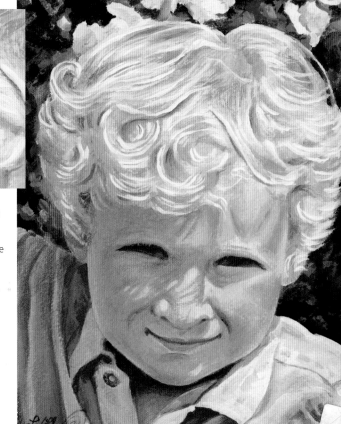

3 Paint tints of Naples Yellow Hue into the hair, softening the harsh shadows established earlier. Taking advantage of the slower drying times of the paints, tint blends of Quinacridone Rose, Naples Yellow Hue, and a little Chromium Oxide Green with Titanium White and work them into the face. After drying, use a stiff, flat brush to texture the hair with Regular Gel Medium.

4 Mix Naples Yellow Hue with either Quinacridone Rose or Chromium Oxide Green and add it to small amounts of Raw Umber to define the darker areas of the hair. Add highlights to the hair with Titanium White. The gel texture will help catch the paint, creating highlights that are almost white. Add more Quinacridone Rose to the lips and cheeks. Adjust the values in the face once more to complete the look of light falling across the child's face and paint your signature with flow release.

Wash properties

Acrylics are so versatile that they can be worked in a manner similar to both watercolors and oils. The softly blended washes characteristic of watercolor can be achieved with acrylics. Some differences do exist, so let's explore them.

While the differences between watercolor washes and acrylic paint washes are significant, careful control of the amount of water used is vital for success in both. Lots of water equals lots of flow in the paint and less water means more precise control in the movement of paint. Practice brings an understanding of water control, both in the brush and on the paper.

As would be expected, wash effects can certainly be used on watercolor paper but may also be applied to canvas with a thin ground that leaves the canvas slightly absorbent, or a special ground manufactured to be absorbent. Each of these produces results with different qualities. Paper is more absorbent than canvas and takes the paint with a greater depth. Textures also affect how the paint settles into the paper or canvas.

The most significant difference between watercolor and acrylics is the fact that acrylics dry permanently. They cannot be rewetted for additional changes like watercolor. This has advantages and disadvantages.

Additional wetting of the paper will not disturb a beautifully smooth dried wash in acrylics. If the paper is still somewhat absorbent, another wash can be applied over part or all of the first one. However, the more acrylic paint goes into the paper and dries, the less the paper is able to absorb water. When the paper becomes sealed with acrylic paint, no more wash effects can be absorbed.

Either opaque or semitransparent acrylic paints can be applied in washes. The semitransparent paints will most strongly resemble watercolor. Opaque acrylics can make excellent washes for backgrounds designed for additional detailed painting once they have dried.

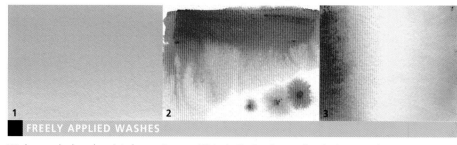

FREELY APPLIED WASHES

Washes can be loosely painted on wet paper. Water in the brush as well as in the paper has to be controlled, even for casual effects. Experimentation gives you the proper feel for it.

1 This example shows a simple wash of Phthalo Green (Yellow Shade) blending from darker at the top to lighter at the bottom of the heavy watercolor paper. The paper was wet enough to look shiny when the paint was applied at the top with a brush and then blended softly into the lower part.

2 An even wetter paper was used in this example of "shooting" in washes. Extremely wet paper allows paint to shoot out in all directions in the wet surface when a loaded brush touches the paper. This paper was lying flat and not tilted to get the Quinacridone Red paint to flow.

3 Three vertical bands of paint, Quinacridone Red, Hansa Yellow Light, and Phthalo Green (Yellow Shade), were allowed to blend together on a wet watercolor paper. The texture shown is a result of the paper texture allowing the paint to settle into the recesses. Smooth paper would give an evenly graduated blend if that were desired.

CONTROLLED WASH AREAS

Applying water to a carefully defined area on the paper allows wash effects to be used in specific areas without spilling into other areas of the painting. Painting the following example in different colors from your palette is a good way to practice. Notice the difference between using a really wet brush and a drier brush loaded with paint on the wet paper. Touching a brush to a paper towel quickly removes excess water for precise control.

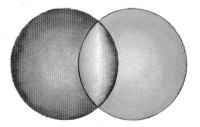

1 Dark pencil lines were used to draw the circles so they would show up clearly. The painted area of the left circle was wet with water before painting Quinacridone Red around the outer edge of the circle. Paint was blended to the center and then lifted in the middle with a paper towel touched to the surface to absorb excess paint and water. A dry brush can also be used for lifting paint in this way.

2 After drying, Phthalo Green (Yellow Shade) was applied in the right circle in the same way as the Quinacridone Red in the left circle. The wash of paint was applied with a smaller brush that left a coarser blend than the smoother wash on the left. Choosing the correct size brush for the effect you want also comes with practice.

3 Once again, the paper was left to completely dry before painting the next step. By now you know that wherever the water lies on the paper, the paint will follow. After precisely painting the football-shaped overlap with water, Quinacridone Red was laid along the right edge and Phthalo Green (Yellow Shade) on the left edge. They naturally blended together toward the middle.

USE THE RIGHT PAPER

For best results, always use 300 lb (638 gsm) high-quality watercolor paper that takes paint beautifully and resists buckling. This cannot be emphasized too much. Painting on thin, poor-quality watercolor paper often convinces the unfortunate artist they cannot handle water media on paper. All that has really happened is that they couldn't handle water media on paper that would be practically impossible for anyone to use.

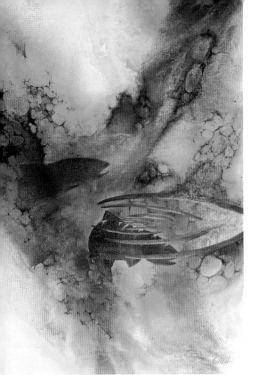

EXPLORING EXAMPLES OF WASH TECHNIQUES

Artists use wash effects in wonderfully varied ways to create compelling artworks with exceptional color. When you look at acrylic paintings, you may find it helpful to notice any wash effects and how they were used. Later, you can apply the effects you need to your own paintings.

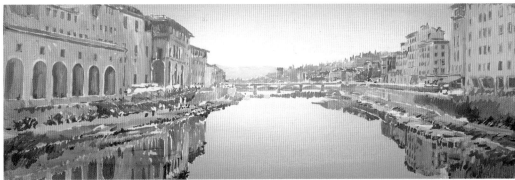

Morning on the Arno **Carol Carter**
Golden-orange washes dominate this serene painting on paper, a great contrast with Green Frenzy. Smoothly blended washes for the sky and water bring a sense of stillness to the scene. Controlled areas of wash effects were used in the buildings and final detail was added with a dry-brush technique over the washes.

Green Frenzy **Loren Kovich**
Wash effects in this painting were applied freely and loosely, allowing accidental blends of several colors. Washes on canvas appear different from washes on watercolor paper. In this painting, additional detail of stylized river rocks, fish, and ripples were painted over the acrylic wash background.

Floor Play **Linda McCord**
Just look at this painting to see what can be done with controlled areas of washes. Each goblet has multiple small washes painted in the colored tops and for the shadows falling across the floor. Some detail was painted with a dry brush, but the entire painting is really a rainbow array of carefully applied wash effects. These washes achieve the appearance of transparent glass and the movement of light through that glass.

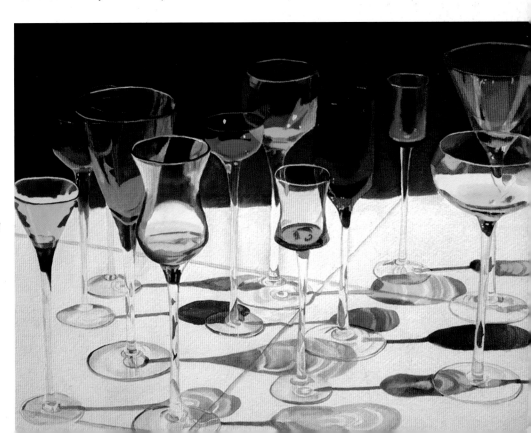

Using texture in paint

While acrylics can be used for wonderful wash effects, sometimes texture is what will give a painting the most impact. Using texture makes possible a different kind of depth and highlights. So, what are the ways we can create texture in acrylics and how can we use them to best advantage?

Heavy-body acrylics can be applied with coarse brushes or palette knives to create textural looks. Gels can be mixed into the paints to alter their texture further, as shown on pages 30–31. You can even mix sand into the paint to add texture.

These are all direct and straightforward ways to create texture in acrylics and they can be used to create enormously varied appearances. Your use of these textures is enhanced by the proper use of color and subject matter. If you are painting a smooth, serene sky, coarse texture may detract from the effect you want to create. But if you are working with more dramatically varied surfaces, texture can be an invaluable tool.

Texture can be created by methods other than mixing gels and sand into the paint. The ground used to prime the canvas or board itself can have additives to start with a textured surface for your painting. Specialty grounds are available that exist only to create unusual textures for paintings.

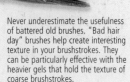

Never underestimate the usefulness of battered old brushes. "Bad hair day" brushes help create interesting texture in your brushstrokes. They can be particularly effective with the heavier gels that hold the texture of coarse brushstrokes.

CRACKLE PASTE AND PALETTE KNIFE

In this example, Crackle Paste and Heavy Gel Medium are applied with a palette knife to paint a leaf lying on a rough rock. The Crackle Paste was applied to the Masonite panel in the background rock area and allowed to cure. A section of it is shown on page 31.

Main palette
Raw Umber
Quinacridone Nickel Azo Gold
Hansa Yellow Light
Titanium White

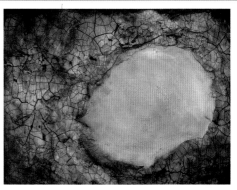

1 After three days of curing (see page 31), brush Raw Umber over the surface carefully and wipe the excess off the lighter areas with a paper towel. This allows Raw Umber to fill the cracks in the ground. Crackle Paste is an extremely fragile ground usable only on rigid substrates and as soon as the paint is dry, apply Soft Gel Medium and allow to dry in three successive coats to stabilize the surface.

GEL LAYERS FOR TEXTURE

An alternative texture is shown in a similar subject in this example. Cerulean Blue adds a complement to the Cadmium Orange, making stronger contrast possible in this painting.

Main palette
Raw Umber
Quinacridone Gold
Quinacridone Burnt Orange
Cadmium Orange Medium
Cerulean Blue
Titanium White

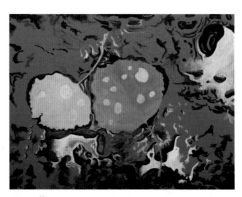

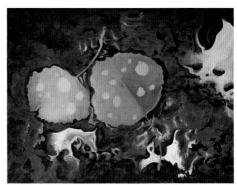

1 Apply a first layer of paint to a canvas with a colored ground using Raw Umber in gesso as shown on page 30. Raw Umber, tints of varying mixtures of Quinacridone Gold and Cadmium Orange Medium, and tints of Cerulean Blue form this paint layer. Notice how flat the painting looks at this stage.

2 Using a "bad hair day" brush (see left), apply a layer of Regular Gel Medium to the dirt and rock background, using brushstrokes to create texture in the desired patterns. After this plain gel layer is dry, apply another layer of paint with flat and round brushes. Add Quinacridone Burnt Orange to parts of the dirt and rock background.

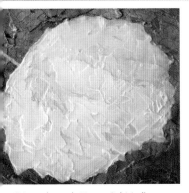

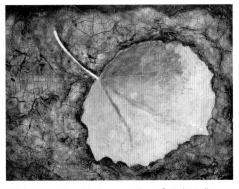

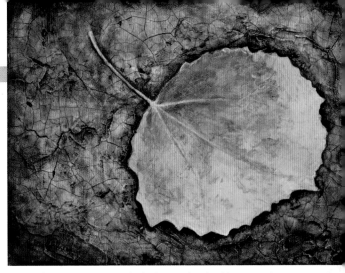

2 Loosely apply Heavy Gel Medium with a palette knife in the leaf area. By using a palette knife application for both the Crackle Paste on the rock background and the gel for the leaf, related textures are created.

3 Paint more Raw Umber over the Soft Gel Medium on the background rock. Underpaint the leaf with softly blended tints of Raw Umber, Quinacridone Nickel Azo Gold, and Hansa Yellow Light. Notice how the gel texture of the leaf adds interest to the blended colors, yet the leaf surface has a distinctly smoother look than the background rock because of those very same soft blends.

4 Make final adjustments to the background rock with Raw Umber. Add additional glazing to the leaf and stem with tints of Raw Umber, Quinacridone Nickel Azo Gold, and Hansa Yellow Medium. All of the texture in this painting was created prior to adding paint layers.

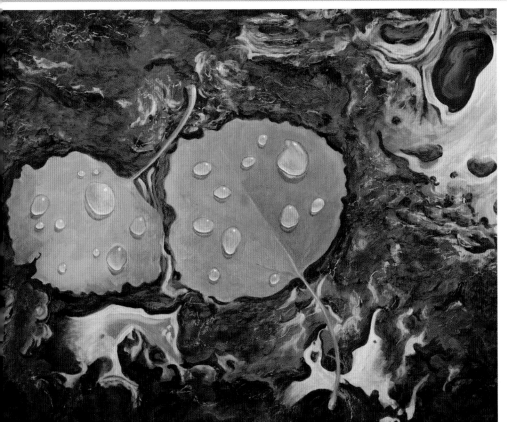

3 After the paint is dry, apply a second layer of Regular Gel Medium with the "bad hair day" brush, taking care to create new patterns of texture over the previous layers. After drying, drag colored highlights over the peaks of the texture with a flat brush. Using multiple layers of gel texture that change with each layer alternated with partial paint layers allows a rich appearance to develop. Leave the leaves and water smooth, and complete the water drops to contrast with the busy background texture.

■ BE VERSATILE WITH TEXTURE

Experiment with different textures combined with the color effects suitable for the subjects of your paintings. Trying various approaches to texture will develop them into natural tools in your arsenal of painting techniques. You will find that selecting a texturing method becomes easy and spontaneous as you continue to practice.

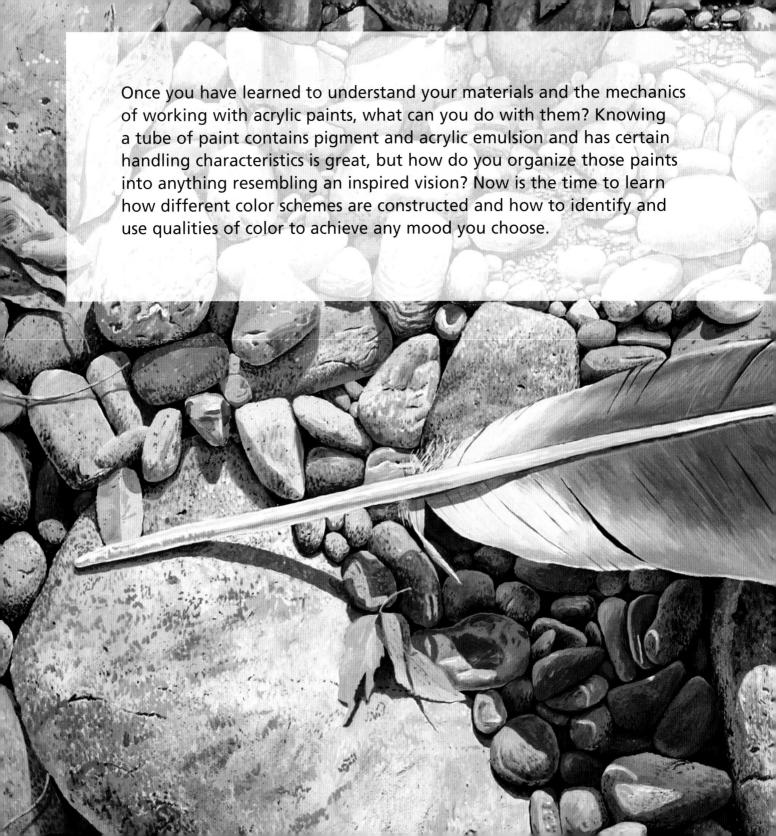

Once you have learned to understand your materials and the mechanics of working with acrylic paints, what can you do with them? Knowing a tube of paint contains pigment and acrylic emulsion and has certain handling characteristics is great, but how do you organize those paints into anything resembling an inspired vision? Now is the time to learn how different color schemes are constructed and how to identify and use qualities of color to achieve any mood you choose.

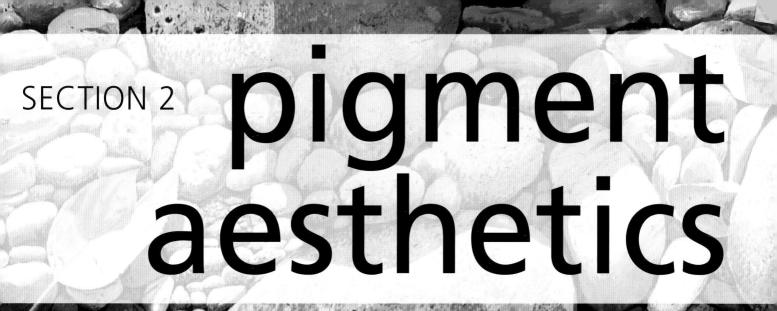

SECTION 2
pigment aesthetics

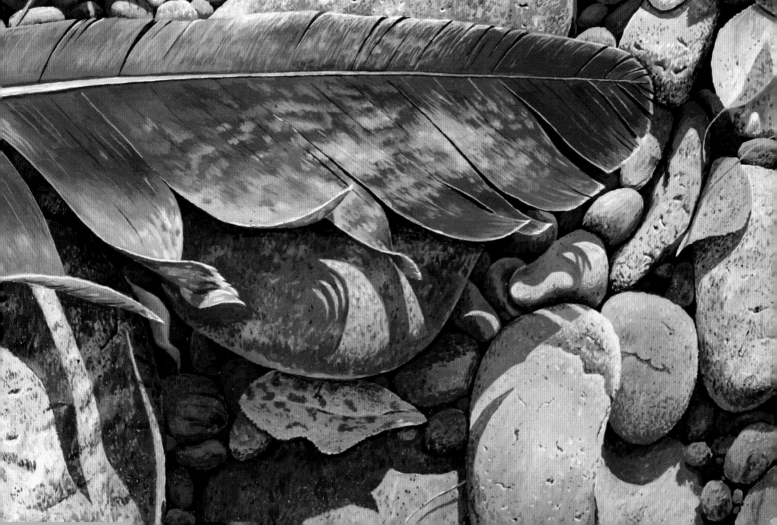

Mixing color on the palette

Mixing color is the key to painting well, but managing an acrylic palette poses some challenges. How to arrange a palette, how to control the pigment mixtures, and how to take proper care of a palette all are important considerations for the artist. So what are some of the best ways to handle a palette?

If necessary you can use a simple paper plate for a palette. Some artists prefer a piece of glass or a butcher's metal tray. But for acrylics, one choice stands out as the most user-friendly solution, the Sta-Wet palette.

The Sta-Wet palette is a lidded plastic tray that holds a thin flat sponge with a sheet of palette paper laid on top of it. Water wicks from the sponge through the paper into the paints placed on the paper. If the piles of paint are fairly shallow and not heaped like

Mount Everest they stay beautifully moist and actually last a couple of weeks or so.

Acrylic paints dry so fast they usually gum up rapidly on other palettes, and "skin"—that horrible dried crust on top of the wet paint. A Sta-Wet palette does not dry out, and if the paints are sitting with the lid removed for an extended time, a gentle mist of water sprayed over the paints keeps them in great shape.

PHYSICAL MIXING: PRIMARY PALETTE

In this example, the three primary colors are placed on the palette and mixed until twelve colors are available. Please note that the colors are placed in a circle on the palette only for your convenience in this book to relate them to the Sundell Color Wheel (see page 17). If this palette was intended for actual use instead of

demonstrating mixing, the paints would be arranged around the outside edge of the palette to allow extra mixing room in the middle. A pile of Titanium White would also be placed in the middle of the palette because it is mixed with nearly everything during the course of a painting.

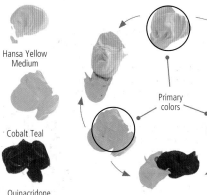

Hansa Yellow Medium

Cobalt Teal

Quinacridone Rose

Primary colors

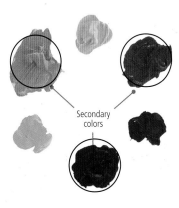

Secondary colors

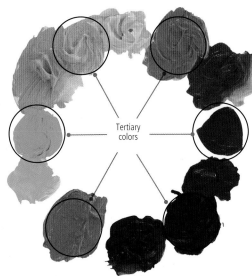

Tertiary colors

Primary colors: Yellow, magenta, and cyan are the standard primary colors from the pigment-mixing color wheel. The ones above are featured in the Sundell Color Wheel for those placements.

Mixing primaries: The secondary colors will be mixed from the primaries. A little pile of each primary has been added to the appropriate placements for the secondary colors. Notice the piles of yellow are larger than the others. Yellow pigments have low tinting strength compared to other pigments, so it takes more yellow to create a balanced mixture. In fact, more yellow will be added during mixing for this reason.

Six-color palette: The piles of paint have been mixed with a stiff, flat brush to make the three secondary colors: red-orange, blue-violet, and a yellow-green. Use a brush instead of a palette knife to reduce the chance of tearing the paper palette. If a hard palette is used, a palette knife works well for mixing.

Twelve-color palette: The tertiary colors—the six colors that fall between the primaries and secondaries—have now been mixed. For each tertiary color, the primary on one side has been mixed with the secondary on the other side. Notice how this approximates the Sundell Color Wheel. A twelve-color palette has now been mixed from the three primary colors.

PHYSICAL MIXING: SIX-COLOR PALETTE

For the six-color palette, the single-pigment paints in the primary and secondary placements on the Sundell Color Wheel have been used (see below). These are all the main colors pictured in the Sundell Color Wheel.

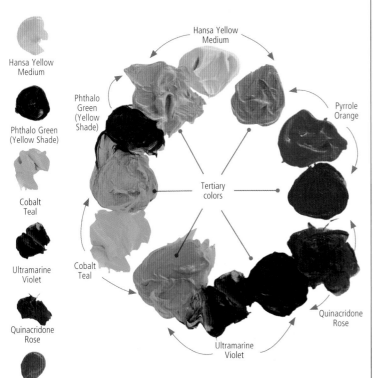

Hansa Yellow Medium

Phthalo Green (Yellow Shade)

Cobalt Teal

Ultramarine Violet

Quinacridone Rose

Pyrrole Orange

Hansa Yellow Medium

Phthalo Green (Yellow Shade)

Pyrrole Orange

Tertiary colors

Cobalt Teal

Quinacridone Rose

Ultramarine Violet

Once again, the tertiary colors have been mixed from the adjacent primaries and secondaries. Notice how much brighter this palette appears than the twelve colors mixed from only the three primary colors (see opposite). Combining pigments reduces chroma, so these single-pigment secondaries are brighter than the mixed secondaries in the primary palette. This makes a good visual example of how the twelve single-pigment paints chosen for the Sundell Color Wheel provide the maximum possible chroma range.

ARRANGING YOUR PALETTE

The best way to arrange the paints on your palette is the way that is most convenient for you for the subject you have chosen. The paints can be arranged on the outside edge of the palette like a rainbow progression of color. However, it may be easier to place colors that you intend to mix a lot next to each other. Colors that will be used extensively should be allowed more room than colors that will only be used occasionally in the painting. White often works best in the middle where it is accessible in all directions.

MIXING NEUTRALS ON THE PALETTE

Sometimes a painting will require a neutral created from a pair of complementary colors in a varied range of mixtures. Mixing color on the palette can make this more easily controllable. This same process can be used for mixing adjacent colors instead of complementary colors.

▶ Ultramarine Violet on the left is mixed in varying degrees with Hansa Yellow Medium on the right. You can pick up any desired variation with your brush and take it to the canvas quickly and easily when the paint is laid on the palette in a range of mixtures like this one.

▶ Since tints of Titanium White are frequently used in painting, adding Titanium White to the range of mixtures can be helpful. Sometimes unevenly mixed colors are desirable for interest in a painting, as shown here in some of the mixed white combinations. If an even mixture is desired, it can, of course, be created on the palette with additional mixing action.

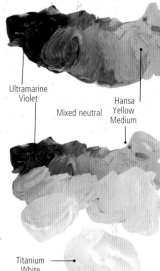

Ultramarine Violet

Mixed neutral

Hansa Yellow Medium

Titanium White

PALETTE CARE

Proper care and cleaning of the palette makes it far easier to focus on the painting instead of complications with the palette itself. Struggling with a palette is an unnecessary waste of time and energy.

▶ After a while, even the best-quality palette deteriorates into a used mess. The one at right was used for three paintings. The waffle pattern comes from the sponge underneath. If that disturbs you, place the sponge smooth side up. Either way works. When the palette is ready for cleaning and renewal like this one, discard the paper palette sheet, clean the sponge if it is still good, and add a new paper palette sheet.

▼ Sponges eventually decay. The one below is stained from lots of use. When left too long, a wet palette grows mold, which turns the sponge into an unpleasant slime. Rinse the sponge in water with borax and a few drops of bleach, then add a few drops of bleach to the water held in the sponge to prevent mold. It only takes a tiny amount of bleach to kill microbes, and permanent pigments remain impervious to bleach. Larger amounts of bleach will, however, make the sponge and paper disintegrate. Borax is a household laundry soap sold as a powder and is available in grocery stores.

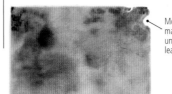

Moldy sponge material washes away under running water, leaving holes.

A badly deteriorated palette needs to have the sponge cleaned or replaced and a new palette paper inserted.

Mixing color wet-into-wet

Mixing color wet-into-wet is a direct and immediate way to manipulate paint that can be greatly satisfying. Most artists use this method in some or all of their work. While creating watercolor effects is covered in Wash properties (see page 34), in this section we will explore ways to mix more textural effects wet-into-wet.

Applying color to the canvas or paper and then adding another color and starting to mix them directly is a great way to create lively brushwork and textures in your paintings. Some of the most exciting painterly effects are achieved by painting wet-into-wet. Getting comfortable with the process allows you to paint with immediacy and strengthens your skill as an artist.

After picking up one color of paint from your palette with a brush and applying it to an area of the canvas, you might want to either wipe the paint off the bristles with a paper towel or use another brush to pick up the next color to avoid leaving unwanted color mixed into the second color on the palette.

Color can be mixed thoroughly on the canvas to make a smooth blend or it can be left partially mixed and show brushstrokes for a painterly effect. Other colors can be added, but combining too many different pigments will make gray or black. Two colors mix well and sometimes a third can be added for emphasis or neutralizing. Mixing more than three colors gets unwieldy. Titanium White is not usually counted as one of those colors as it can be used to make lighter tints with any mixtures.

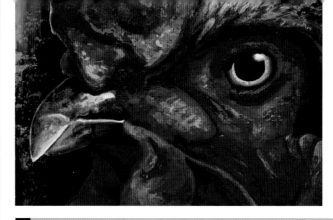

This detail from Royal Rooster *shows the rich color effects possible from mixing wet-into-wet. Almost all the painting in this detail was done in that manner, except for the blue-violet accents added after drying. The comb, face, and wattles used Permanent Red, Cadmium Orange Medium, Quinacridone Rose, Anthraquinone Red, Indanthrone Blue, and Titanium White.*

MIXING TWO PIGMENTS

The following examples show two colors being mixed wet-into-wet on heavy watercolor paper. Each step was photographed during the mixing process to show the lively way in which the look changes with this direct approach.

As a simple example, Cobalt Teal is mixed with Titanium White in a soft blend.

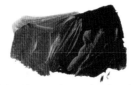

Quinacridone Magenta was heavily applied and a little Hansa Yellow Medium mixed directly into it, leaving distinct brushstrokes of the yellow paint throughout.

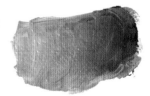

For a more textural look, Hansa Yellow Medium is thickly applied and partially mixed into Phthalo Green (Blue Shade), providing a graduation of color across the swatch. The flat Taklon brush effectively moves the thick paint and mixes it further.

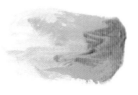

While still wet, more Cobalt Teal is brushed into the previous blend, adding stronger value contrasts and painterly brushstrokes for emphasis.

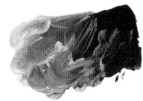

Additional Hansa Yellow Medium is added. Larger quantities of the lower tinting strength yellow are needed to make a brighter mix with the Quinacridone Magenta.

Working the paint with the flat brush blends it more evenly and makes the texture much less pronounced.

MIXING THREE PIGMENTS

Mixing three pigments, particularly if two of them are complements, can produce neutralized grays. Titanium White can further modify the resulting mixtures.

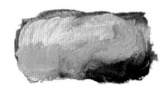

The swatch is first painted with Quinacridone Gold tinted with Titanium White. Phthalo Green (Yellow Shade) is painted in the lower right corner and blended upward and across with Titanium White.

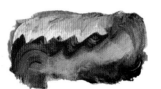

Quinacridone Rose, the complement to Phthalo Green (Yellow Shade) is painted into the wet mixture. Some neutralizing toward gray is visible in the brushstrokes.

MIXING TWO COLORS WITH A TINT

Another common need in mixing color wet-into-wet is to create lighter tints of the mixture. In the following examples, Titanium White is used. Zinc White is not as strong in tinting strength and is not as opaque. Buff Titanium would create a lower-chroma tint.

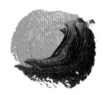

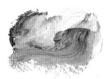

Indanthrone Blue, an intense pigment with great tinting strength, has Hansa Yellow Medium mixed into the left and across the middle, without a lot of effect on the powerful dark value of the Indanthrone Blue.

Yellow Ocher meets Raw Umber in this swatch painted in earth tones.

Cobalt Blue and Titanium White are painted in an irregular mixture showing brushstrokes and strong value contrasts.

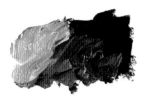

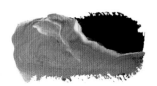

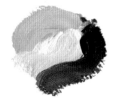

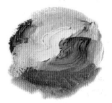

Quinacridone Violet is mixed in a loosely graduated blend with Titanium White. Brushstrokes are left clearly visible.

By adding Titanium White to the area where the Hansa Yellow Medium was added, the mixture is greatly lightened and we see a blue-green cast to the color.

Titanium White added to the Yellow Ocher lightens it. The white is also used to alter the values in the Raw Umber. A patch of nearly white paint divides the Raw Umber from the lightened Yellow Ocher.

The mixing wet-into-wet continues with Cobalt Blue and Titanium White. Heavier texture appears in the swatch.

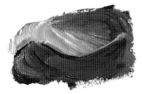

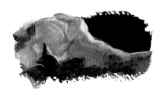

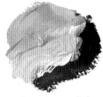

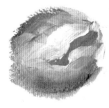

For a different look, more Titanium White is added, reducing values in the swatch but still keeping the loose brushstrokes visible. Then Quinacridone Rose is applied across the bottom half in a slightly more smoothly blended area of color.

More Indanthrone Blue is added to the lighter mixture to add contrasting values in the brushstrokes.

Additional Yellow Ocher is applied to add a painterly effect in the brushwork.

Ultramarine Violet is painted into the wet swatch, giving a new look to the mixture.

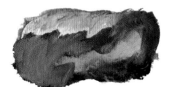

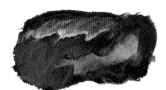

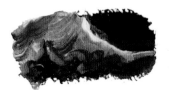

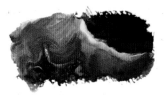

The brush is used to blend the Quinacridone Rose into a neutralized gray. More Phthalo Green (Yellow Shade) is added during the process.

To increase the contrast of the complements, Quinacridone Rose is painted across most of the wet Quinacridone Gold tint. The neutralized gray area somewhat subdues the complementary contrast of Quinacridone Rose and Phthalo Green (Yellow Shade).

Pyrrole Orange is liberally applied to the wet swatch of Indanthrone Blue with a tint of Hansa Yellow Medium shown in the previous section on mixing two colors with a tint. Pyrrole Orange is the complement of Indanthrone Blue.

Additional mixing with the flat brush produces some neutralized grays in the swatch.

Mixing color with layers and glazes

One of the most outstanding effects of acrylic paints is the glowing luminosity that can be created with glaze mediums and thin layers of paint. The action of light moving through multiple semitransparent layers can be magical. By patiently adding layer upon layer of these glazes, an amazing richness emerges on the canvas.

Since acrylic paint needs to be applied heavily enough to dry into a durable film, thinning paint with water to apply a thin layer of color can have disastrous results. The paint tends to be too thin to form a film during drying and can be rubbed away by accident in handling.

To avoid this, artists use an acrylic glazing medium or gel medium to thin the paint (see page 30). Most of the mediums on the market are slightly white before they dry to a clear film, so correctly estimating the strength of the color during mixing requires

a little practice. Fortunately, the process of building a depth of color through multiple layers of glazes works well with pale mixtures that gradually appear richer and darker as multiple layers are added. This gives the ability to easily control the stopping point when the color has reached the desired intensity.

Matte or satin glazes and mediums contain titanium and they are slightly opaque, even when dry. Using glossy glazes or mediums eliminates this effect. If a matte or satin final surface is wanted, varnish can be used to accomplish it without as much interference to the clear depth of the accumulated layers.

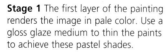

PAINTING WITH LAYERS AND GLAZES

A glance at the placement of the palette selections for this painting and where they fall on the Sundell Color Wheel (see page 17) reveals a tetradic palette (see page 60). The only exception is with Raw Umber, a paint used in small amounts to neutralize green mixtures in the painting. This particular color combination works extremely well with the natural colors of the flower and leaves in the painting.

| Ultramarine Violet | Dioxazine Purple | Quinacridone Rose | Phthalo Green (Yellow Shade) | Hansa Yellow Medium | Raw Umber | Titanium White |

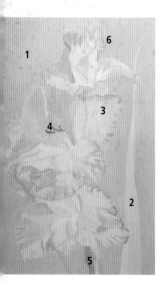

Stage 1 The first layer of the painting renders the image in pale color. Use a gloss glaze medium to thin the paints to achieve these pastel shades.

1 Use Ultramarine Violet for the background.

2 Phthalo Green (Yellow Shade) establishes the leaves and stem.

3 Quinacridone Rose and Ultramarine Violet form the petals with a few splashes of Hansa Yellow Medium.

4 Paint the stamens in Ultramarine Violet that has not been thinned in glaze medium.

5 In this initial layer, some of the green areas of the stem and leaves are darker, since they will be in shadow in the final painting.

6 A few edges of the petals have a stronger colored edge as well because that is characteristic of this flower.

Stage 2 Continue painting with the previous glaze mixtures and develop the forms of the flower and leaves further. Use as many layers as you need without rushing the increase of color. This stage of the painting is fairly ugly, which is sometimes necessary. Building layers may require steps that are individually unattractive, but as other color is applied, the value of those foundation layers becomes evident.

1 Include a tiny amount of Raw Umber in the shadows of the leaves and stem.

2 In the background, introduce glazed layers of Hansa Yellow Medium, alternating with the Ultramarine Violet layers to partially neutralize the Ultramarine Violet.

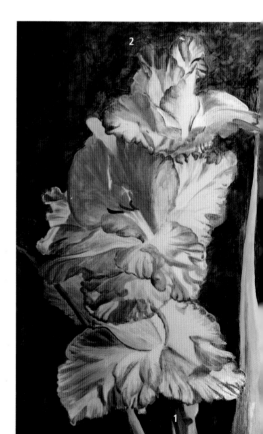

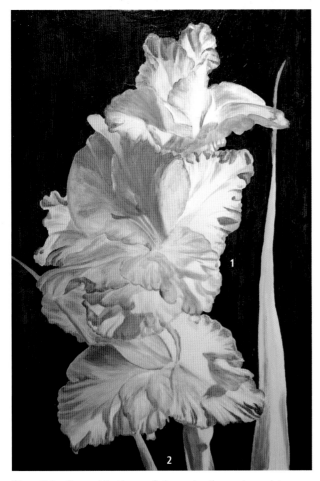

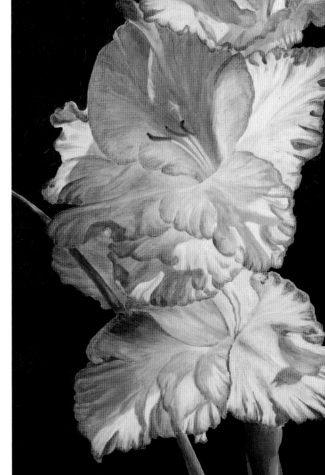

Stage 3 Continue adding layers of glaze using the previous mixtures. The values in the flowers need to be defined with multiple layers of glaze. The leaves take on a smoother glowing look.

1 Create a dramatic shift in the background by switching to Dioxazine Purple. This pigment is powerful and dark, so keep it thinned in the glaze medium and apply it in vertical strokes over the uneven Ultramarine

Violet and Hansa Yellow Medium layers. Allow a little of those prior layers to show so that the background has some life to it.

2 Add more blended layers of Dioxazine Purple to create rich, dark shadow across the bottom of the background. This helps bring the painting closer to the intended final appearance.

Stage 4 Continue developing the glazes as described at right to complete the painting. Some artists work with 20, 30, or even more layers of these glazes, so do experiment. The radiance that results is not matched by any other technique.

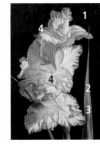

1 Continue developing the depth in the background with more Dioxazine Purple. Then apply a glaze of Hansa Yellow Medium over the background.

2 Complete the leaves with delicately applied glazes of Phthalo Green (Yellow Shade) mixed with a little Raw Umber.

3 For the final highlights in the leaves, a slight tint of the Phthalo Green (Yellow Shade)

and Raw Umber mixture can be painted in soft streaks that follow the form of the leaves and stem.

4 Bring the blends of the flowers into dramatic contrast by deepening the Ultramarine Violet shadows and the strong Quinacridone Rose edges on the petals. The Hansa Yellow Medium splashes of yellow blend into the petal edges and the shadows.

For a few areas of the flowers, particularly the upper flower, mix Hansa Yellow Medium with Quinacridone Rose into glazes for the petal areas that have an orange color cast.

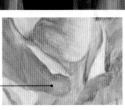

Add a sharp emphasis to the petal edges with either Quinacridone Rose or Quinacridone Rose mixed with a little Hansa Yellow Medium.

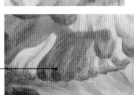

Comparison of color schemes

Artists who first begin to learn about color schemes are often surprised to learn that the paintings they most admire follow specific color schemes. Using paints selected by their placement and relationships on the color wheel evokes distinctive harmonies and emotions. So how do you employ these color schemes in your own work?

1 **To create a specific mood or atmosphere through the controlled use of color.**
By selecting a suitable color scheme, the colors that most easily create a certain mood or atmosphere can be emphasized to their best advantage in the painting.

COLOR SCHEMES OVERVIEW

Monochromatic color scheme	Complementary color scheme
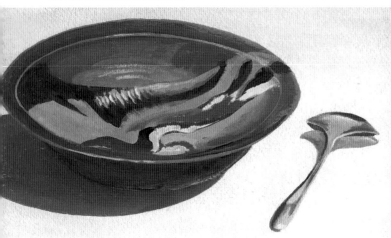	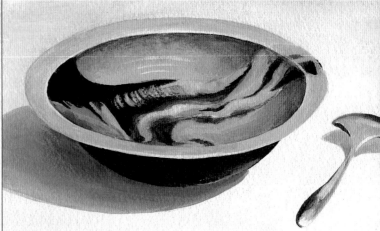

Ultramarine Blue

Titanium White

A monochromatic color scheme uses a single paint from the Sundell Color Wheel (see page 17) plus Titanium White for tinting.

The monochromatic color scheme is invaluable for exploring value in a painting. The ability to perceive light and its reflective behaviors comes into sharp focus when painting with an emphasis on values.

When using a dark pigment with powerful tinting strength, such as the Ultramarine Blue used here, you can create a great range of values. A pigment such as Hansa Yellow Light provides a much narrower range of values, since that pigment cannot go darker in value than the mid-range on the value scale.

Blue

Cadmium Orange Medium   Ultramarine Blue   Titanium White

A complementary color scheme offers the strongest contrast possible, since it uses colors opposite each other on the Sundell Color Wheel. Opposing colors also neutralize each other when mixed, which allows useful variations in chroma.

By using only two opposing colors in the painting, one of them can be emphasized to create mood in a highly specific way. In this example, Cadmium Orange Medium dominates and is supported by Ultramarine Blue. Modify the Ultramarine Blue by mixing with small amounts of Cadmium Orange Medium to neutralize it, or tint with Titanium White.

For further explorations, paint with Ultramarine Blue as the dominant color. Try other pairs of complements from the Sundell Color Wheel. Remember the list of substitute colors on page 17 adds even more possible combinations to test.

Orange

Blue

2 **To create a color harmony throughout the painting by the use of a limited palette.**
By using a clearly related and limited palette, the resulting mixtures in the painting maintain a natural color harmony. No discordant hues appear in the work.

3 **To use color schemes to deeply explore hue and chroma relationships.**
Discover how certain hues in a color scheme can be emphasized and how other hues in that same color scheme can support that emphasis. Mixtures that alter chroma play into this dynamic in the painting as well.

4 **To use color schemes to deeply explore value relationships.**
By using extremely limited color schemes, such as a monochromatic color scheme, working with the paint becomes a process of establishing and refining values. Some artists use this as a basis for developing the first layer of a painting, applying a wider color range later in the work.

5 **To develop a more powerful use of the full palette by understanding the nuances of relationships used in color schemes.**
An informed understanding of the full palette comes after thorough exploration of color schemes. Certain aspects of color relationships from color schemes begin to naturally arise when using the full palette, making the painting more effective.

Analogous color scheme

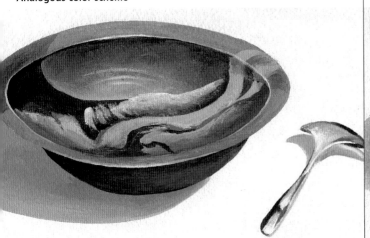

| Ultramarine Violet | Ultramarine Blue | Cobalt Teal | Titanium White |

An analogous color scheme employs three to four adjacent placements on the Sundell Color Wheel. This example shows Ultramarine Violet, Ultramarine Blue, and Cobalt Teal. Using adjacent colors makes a smooth color harmony without any complementary contrasts. Value contrasts, however, are vital to the success of an analogous painting.

Cool or warm colors may be chosen to establish mood. In this case, cool colors are dominant. Consider how this painting would look if painted with a warm trio of Hansa Yellow Medium, Cadmium Orange Medium, and Pyrrole Orange. For further study, try a series of paintings using different sets of analogous colors.

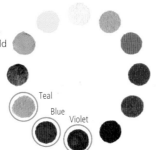

Six-color scheme

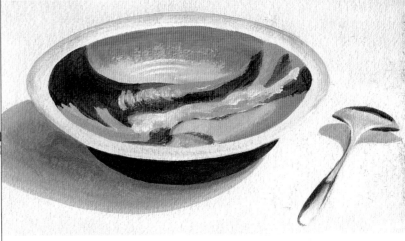

| Hansa Yellow Medium | Pyrrole Orange | Quinacridone Rose | Ultramarine Violet | Cobalt Teal | Phthalo Green (Yellow Shade) | Titanium White |

A six-color scheme uses a palette of the three primary colors plus the secondary placements midway between them. This means three pairs of complementary colors are included, making a variety of neutrals possible. This color scheme has less natural harmony inherent in the color selections than the more limited-palette color schemes.

In this example, some neutrals are mixed and tinted, but strong color is emphasized. By using more neutrals, a much more subtle painting can be created. Try variations in the amount of neutrals used and in the choice of high-chroma color emphasis. This color scheme gives an enormous range of possibilities.

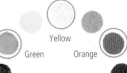

Primary color scheme

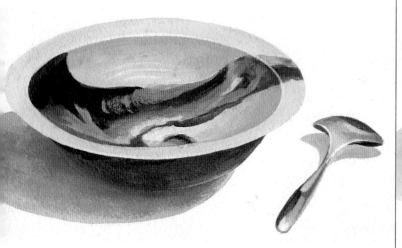

| Hansa Yellow Medium | Quinacridone Rose | Cobalt Teal | Titanium White |

A primary color scheme consists of the three pigment primaries. These high-chroma paints provide an extensive range of mixing options. Keeping the palette limited to three colors maintains a harmony throughout all the potential mixtures.

This example combines Hansa Yellow Medium, Quinacridone Rose, and Cobalt Teal with Titanium White for tinting. Try a series of paintings that each emphasize a different primary with varied mixtures of the supporting primaries. This can be a rewarding exercise in color play.

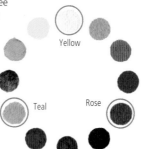

Yellow

Teal   Rose

Split-complementary color scheme

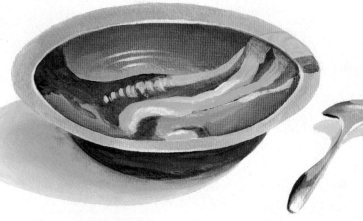

| Quinacridone Rose | Phthalo Green (Blue Shade) | Phthalo Green (Yellow Shade) | Bismuth Yellow | Titanium White |

A split-complementary color scheme is a combination of the complementary and analogous palettes. Three adjacent colors and the complement of the middle color are selected from the Sundell Color Wheel. Neutrals can be achieved with this palette by mixing the complementary pair. This lovely color scheme brings a harmony with the analogous colors accented by the vibrant contrast of the complement.

With twelve adjacent trios and their middle complements available, you can explore a host of possibilities in a series of paintings. The number of options increases dramatically when you also use substitute colors from the list on page 17.

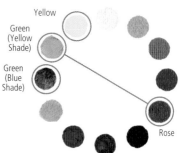

Yellow

Green (Yellow Shade)

Green (Blue Shade)

Rose

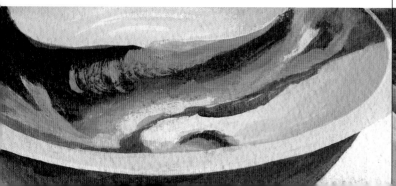

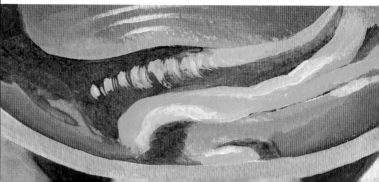

Tetradic color scheme

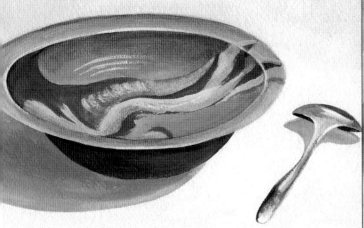

| Cadmium Orange Medium | Quinacridone Rose | Ultramarine Blue | Phthalo Green (Yellow Shade) | Titanium White |

A tetradic color scheme is particularly distinctive because it employs two pairs of complements that are separated by at least one placement on the Sundell Color Wheel. This unusual set of color relationships may be difficult to use unless one color is chosen as the dominant color.

While tricky to master, the results can be visually arresting in ways other color schemes do not accomplish. Try using one tetradic color scheme in four separate paintings, each emphasizing a different color within it. Then try another selection of tetradic colors and do another series of four paintings. Remember, the list of substitutes on page 17 also expands your options.

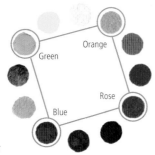

Orange
Green
Rose
Blue

Tertiary color scheme

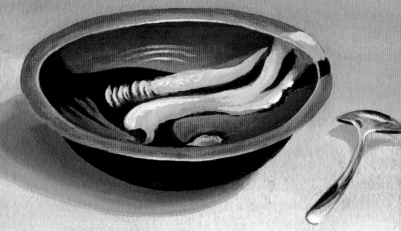

     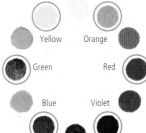

| Cadmium Orange Medium | Naphthol Red Medium | Quinacridone Violet | Ultramarine Blue | Phthalo Green (Blue Shade) | Bismuth Yellow | Titanium White |

A tertiary color scheme is made up of the colors between the primary and secondary placements on the Sundell Color Wheel. This makes another distinctive palette. Like the six-color palette, it includes three pairs of complements, offering a good range of neutrals as well as the lively contrasts of the complements themselves.

Due to the diverse colors in this palette, emphasizing one color or one pair of colors helps make the palette work well. In this example, Naphthol Red Medium is the most pronounced color used but mixtures of the other colors, particularly the neutrals, make a melodious supporting palette. Explore as many different options with this palette as you can imagine, extending your understanding of these color relationships.

Yellow
Orange
Green
Red
Blue
Violet

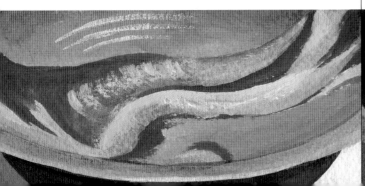

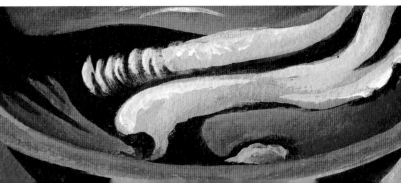

Primary palette

A primary palette—three basic colors that can mix all the other colors—sounds simple enough. In practice, this proves to be far more complex.

Additive color describes how light mixes to create brighter and brighter colors until becoming white, and subtractive color describes how pigments mix, absorbing more and more light until enough combined pigments become black. This is described in more detail on page 9.

Because additive color becomes increasingly brighter, the primaries are darker hues, as mixing them creates the brighter hues. Mixing the brighter hues cannot create darker hues in additive color. The opposite holds true for subtractive color, resulting in two different sets of primary colors.

Yellow, magenta, and cyan are the primaries in the Sundell Color Wheel.

Once we start working with actual pigments, the subject becomes even more complicated. The idea behind primary colors is that they cannot be broken down further because they are the most basic colors. With that in mind, all single-pigment paints could legitimately be considered primary colors, since no single-pigment paint can be broken down any further.

The important principle to keep in mind is that mixing single-pigment paints adjacent to each other on the color wheel is going to result in brighter colors than mixing multiple-pigment paints, due to the subtractive nature of pigment color.

To properly understand color handling it is helpful to start with minimal palettes and discover with practical experience how they work. Mixing the three primaries of yellow, magenta, and cyan teaches us a great deal. Refer back to page 40 in Mixing color on palette to see the three paints from the primary positions on the Sundell Color Wheel sequentially mixed to create a palette of twelve colors. Try this for yourself and then create a painting with that palette.

Hansa Yellow Medium

Quinacridone Rose

Cobalt Teal

PRIMARY PALETTE AND SUBTRACTIVE COLOR

In order to work effectively with our primary palette of yellow, magenta, and cyan, we have to clearly understand how subtractive color works in the pigment color wheel. Since our paint does not radiate light but reflects it, the pigment color wheel works quite differently from the light color wheel. Paint absorbs all the light except the wavelengths of light that our eyes and brain translate into color.

Magenta paint absorbs all of the wavelengths except the ones we see as magenta. This is true for all other hues.

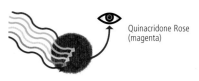

Quinacridone Rose (magenta)

When we mix magenta and cyan paints, not only does the mixture turn blue-violet, but this blue-violet is not as bright as the magenta and cyan paints separately. This is because when magenta paint is mixed into cyan, it still absorbs everything but the magenta hue, including some of the cyan hue the cyan paint would reflect if it wasn't mixed in with the magenta, and vice versa.

Quinacridone Rose + Cobalt Teal = Blue-Violet

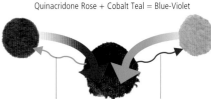

When mixed, each of the hues absorb a little of the other, making the result less bright.

The more pigments you add to the mixture, the more light will be absorbed in the mixture. If you add enough different pigments, the mixture turns black because all of the light will be absorbed, or subtracted. In this example, yellow has been added to magenta and cyan, which makes a dull, neutralized color that is not yet black.

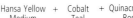

Hansa Yellow Medium + Cobalt Teal + Quinacridone Rose = neutral

USING A PRIMARY PALETTE TO MIX NEUTRAL GRAYS

Bern Sundell used the capability of a three-primary palette in mixing neutral grays to good advantage in *Leather and Steel*. Yet he used enough colorful accents as well as variations in the neutrals to keep the painting rich and interesting instead of dull and lifeless. Notice that the gray background is not left flat and expressionless either but shifts according to the light.

Main palette
Hansa Yellow Medium, Quinacridone Magenta, Cerulean Blue, and Titanium White

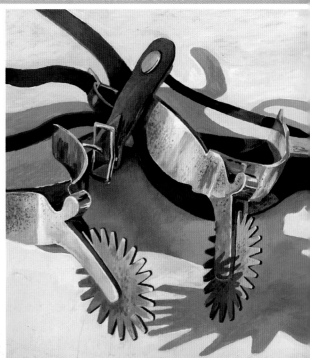

WHY USE ONLY THREE PRIMARIES?

With the wonderful array of paints available, why would you want to limit yourself to only three paints? Actually, there are some excellent reasons to do so.

• Achieve a deep understanding of how those three paints mix without being distracted by other colors and their effects, which may be surprising.
• Create a color harmony in your painting that comes from using closely related mixtures.
• Focus on learning to handle values without being distracted by myriad paint-mixing complications.
• Learn to create simple and direct effects.
• Sequentially explore different primary combinations by substituting primaries from the list on page 17 and gain a deep understanding of those alternative mixtures.

Or, best of all, you may want to just paint something wonderful with minimal complexity. Sometimes the greatest mastery is found in the greatest simplicity.

COLOR WHEEL MIXED WITH JUST THREE PRIMARIES

Yellow, magenta, and cyan are the primaries in the Sundell Color Wheel. The specific paints chosen for those placements are shown at right, which are all single-pigment paints. See page 17 for more on the Sundell Color Wheel.

To experiment with variations of this particular primary palette, you can consult the list of substitutes on page 17 and try different combinations of primaries. For example, if Cerulean Blue (also a single-pigment paint) is used instead of Cobalt Teal, the blue becomes much stronger, as shown in the example left.

It is not recommended to use multiple-pigment paints for primaries in a three-primary palette, as the resulting mixtures will lose more brilliance than if single-pigment paints were used.

Quinacridone Rose + Cerulean Blue = **blue-violet** (secondary color)

Quinacridone Rose + blue-violet (i.e. the above mix) = **red-violet** (tertiary color)

Blue-Violet (i.e. the top mix) + Cerulean Blue = **blue** (tertiary color)

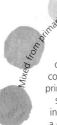
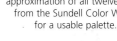
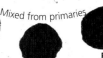

1 Yellow Hansa Yellow Medium

Primary

Mixed from primaries

Mixed from primaries

By using the instructions in Mixing color on the palette on page 40 for mixing a twelve-color palette from the three Sundell primary paints and placing the mixed secondaries and mixed tertiaries in their appropriate placements on a color wheel, we see a reasonable approximation of all twelve colors from the Sundell Color Wheel for a usable palette.

Primary

3 Cyan Cobalt Teal

Mixed from primaries

2 Magenta Quinacridone Rose

Blue

Blue-violet

Red violet

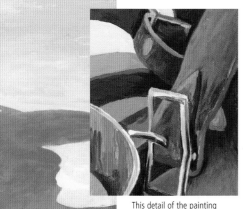

This detail of the painting reveals some of the color effects used in the metal to give the reflective quality of the material a colorful accent. Variations in the earthy brown neutrals of the leather straps continue these effects in a quieter way.

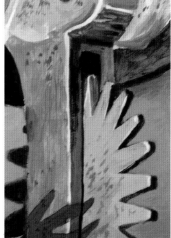

This detail of one of the spurs shows the interesting use of color in the metal as well as the variations in the earth tone and neutral grays. Crucial to the success of a restricted palette is the ability to evoke color variations to command the viewer's attention. Strong value contrasts, chroma variations, and shifts in hue all contribute to the final result.

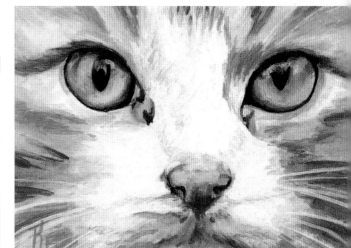

Fluff **Kiana Fecteau**
Since the primary palette includes the three brightest hues in the color wheel, a light and lively painting can be created with them. Mixed neutrals are hardly noticeable in this work as our eyes are drawn to the distinctive mixed-green eyes and contrasting magenta nose of this cat. The yellows and soft mixed oranges of the fur around the eyes enhance the overall effect. Cyan was used only in mixtures in this painting.

Six-color palette

We saw on the previous pages how a primary palette can be used to approximate almost any color needed in a painting. However, a palette of six single-pigment paints will provide an even greater range of brilliance and mixing power because the secondary colors in it are not mixed from the primaries. With the proper selection of pigments, six colors plus Titanium White can provide all some artists ever want to use.

After working with three primary colors, expanding to a six-color palette opens the door to even more varied color-mixing possibilities. The six-color palette is most commonly composed of three primary colors and three secondary colors, preferably all single-pigment paints for maximum mixing power. These six paints can be mixed to add the six tertiary colors to the palette as well. For an example of the primaries and secondaries in the Sundell Color Wheel being mixed to make the six tertiary colors for a twelve-color palette, please review page 41.

As with the primary palette, alternative pigment substitutes can be chosen from the list on page 17. It is wise to experiment with variations in this palette before settling upon your favorites. You may find the palette you want to use most often this way.

BUILDING THE SIX-COLOR PALETTE

The primaries of yellow, magenta, and cyan are circled (with the dark ring) along with the secondaries of red-orange, blue-violet, and yellow-green (in the pale ring), the basis for the six-color palette. The positions of the mixed tertiaries are in numbered circles. One possible mixing option for each tertiary position is shown below and the mixes are bright and vibrant, as single-pigment paints have been used.

1 Hansa Yellow Medium + Pyrrole Orange = Yellow-orange

2 Pyrrole Orange + Quinacridone Rose = Red

3 Quinacridone Rose + Ultramarine Violet = Red-violet

4 Ultramarine Violet + Cobalt Teal = Blue

5 Cobalt Teal + Phthalo Green (Yellow Shade) = Green

6 Phthalo Green (Yellow Shade) + Hansa Yellow Medium = Green-yellow

Backyard Trout **Bern Sundell**

Even with a six-color palette, it is vital to consider the subject and mood of your painting before you finalize your paint selection. The palette shown below lends itself well to a natural-looking landscape, where low-chroma blues, greens, and neutrals are required.

Main palette
Cerulean Blue
Chromium Oxide Green
Yellow Ocher
Pyrrole Orange
Quinacridone Rose
Ultramarine Violet
Titanium White

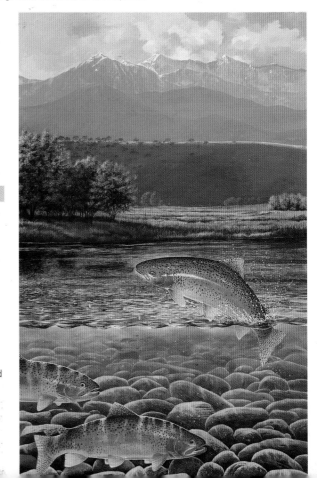

SPLIT-PRIMARY SIX-COLOR PALETTE

The split-primary palette is an archaic and forced palette model that is based on the now discredited theory that red, yellow, and blue should be considered primary colors (see www.handprint.com). Each of these supposed primaries is divided into a cool and a warm version, so the three primaries end up being represented by six paints instead of three paints.

The confused thinking behind the split-primary palette has its basis in the belief that paints are impure. The same "impurity" ascribed to paint is also inherent in how our eyes perceive color, because not only do some pigments reflect light across all wavelengths, but the individual cones in our eyes register multiple wavelengths as well. In other words, "pure" color is strictly a figment of the imagination without any basis in reality.

Relating the typical split-primary palette to the Sundell Color Wheel, it could largely be duplicated by renaming placements green-yellow and yellow as a primary, placements red and magenta as a primary, and placements blue and cyan as a primary. There is nothing at all wrong with working with those paint combinations if you so choose, but it is an arbitrary choice, not one founded on current scientific understanding of color.

SPECIALIZED USAGE OF THE SIX-COLOR PALETTE

While the six-color palette taken from the Sundell Color Wheel (see page 17) is capable of an extensive range of colors for a variety of subjects, sometimes it is helpful to choose a really specialized six-color palette for a specific painting project.

To paint the portrait of an outdoorsman who loves to fish in the Bahamas, the author selected one of these specialized palettes. The goal was to render high-key colors commonly seen in the Bahamas, as well as the tanned face of the angler.

Substitutes for the six-color palette in this painting were chosen as follows: Naples Yellow Hue, Quinacridone Burnt Orange, Quinacridone Magenta, and Indanthrone Blue. Unchanged were Cobalt Teal and Phthalo Green (Yellow Shade) and the usual Titanium White. Naples Yellow Hue is not a typical selection for a six-color palette as it is a multiple-pigment mixture, but it works well with the other colors to make the necessary skin tones.

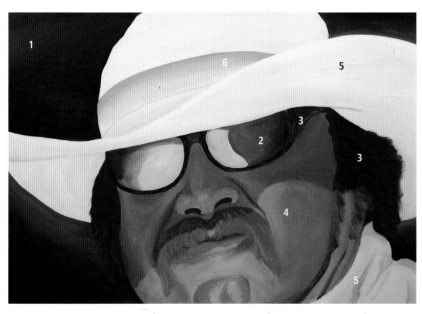

Stage 1 The initial layer of paint establishes the main areas of the painting.

1 Use Indanthrone Blue in the background and also tinted for part of the sunglasses.

2 Add tints of Cobalt Teal to the sunglasses.

3 Paint the hair and sunglasses frames with a mixture of Indanthrone Blue, Quinacridone Burnt Orange, and a little Naples Yellow Hue.

4 Begin the skin with varying mixtures and tints of Naples Yellow Hue, Quinacridone Burnt Orange, and a little Indanthrone Blue.

5 Paint the shirt in tints of Phthalo Green (Yellow Shade) and the hat in tints of Naples Yellow Hue.

6 Paint the hatband in tints of Quinacridone Magenta.

Naples Yellow Hue / Phthalo Green (Yellow Shade) / Titanium White / Quinacridone Burnt Orange / Cobalt Teal / Indanthrone Blue / Quinacridone Magenta

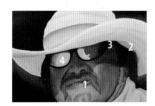

Stage 2 Continue working over the painting to intensify the colors.

1 Add small amounts of Quinacridone Magenta to the skin tones, particularly in the lips. Paint most of the skin wet-into-wet with drying extender added to the mix to facilitate the smooth blends.

2 Brush a little Quinacridone Burnt Orange into the shadowed areas under the hat brim and then paint with glazes of Naples Yellow Hue.

3 Add Phthalo Green (Yellow Shade) to the sunglasses frame mixture to make a distinct black.

4 After painting the lenses again, add highlights as a final touch.

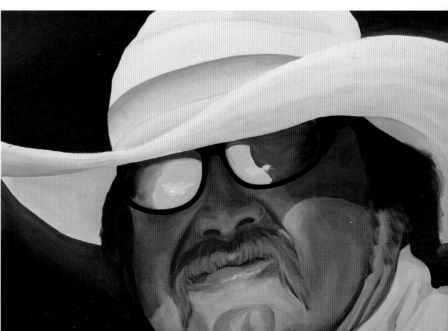

Analogous color palette

Working with the analogous color palette offers many different options, but each painting created with such a palette will be founded on closely related colors. Painting with this palette is like creating art with a slice of the rainbow. The colors merge into one another in a harmonious way and naturally delight the eye. This offers a powerful way to establish specific moods with controlled use of color.

Any three adjacent colors from the Sundell Color Wheel (see page 17) can be used for the simplest analogous palette. Obviously the mood of a painting done with yellow-orange, red-orange, and red is going to have a hot intensity that does not appear in a painting done with blue-violet, blue, and cyan. Initial palette selections play a major role in establishing the mood of an analogous color scheme. Moods can be further adjusted by the choice of high- or low-key pigments and by the choice of high- or low-chroma pigments. The yellow-orange, red-orange, and red analogous color palette previously mentioned will blaze in high-key or high-chroma pigments. This will alter into a deeply smoldering mood if low-key or low-chroma colors are chosen.

LOOSE ANALOGOUS PALETTE

A looser analogous color palette can be constructed with three colors with a missing step between them. This palette cannot be extended to a fourth color, since that would be the complement of the first color in the selection. This palette offers more diversity than using three adjacent colors.

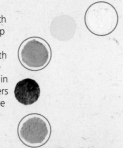

USING AN ANALOGOUS PALETTE

This loose-leaf cabbage head provides the opportunity to paint a range of greens, extending from a grayed blue-green to brighter yellow-greens. The Perylene Green—used in the darkest shadows of the leaves—is so dark that a high contrast in values can be easily achieved.

Mixing batches of different combinations on the palette makes it easier to select the most suitable mixture for any given area in the painting. For example, mix a lot of Cerulean Blue, a little Chromium Oxide Green, and a little Raw Umber for a basic grayed green. Add varying amounts of Titanium White to create a range of those grayed greens.

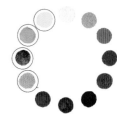

Cerulean Blue	Chromium Oxide Green	Perylene Green	Phthalo Green	Raw Umber	Bismuth Yellow	Titanium White

Stage 1 At this stage, establish the basic shapes and values of the leaves.

1 Begin the painting by applying Perylene Green in the upper background.

2 The outer leaves receive varying mixtures and tints of Cerulean Blue, Chromium Oxide Green, and a tiny amount of Raw Umber.

3 The inner leaves receive varying mixtures and tints of Phthalo Green (Yellow Shade), Chromium Oxide Green, and even less Raw Umber.

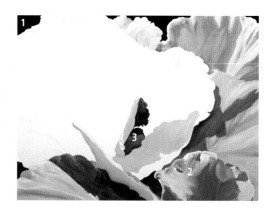

Stage 2 More complex variations in color patterns in the leaves appear in the middle and upper-back leaves.

1 Dark shadows, gray-greens, and brighter yellow-greens intermingle. The variations are due to the fact that the leaves are backlit and the light shining through parts of the leaves makes a dramatic color shift as well as dark shadow areas.

2 For the brighter yellow-greens, mix Phthalo Green (Yellow Shade) with a little Chromium Oxide Green and a tiny amount of Raw Umber for the basic yellow-green. Add Titanium White as required for the desired tints.

3 Establish shadow areas with different mixtures than those used in the brightly lit areas. The deepest shadows typically have more Raw Umber and/or Chromium Oxide Green and use very little or no Titanium White.

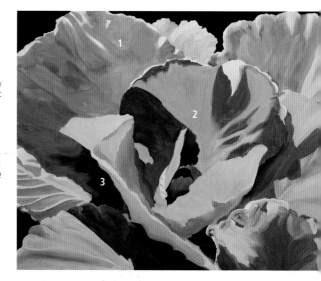

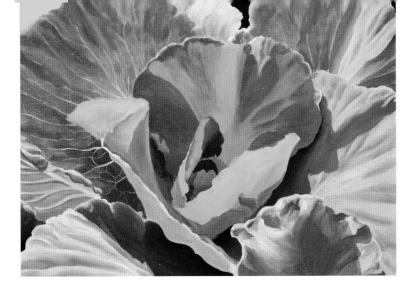

Stage 3 Introduce Bismuth Yellow into the mixtures in this stage of the painting. Bismuth Yellow with small amounts of the gray-green mixture can be used for the brighter veins in the backlit leaves. Add at least one more layer of paint to all of the leaves to soften the blends and create suitable value contrasts.

The veins with the most yellow in the mixture are in the backlit areas of the leaves.

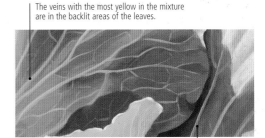

Stage 4 Complete the painting by further adjusting the blends of the mixtures and value contrasts in the leaves. The veins in the leaves have a surprising diversity of color. Some are almost a bluish-gray that verges on white, others are pale yellow, and the rest are variations in between those.

The blue-gray veins appear where the light slants across the leaf.

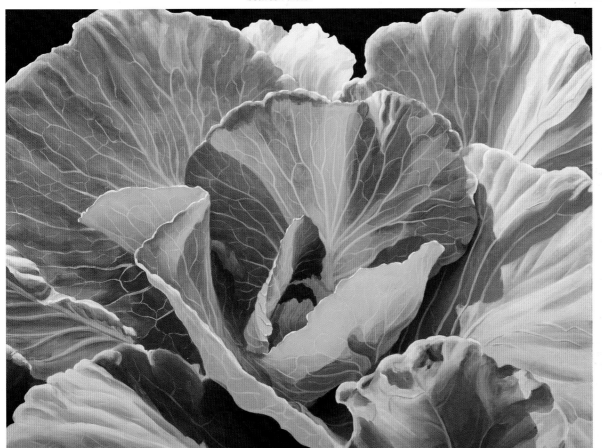

1 Paint a little Perylene Green into the darkest shadows of the leaves. Other than that, Perylene Green is not used extensively in these leaves.

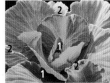

2 The final step is to add the white highlights. Small linear accents of Titanium White—thicker in places, thinner in others, and sometimes skipping altogether—bring the edges of the leaves into sharp relief. The resulting strong value contrasts make this painting highly three-dimensional.

Complementary palette

For maximum brilliance and contrast, artists choose to combine complementary colors. If you pay attention, you are likely to find one or more pairs of complements in many of the paintings you see simply because they add such vibrant qualities. Choosing the right complements and then handling them in the way best suited to your subject is well worth studying.

THE CHARACTERISTICS OF COMPLEMENTARIES

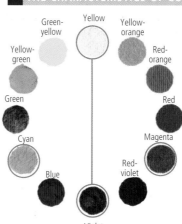

Green-yellow • Yellow • Yellow-orange
Yellow-green • Red-orange
Green • Red
Cyan • Magenta
Blue • Red-violet
Violet

A complement for any color is found by the easy process of looking on the Sundell Color Wheel and locating the color opposite it. Theoretically these two colors will mix to a neutral gray, although variations in the chemistry of mixing pigments makes that slightly variable. If we choose yellow, the complement is blue-violet. We also know that blue-violet can be mixed from the cyan and magenta primaries. Since yellow is also a primary, a mixture made with a complementary pair can be considered a mixture of all three primaries.

The main reason complements are chosen for paintings so often is that the two colors look exciting when placed next to each other. If a painting is done with a great deal of one color and a few hits of its complement are added, it is like putting little exclamation marks in the painting.

In order to maximize the contrast, choose a strongly warm color that opposes a cool complementary color. Contrasts are the lifeblood of paintings so knowing how to increase them is very useful.

TWO APPROACHES TO RED AND GREEN COMPLEMENTS

These two paintings are examples of differing ways of using complementary pairs of red and green. Each is effective in creating a strong contrast and interest in the painting.

Royal Wulff **Bern Sundell**
The overwhelmingly dominant color in this painting is green. A few earth tones and Titanium White were used, but the eye is drawn to the red accent used in the body of the fly to make the fly leap off the background. A shadow painted under the fly adds to this effect, as do the brilliant highlights. However, the main power of this painting is carried by the lively punch of that bright Cadmium Red Medium body against the deep green background.

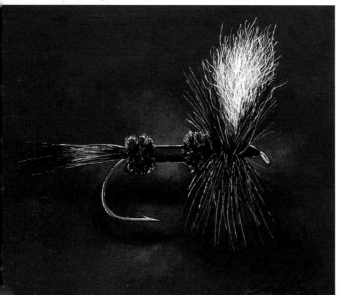

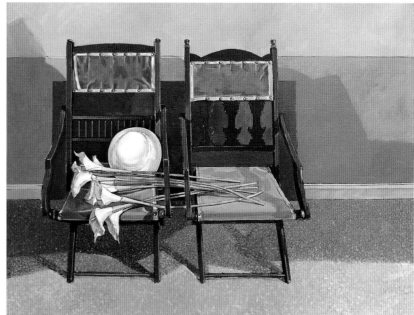

The Two Red Chairs **John Sprakes**
This painting uses the complementary pair along with various grayed neutrals. Those neutrals help make the complements appear even brighter. Another factor in this painting is that both the red and the greens have been used in a range of mixtures with each other.

Notice the shadows in the red wood that can be created by mixing red with a green. Notice the green panel behind the chairs that has been neutralized with some red in places. Shadows on the upholstery of the chairs also show this neutralizing effect.

APPROACHING YELLOW AND BLUE-VIOLET COMPLEMENTS

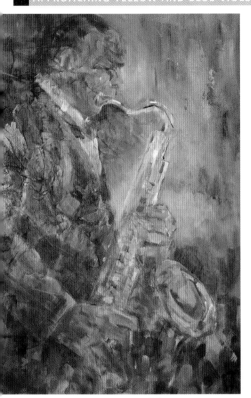

Exploring a variety of ways to use complementary pairs adds more options to the artist's arsenal of techniques.

The Saxophonist
Sera M. Knight
The artist has taken another approach yet to the use of complementary colors in this painting. The paint was applied in broken color with plenty of blue-violet. The saxophone was loosely painted with yellow in broken color along with a few other areas that serve as accents. One can almost translate the yellow in the painting into the notes of the saxophone itself.

A CAUTIONARY NOTE

Using more than one pair of complements in a painting can add more contrast and brilliance. Two pairs is often very effective. Depending on the colors selected, three pairs can also work well. But using too many pairs of complements in equal amounts can make it hard for the eye to register the colors without confusion. This flower of life painting is a clear example of what happens when this is done—all six pairs of complements in the Sundell Color Wheel (see page 17) appear in this painting. If using multiple pairs of complements, use your judgment to make sure the amounts and placements of those colors emphasize some of them and deemphasize others for most effective use.

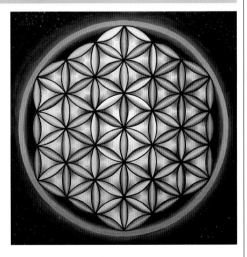

USING DIFFERENT KINDS OF COMPLEMENTS

Most of the time artists use a color wheel based on mixing pigment colors. A pigment (subtractive) color wheel has different positions for the hues than the light (additive) color wheel. Yellow, for example, opposes blue-violet on the Sundell Color Wheel, but opposes blue in a light color wheel (see page 9). A defining feature of pigment color wheels is that opposing complements fully absorb each other's color as a natural result of subtractive color, resulting in the lowest-chroma neutral gray mixtures. This does not happen in the light color wheel where mixing colors always increases brightness. Both pigment and light color wheels work well, but not at all in the same ways.

1 Paint French Ultramarine Blue and Titanium White onto heavy watercolor paper. This painting sets yellow against two kinds of complements—blue from a light-mixing color wheel and blue-violet from the pigment-mixing Sundell Color Wheel.

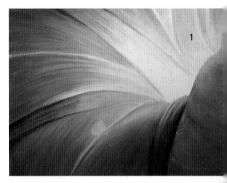

2 After the initial paint layer has dried, paint tints of Hansa Yellow Medium into the center of the morning glory flower. By not allowing the yellow and blue paints to mix while wet, the inevitable green mixtures will be avoided. Complete the flower with a little Ultramarine Violet in the water drops and Dioxazine Purple in deep shadows of the petals.

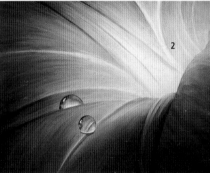

FIVE REASONS TO USE COMPLEMENTARY COLORS

1 Complementary colors are easy to use for strong color contrasts in painting.

2 Complementary colors increase the effectiveness of warm/cool contrasts.

3 The carefully applied placement of a complementary color is a good technique for making powerful accents.

4 Complementary colors can be mixed to provide neutral grays that can be adjusted to favor one color or the other, adding liveliness to a composition that also uses one or both of the complementary colors at full strength.

5 Complementary colors can be used to direct the viewer's eye through the painting by creating intensity where needed.

Split-complementary palette

The split complementary palette offers the harmony of the analogous palette combined with the vigor of the complementary palette. The complement can provide a sharp accent or provide a neutral mixture, depending on the objectives of the artist.

Using three analogous colors along with the complement of the middle color creates a split-complementary palette. The middle color of the three analogous colors is known as the key color. The complementary color can be used to spice the palette either with contrasting accents or to create neutralized colors not available in the analogous palette alone.

A variation on the typical split complementary palette involves omitting the key color, the middle color of the analogous trio. This extremely limited palette loses both the direct complementary vibrancy and the neutralized color possible from mixing the two complements.

A warm or cool trio of analogous colors for the split complementary palette can be chosen to establish a variety of moods. The color temperature of your paints is an important tool for creating emotional impact.

Changing the key of the colors used in the split complementary palette allows even more flexibility for creating a variety of moods. A low-key palette will create a quieter mood than the corresponding high-key palette.

The split-complementary palette can achieve hot, lively, vibrant effects or somber, deeply introspective feelings and everything in between them with simple changes of key and temperature. Take one subject and paint it in several variations of a split-complementary palette and observe the results.

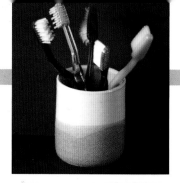

Using a subject that allows easy color variations but that carries no great emotional content of its own quickly reveals how color choices affect the emotional feel of a painting. A cup of toothbrushes lets us explore the split-complementary palette and create different moods with it.

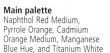

Warm low key Fiery reds and oranges dominate this painting with only hints of the cool Manganese Blue Hue complement to be seen. The background is deep and intense despite the use of neutralized color made from mixing the complements. Due to the low color key (see page 64), the mood of these reds and oranges is darkly smoldering rather than a blazing inferno. If Manganese Blue Hue were more prominent in this painting, the reds and oranges would appear even more forceful. Adjustments in the amount shown of the single opposing complement will greatly modify the final mood of a painting, so choose carefully as you paint.

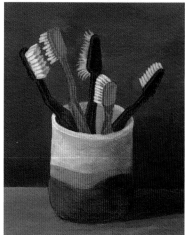

Main palette
Naphthol Red Medium, Pyrrole Orange, Cadmium Orange Medium, Manganese Blue Hue, and Titanium White

Warm high key The diagram on the color wheel is the same for this painting as Warm low key (see above), but different paint selections have been made for those placements. Quinacridone Red and Cobalt Teal Blue were chosen instead of Naphthol Red Medium and Manganese Blue Hue. This results in a palette that can easily be painted in a higher key. The reds and oranges still dominate, but very few neutrals appear in the work. The single opposing complement, Cobalt Teal Blue, has been used extensively in the background. Notice how bright and lively this combination looks. The painting has an expansive and joyful quality as the pure, clear color was allowed to sing.

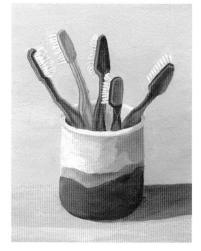

Main palette
Quinacridone Red, Pyrrole Orange, Cadmium Orange Medium, Cobalt Teal Blue, and Titanium White

Cool low key

The mood abruptly shifts in this version of the toothbrushes. Cool blues and purples dominate with very little of the Cadmium Orange Medium complement to be seen. The background is dark and neutral, painted with a mixture of Cadmium Orange Medium, its complement Ultramarine Blue, and the adjacent Ultramarine Violet. Some people automatically equate a dark subdued color scheme with sadness and depression, but it is worth taking a second look here. This color scheme can be used to evoke the magic of moonlight, that tranquil peace the stillness of the moon brings. A meditative quiet pervades this painting.

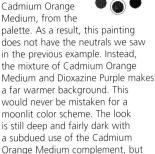

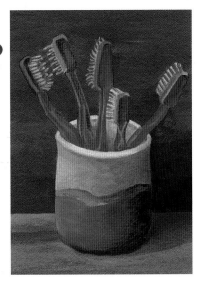

Main palette
Manganese Blue Hue,
Ultramarine Blue, Ultramarine
Violet, Cadmium Orange
Medium, and Titanium White

Cool full key

Cool blues set the tone for this painting, but it has a completely different mood from the Cool low key version. The combination of both high-key and low-key color gives a lively lilt to the mood. Using both Cobalt Teal Blue and Manganese Blue Hue from the cyan placement on the Sundell Color Wheel increases the sense of variety in the play of color. The neutrals are lighter and bluer than in the Cool low key version as well.

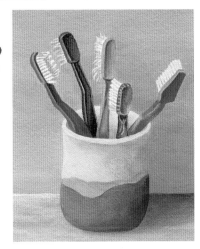

Main palette
Cobalt Teal Blue,
Manganese Blue Hue,
Ultramarine Blue,
Cadmium Orange Medium,
and Titanium White

Low-key limited palette

This starkly limited palette omits the key color, the complement of Cadmium Orange Medium, from the palette. As a result, this painting does not have the neutrals we saw in the previous example. Instead, the mixture of Cadmium Orange Medium and Dioxazine Purple makes a far warmer background. This would never be mistaken for a moonlit color scheme. The look is still deep and fairly dark with a subdued use of the Cadmium Orange Medium complement, but a warmer vigor emerges.

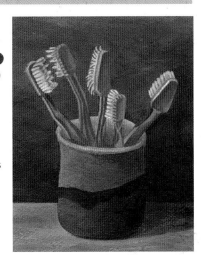

Main palette
Manganese Blue, Dioxazine Purple, Cadmium
Orange Medium, and Titanium White

CHOOSING COMPLEMENTS FOR PAINTING NEUTRALS

Neutrals in a painting can be used to emphasize brilliant colors or to further enhance a low-key emphasis. Light-colored neutrals can add an airy look while dark-colored neutrals may bring a more reflective and thoughtful mood to a painting.

Ideally any pair of opposing complements from the color wheel mixes to a neutral gray. However, we are working with actual pigments in our paints and those chemistries do not always produce the ideal gray in every combination on the wheel. Testing any specific pair of paints quickly shows the way they will work together.

In addition to those unavoidable variations, we can also deliberately mix neutrals that lean more heavily to one side or the other of the complementary opposition. This can be helpful for emphasizing a mood in a painting.

In the process of selecting your palette for a split complementary painting that will use neutrals, test your opposing complements to see if their mixture will create the look you want. Work with the possible variations until you find the combination that suits the appearance you want to create.

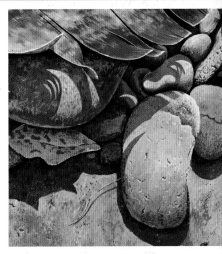

Going to the color wheel to find complements does not help the painter confronted with a subject that is already neutral in color in direct light. *October Gifts* (detail) by Bern Sundell presents this difficulty and the solution as well. In this example, shadows of the feather fall across the irregular, curving shapes of the rocks, following those shapes. By shifting to a lower color key, convincing shadows were created without losing their subtleties of color (see pages 64–65). The sunlit area of the large rock was painted with Ultramarine Blue, Raw Umber, and Titanium White. The shadows have more Ultramarine Blue and considerably less Titanium White in the mixture.

Tetradic color palette

The tetradic color scheme can be a challenge to use effectively. Yet, if you look closely at paintings that catch your eye with an unusual—perhaps even jarring—color balance, you will often find a tetradic color scheme lurking in the paint. Handled with skill, this palette can make a painting with an arresting appearance and unique appeal.

The tetradic color palette is composed of four colors that make two complementary pairs separated by at least one step on the Sundell Color Wheel. If only one step separates the two complementary pairs, a rectangular pattern on the color wheel results. If two steps separate the two complementary pairs, a square pattern is seen.

We more commonly relate to the color wheel in a triadic sense, with the three primaries and their mixing derivatives, the secondary and tertiary colors. However, dividing the wheel into four instead of three is perfectly reasonable. Using a tetradic color scheme composed of single-pigment paints is roughly equivalent to using a four-color primary set.

One of the keys to effective use of the tetradic color palette is establishing an emphasis in the palette. Choosing either a warm or cool emphasis helps steady the viewer's eye rather than leaving it lost in an equal balance between all four colors.

Rather than emphasizing warm or cool, sometimes one color of the four is allowed to dominate the painting. Deliberate variations in chroma can also help to accomplish the desired emphasis. Whatever solution is found, creating a visual imbalance in the four colors of the palette is vital.

USING THE SQUARE TETRADIC PALETTE

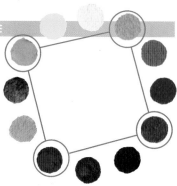

In a square tetradic color palette, all of the color mixtures created to fill the spaces on the color wheel between the four colors chosen for the palette will be dulled by the same amount, as each side of the square has two color placements to be mixed. For example, in the diagram of the square tetradic color palette, blue and magenta mix to make blue-violet and red-violet on one of the sides of the square, yellow-orange and magenta mix to make red-orange and red on another, and so on around the wheel. As we know, colors closer together on the color wheel generally make brighter mixtures than colors farther apart on the color wheel.

Warnish, Skye **Jim Woodman**
This painting uses the square tetradic color palette shown above. The complementary pairs are yellow-orange/blue and magenta/yellow-green. Warm colors clearly dominate. While a red-orange can be mixed from single-pigment yellow-orange and magenta paints, the brilliance of the foreground red-orange implies it is not such a mixture. However, the overall color scheme does fit the idea of a tetradic color palette. The small patch of magenta on the far hill provides a sharp contrast with the yellow-green roof of the building, creating the main interest in the painting.

Main palette
Cadmium Orange Medium, Pyrrole Orange, Quinacridone Magenta, Ultramarine Blue, Green Gold, and Titanium White.

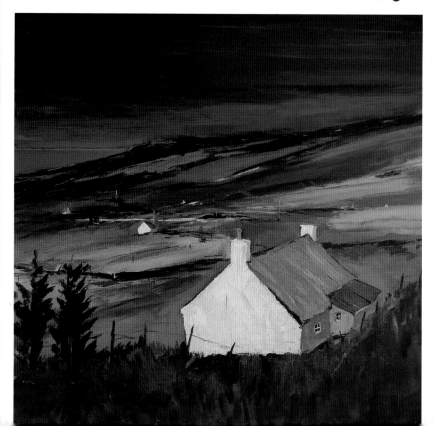

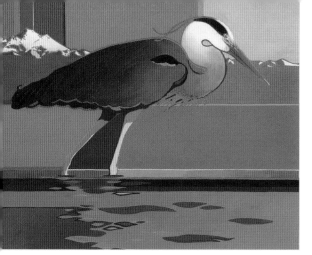

Autumn Heron **Jennifer Bowman**
A drastically contrasting style of painting is used in this work. Warm colors dominate despite the expanses of cyans and blue-violets in the background. Even the yellow chosen for the palette is a warm, rich yellow instead of a light, bright yellow. The rusty red-orange of the heron also makes the warm emphasis unmistakable. Neutral mixtures are largely absent, emphasizing strong color throughout the painting.

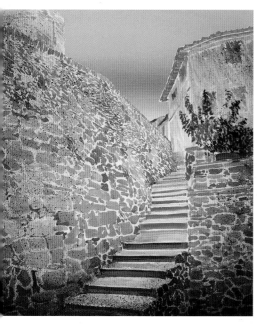

A View Worthy of the Climb **Carol Carter**
Yet another way to use this rectangular tetradic color palette is shown here. Rather than emphasizing either cool or warm colors, warm colors are stronger in the foreground and cooler colors lead us into the distance, where they dominate. Neutral mixtures are used in the rockwork and buildings effectively. Chroma variations are important in this work, with a deep, dark red-orange across the bottom of the painting opposing high-key cyans.

COMPARING RECTANGULAR TETRADIC PALETTES

Looking at three different ways of handling similar palettes allows you to see the varied potentials of tetradic color palettes. The same rectangular tetradic palette dominates each one of the paintings on this page. The artists chose differing substitute paints for the placements on the Sundell Color Wheel but used the same basic tetradic color relationships. The complementary pairs common to all three of these paintings are yellow/blue-violet and red-orange/cyan.

Notice the way a rectangular tetradic color scheme changes the mixing possibilities compared to a square tetradic color scheme. With a square tetradic color scheme, the missing steps on each side can be mixed so that all the mixed colors have similar loss of chroma from mixing. With the rectangle, the blue-violet and cyan placements mix to a high-chroma adjacent step for blue between them, as do the yellow and red-orange placements in mixing the adjacent yellow-orange. But on the long sides of the rectangle, three steps appear, ensuring lower-chroma mixtures for those placements because of the extra distance between cyan and yellow as well as red-orange and blue-violet.

Main palette
Cadmium Yellow Medium
Quinacridone Burnt
  Orange
Ultramarine Violet
Cobalt Turquoise
Titanium White

Artist Afternoon **Bern Sundell**
Cool colors are the emphasis in this painting, although warm colors are used to good dramatic effect. Cool and warm colors used in close proximity create a vibrant appearance, an effect that lends itself to the use of the rectangular tetradic palette. The artist employed substantial use of neutrals in this painting with high-chroma color holding the main stage.

Main palette
Cadmium Yellow Medium
Pyrrole Orange
Ultramarine Violet
Cobalt Teal
Titanium White

Main palette
Yellow Ocher
Quinacridone Burnt Orange
Ultramarine Violet
Cerulean Blue
Titanium White

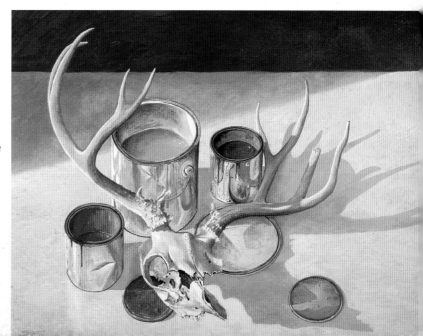

Tertiary palette

The tertiary color palette is often overlooked, but using it can produce some surprisingly vibrant paintings. The eye is naturally drawn to distinctive and unusual color combinations, so this is an excellent palette to explore to broaden the appeal of your paintings.

THE TERTIARY PALETTE

The traditional tertiary color palette runs more to browns and grays as the colors were mixed from all three primaries, neutralizing them. But the contemporary tertiary color palette is altogether different because it is created by mixing a primary with a nearby secondary.

Mixed tertiaries or single-pigment paints? Each tertiary color is mixed from the primary color and the secondary color adjacent to its placement on the Sundell Color Wheel. Using mixed tertiaries is one way to set up your palette for painting. However, it will usually be preferable to use single-pigment paints to give the greatest chromatic range of possibilities for mixing while painting. You can select tertiary paints for your palette from the Sundell Color Wheel and also from the list of substitutes on page 17.

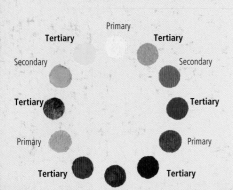

USING A TERTIARY PALETTE

The tertiary palette for *Bowl of Apples* by Bern Sundell is composed of the single-pigment paints below. You will note that two different red paints are used for the red placement on the color wheel. Cadmium Red is an opaque red but Naphthol Red Medium is more transparent. This gives a useful flexibility in the ways you can apply red in the painting.

Cadmium Orange Medium

Cadmium Red Medium

Naphthol Red Medium

Quinacridone Violet

Ultramarine Blue

Phthalo Green (Blue Shade)

Bismuth Yellow

Titanium White

Stage 1 Sketch the outlines of the shapes on the canvas. Mix Ultramarine Blue with Quinacridone Violet and Phthalo Green (Blue Shade) to paint the dark background.

1 Apply a pale tint of Bismuth Yellow for the table top.

2 Use varying tints of Ultramarine Blue for the shadow of the bowl and the interior stripe and shadows inside the bowl.

Stage 2 Apply another layer of paint using the previous mixture in the background.

1 Paint pale tints of Bismuth Yellow and Cadmium Orange Medium on the table top. Add in a tiny amount of Phthalo Green (Blue Shade) to the mixture in the lower left corner.

2 Continue refining the apple in the bowl, painting a mixture of Bismuth Yellow, Phthalo Green (Blue Shade), and Titanium White in part of the yellow area of the apple.

3 Repaint the rest of the apple using the previous palette. Add small white highlights to the apple.

4 Paint the apple on the right with the same paint mixtures used for the apple in the bowl.

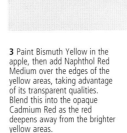

3 Paint Bismuth Yellow in the apple, then add Naphthol Red Medium over the edges of the yellow areas, taking advantage of its transparent qualities. Blend this into the opaque Cadmium Red as the red deepens away from the brighter yellow areas.

4 Apply Quinacridone Violet in the deepest shadows of the apple.

5 Add a little Ultramarine Blue to some of the red mixture and paint it on the interior of the bowl on the right to show the reflection of the apple on the shiny surface of the bowl.

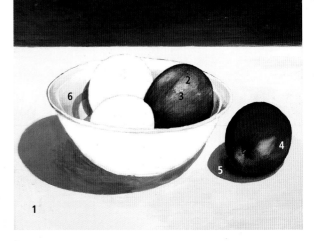

5 Apply varying tints of Ultramarine Blue for the shadow of the apple on the table. After drying, refine the shadows on the table with a tint of Ultramarine Blue mixed with a little Naphthol Red Medium.

6 Continue developing the interior of the bowl with tints of Ultramarine Blue.

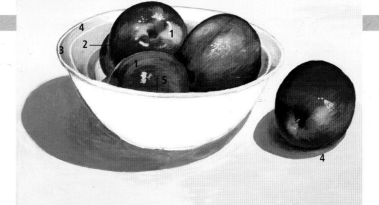

Stage 3 Continue adjusting the dark background. Lighten it with a tint of Ultramarine Blue and Naphthol Red Medium so it does not overwhelm the bowl of apples.

1 Paint the remaining two apples in the bowl using the same mixtures as used in the first two apples.

2 Notice the lighter area on the upper-left apple next to the inside of the bowl. Light is reflecting between the apple and the shiny interior surface of the bowl.

3 Paint varying tints of Naphthol Red Medium inside the bowl to show the reflections of the apples. Mix Cadmium Red with Cadmium Orange Medium and paint an accent line along the curved side of the bowl and along the lip on the left.

4 Add a tint of Phthalo Green (Blue Shade) to the interior of the bowl and the shadow of the apple on the table.

5 Paint small touches of Ultramarine Blue with a little Naphthol Red Medium and Titanium White into selected areas of the apples to show reflections from the blue of the bowl.

In this detail, notice the painterly play with the color in the bowl and on the apples. The freedom of these brushstrokes takes lovely advantage of the tertiary color palette, resulting a vibrant and lively still life.

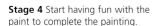

Stage 4 Start having fun with the paint to complete the painting.

1 Paint the Ultramarine Blue stripes on the outside of the bowl, then add varying tints of Ultramarine Blue with Phthalo Green (Blue Shade) or Bismuth Yellow to fill the outer shape of the bowl.

2 Paint the Ultramarine Blue shadow on the right side of the bowl and add Cadmium Red to show the reflection of the nearby apple.

3 Paint a slight Cadmium Red and Cadmium Orange Medium mixture along the edges of the bowl as a lively accent.

4 Repaint the shadows on the table top with more Ultramarine Blue and Naphthol Red Medium in varying tints. Remember to put the darkest shadow where the bowl or apple touches the table. Paint a tint of Phthalo Green (Blue Shade) across the shadows near the front edge.

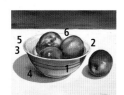

5 Add a little Bismuth Yellow to the lip of the bowl.

6 Add small touches of Phthalo Green (Blue Shade) or the Ultramarine Blue and Naphthol Red Medium tint to the apples. Paint the final Titanium White highlights on the apples.

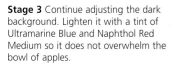

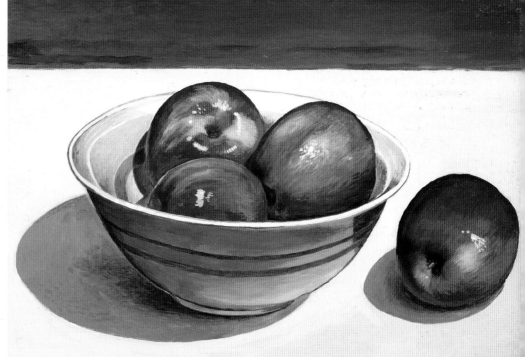

High and low color key

High-key colors do what you would expect from the name—they hit the high, bright notes, while low-key colors provide the deep, dark rumble. You can make your paintings really sing with the high-key colors, while the low-key colors bring depth and power to your work.

High-key colors are high-chroma paints and may be tinted with Titanium White to accentuate their lightness. Typically a high-key color does not drop below the mid-range on the value scale. High-key colors are usually cheerful, energetic, and express a zest for life.

Low-key colors fall in the lower range of the value scale and are often low in chroma as well as dark in value. Low-key colors are excellent for conveying dim lighting and quietly introspective or even melancholy moods.

Selecting paints that have bright, high-chroma pigments from the Sundell Color Wheel with the list of substitutions on page 17 provides a specialized high-key palette for painting high-key color. Alternatively, selecting low-chroma pigments that may also be dark in value results in the specialized low-key palette.

While paintings can be created exclusively in either high or low key, more frequently, both are employed to allow a full color key in the painting. This makes it possible to have a wide value range, which is important in establishing the underlying structure and typically makes a more successful painting.

When you make decisions about your palette for a painting, carefully consider the mood you wish to create and the choices in high or low color key that will support that mood most effectively. With practice, you will easily identify what emphasis in color key will work best for your purpose.

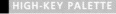

HIGH-KEY PALETTE

1. Hansa Yellow Medium PY73
2. New Gamboge PY153
3. Quinacridone Coral PR209
4. Naphthol Red Light PR112
5. Quinacridone Rose PV19
6. Cobalt Violet Hue PV19, PR122, PW4, PV23
7. Ultramarine Violet PV15
8. Cobalt Blue PB28
9. Cobalt Teal PG50
10. Permanent Green Light PY3 PG7
11. Phthalo Green (Yellow Shade) PG36
12. Cadmium Yellow Light PY35

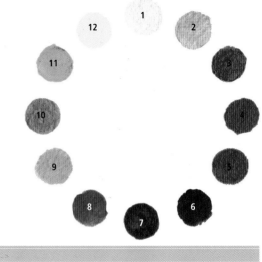

LOW-KEY PALETTE

1. Yellow Ocher PY43
2. Raw Sienna PY43
3. Quinacridone Burnt Orange PO48
4. Anthraquinone Red PR177
5. Perylene Maroon PR179
6. Alizarin Crimson Hue PR122, PR206, PG7
7. Indanthrone Blue PB60
8. Anthraquinone Blue PB60
9. Cerulean Blue Deep PB36
10. Perylene Green PBk31
11. Chromium Oxide Green PG17
12. Rich Green Gold PY129

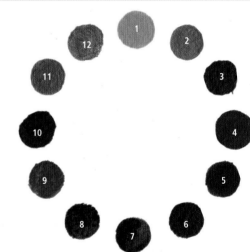

COMPARING HIGH-KEY, LOW-KEY, AND FULL-KEY COLOR

Be alert in your daily life and practice identifying high- and low-key colors wherever you go. Becoming more aware of light and its effect on the color of your surroundings will bring new strength and variety to your paintings. A helpful practice is to paint a subject solely in high-key color and then paint the same subject solely in low-key color. By the time you paint this subject in full-key color, i.e. a combination of the two, a new ease will have entered your work.

Low-key values   High-key values

Desert Song Frederick G. Denys

Full-key color provides a wide range of values and chroma in the landscape, allowing dramatic color to unfold in the painting. A passing cloud leaves a shadow across the middle of the painting, the area dominated by low-key color. Dark silhouettes of saguaros stand in sharp contrast against the brilliant high-key mountains that blaze in direct sunlight. The foreground coloration is handled with more subtlety, but still plays high-key color against low-key color. Technical mastery of the palette makes such richness in color possible.

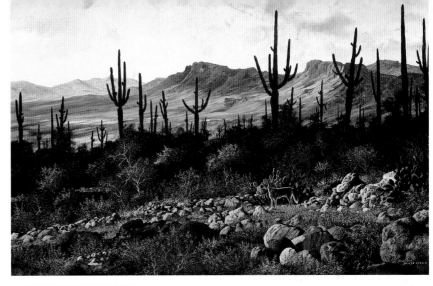

 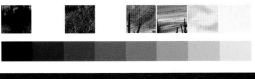

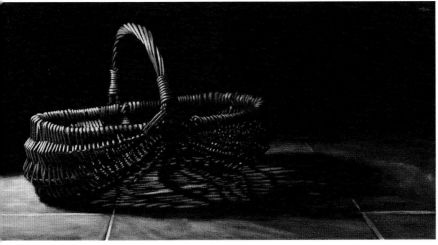

Floored Light Joseph Krawczyk

Low-key colors dominate this painting most emphatically. Even the highlights on the basket are muted, painted with neutralized yellows. The background is swallowed in darkness, a deep brown almost going black. The tiles are painted in low-chroma reds and a little neutralized yellow-orange. These dramatic value contrasts convey a strong sense of the light falling through the open weave of the basket. In the highly dimensional and tactile space of this painting, the viewer can almost feel the hard fibers of the basket and the smoothness of the tiles. Consider how the power of this painting would largely evaporate if the basket and tiles were painted in high-key colors.

Steelhead Flies Bern Sundell

This painting is clearly dominated by high-key colors. Light, bright, and lively, the high-key effect is increased by the broken color lines with white accents in parts of the flies. The colors mostly remain saturated, even in the lighter values. A few low-key dark colors appear in the hooks, bodies, and dressings of the flies. However, they do not overpower the high-key color and instead provide a supporting framework. Imagine the difference it would make if the high-key shadows on the table top were painted in low-key colors. The mood of this painting would change drastically.

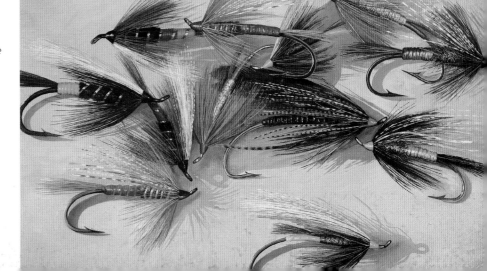

Luminosity in color

Luminous, glowing color in a painting holds the viewer's attention in the most gratifying way. The magic of light illuminating the canvas can be absolutely unforgettable. So how does the artist achieve such effects with color, bringing the hidden luminosity of piles of paint on the palette into this stunning imagery on the canvas? The nine methods for painting in luminous color are highlighted on the grayscale thumbnail of each finished painting to give you a few pointers.

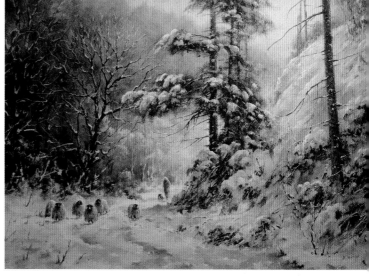

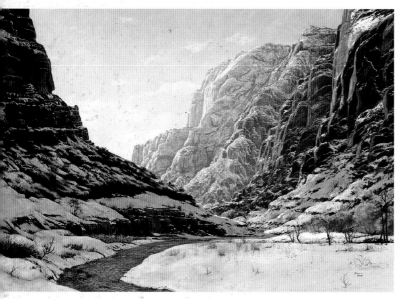

▲ *The Last Strays* **Joe Hush**
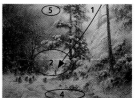
The luminosity in this painting is quietly romantic with the diffused evening light. The soft blends of color (4) effectively establish this mood. We still have a strong sense of the source of light (1) with the glowing sky and the shepherd backlit as he comes around the corner behind the sheep (2). This painting relies heavily on the use of warm and cool colors with cool lavender shadows in the snow dominating the scene, accented by smaller areas of warm yellows and oranges (5).

◀ *Sudden Snow* **Frederick G. Denys**
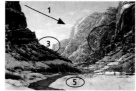
This snowy landscape conveys a strikingly different mood than the above painting. Blends are soft, but this painting has a crystalline clarity of light that creates powerful value contrasts (3). This artist also utilizes the contrasts of warm and cool colors with soft, subdued cool blues in the snow, stream, and sky against the powerful warm red rock formations (5). The angled light adds to the luminosity of this painting (1).

NINE METHODS FOR PAINTING LUMINOUS COLOR

If you practice looking for each of these nine methods in each painting you see, after a while you will naturally know which ones you need to use when planning paintings of your own.

1 Establish the light source
Confusion about the source of light does a painting no good at all. Flat, undifferentiated light is also detrimental. Consistent angled lighting that brings shadows into the composition also brings interest into the color and offers the potential for creating a luminous glow.

2 Use distinctive backlighting
When the angle of light comes from behind the subject, a halo of light naturally appears around it. This enhances almost anything you choose to paint. Flowing hair takes on a romantic appearance, flowers glow with a new radiance, and living creatures look vibrant.

3 Establish strong value contrasts
Luminosity suggests brilliant light, and a painting of brilliant light will look flat and featureless without strong shadow areas to differentiate the bright areas and emphasize their importance.

4 Apply smooth blends of color
Coarse handling of color transitions does not convey the liquid beauty of glowing light. The use of smooth blends of color helps convey the radiance of light flowing around the subject.

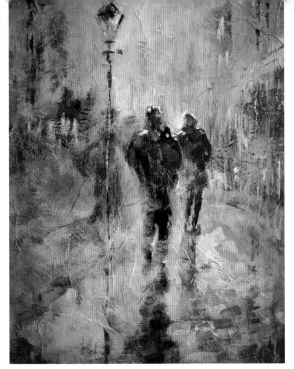

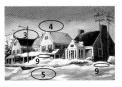

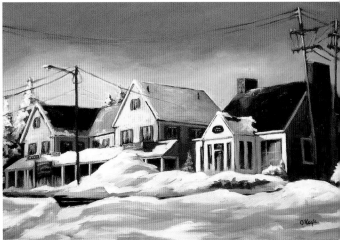

Winter Warmth
Lou O'Keefe
A brilliant sunset illuminates this row of houses in the snow. Notice the soft blends in the sky in particular (4). The snow reflects the warm yellow of the sunset but the shadows of the snow are cool cyans and blue-violets (5). Strong value contrasts are also evident in this painting (3). Brilliant white highlights add to the sense of luminosity created by the powerful warm and cool colors in this scene (9).

Misty Day **Sera M. Knight**
Wet, reflecting surfaces throw light in all directions in this painting, a somewhat diffuse scattering of warm and cool colors (5). The backlit couple walk into a pool of light from the lamp (1). The partially neutralized background colors let the hits of high-key and high-chroma accents really vibrate. The luminosity in this painting comes from a loose play with color in the diffuse reflected light (6).

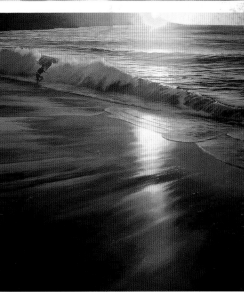

Meor Light **Paul Geraghty**
Dramatic, angled backlighting is the main factor creating luminosity in this painting (2). A hot yellow sun sets on the horizon, sending rays of light across the water and wet sand (1). Cool blues and purples in the water contrast with the warm, reddish-orange in the reflected light on the wet sand, in the crashing wave, and on the horizon (5). The backlit wave shows its transparency with that reddish-orange glow where the sunlight passes through it. The top edges of the wave have brilliant highlights to complete the strong value contrasts in the painting (9).

5 Juxtapose warm colors with cool colors
The contrast between warm and cool colors inherently adds luminosity to a painting. This can be done with dramatic contrasts but may be even more effective with subtle handling. A delicate shimmer can appear where pale tints of warm and cool colors are placed next to each other.

6 Include areas of reflected light
Luminosity is about glowing, flowing light, so areas of reflected light communicate this quite well visually. Along with light radiating through a partially transparent object such as a colored glass vase or a flower petal, this delicate expression of the movement and transformation of light adds luminosity to the painting.

7 Apply the paint in multiple layers of glazes
The physical structure of thin, partially transparent layers of paint suspended in glaze medium or gel medium creates a form of luminosity due to the refraction of light within those layers. Review the section on Mixing color with layers and glazes on pages 44–45 for more information.

8 Use neutrals to accent bright color
Soft neutrals make high-chroma color really sing and vibrate, which can be an excellent tool for creating luminosity. A pale gray is ideal for this effect, but any neutralized or partially neutralized color can be used.

9 Accent with brilliant highlights
Small Titanium White highlights add a lovely sparkle to a painting. These highlights maximize the value contrasts in the painting and emphasize the quality of light, greatly enhancing the luminosity of the image.

Color value

Color is a three-legged stool, with hue, value, and chroma as the three legs. Yet, unlike a wooden stool, color can stand on only one of those legs, the one pertaining to value. The eye still perceives values when hue and chroma have largely vanished from vision in low light. Value creates the main structure of color in our minds, although we pay more attention to hue and chroma.

ESTABLISHING PIGMENT VALUE

Swatches from the Sundell Color Wheel (see page 17) are placed to match the value scale. You can see the colors at the top of the color wheel are lighter in value than the colors at the bottom of the color wheel. The brain registers yellow-reflecting colors as lighter than blue-reflecting colors. Yet this is trickier than it looks, because the Cobalt Teal is significantly lighter than you might expect and the Phthalo Green (Blue Shade) is much darker than you would predict from their positions on the color wheel. These are actual pigments, not light, so variations such as this should be expected. Try testing your own paints to see where they fall against a value scale by converting paint swatches like the ones below to a black-and-white photocopy or grayscale image on your computer.

By converting swatches of paints from the Sundell Color Wheel to black and white, it is possible to establish their values.

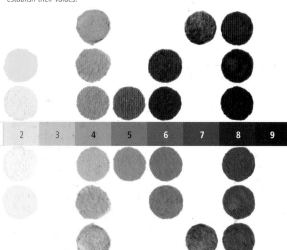

THE VALUE SCALE

A nine-step value scale (above) with step one as white and step nine as black is commonly used to illustrate value. With practice you can identify the value of the colors you are applying to your canvas.

Artists use different techniques to see values in their paintings. Some use a piece of red Plexiglas or film to view their painting. Others squint to reduce the available light coming into the eye so they can more readily perceive values alone. Photographing the painting and converting to black and white or making a black-and-white photocopy is another method. Quite often a problem with values will suddenly appear in the fundamental structure of your painting. This can be a lack of contrast or an imbalance in either light or dark values. You might then correct your difficulty by changing the color values in the problem area.

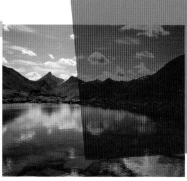

Assessing values on location
If working on location, it is not possible to make black-and-white photocopies, and an image on a camera would be too small. Take a piece of red Plexiglas or film and hold up to the view to eliminate colors and show the tones. Note: If your subject includes a lot of red you will need to use another color film, since the film will hide objects of a similar color.

HOW DARKENING OF ACRYLIC PAINTS IN DRYING AFFECTS VALUE

Acrylic paints darken as they dry, and this must be understood before using values in painting acrylic color, since what you see when painting does not reflect the final result. Most acrylic paints use a whitish emulsion that dries clear. This makes the color appear darker when dry because the whitish appearance of the wet emulsion no longer obscures the true color. Lighter-value paints will show less color shift in drying than darker-value paints because not as much dark color is obscured while wet.

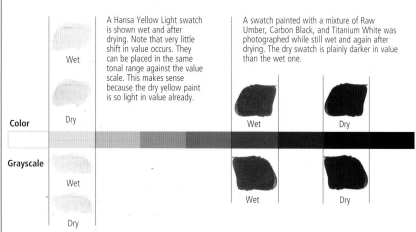

A Hansa Yellow Light swatch is shown wet and after drying. Note that very little shift in value occurs. They can be placed in the same tonal range against the value scale. This makes sense because the dry yellow paint is so light in value already.

A swatch painted with a mixture of Raw Umber, Carbon Black, and Titanium White was photographed while still wet and again after drying. The dry swatch is plainly darker in value than the wet one.

Matching the wet and dry swatches to the nine-step value scale is revealing. The visual above shows the placement of the two pairs of swatches converted to grayscale. While the Hansa Yellow Light shifted less than one step in drying, the Raw Umber mixture darkened a full two steps on the value scale. With this knowledge you will find it easier to mix a lighter-looking paint to match a dried area of your painting when you need to retouch it. Experiment with other paints in your palette.

Artists use different techniques to see values in their paintings. However, the best way to become instinctively comfortable with handling values is to paint an entire series of monochromatic paintings. After completing enough of them, you will internalize the process of identifying values so you naturally use them properly in your paintings when you add other colors to the palette. Study the examples shown on this page and then create your own series of monochromatic paintings to master values.

Barn Owl **Paul James**
This painting is not strictly monochromatic, but it verges on it. Strongly defined values create a distinctive composition in this work. The notch in the upright timber and the owl hold the lightest values, effectively making the owl the focal point of the painting. To handle values this well requires a solid understanding of light, shade, and shadow as well as acrylic paints themselves. In this painting the values reduce contrast by becoming darker as the painting recedes into the distant corners of the barn.

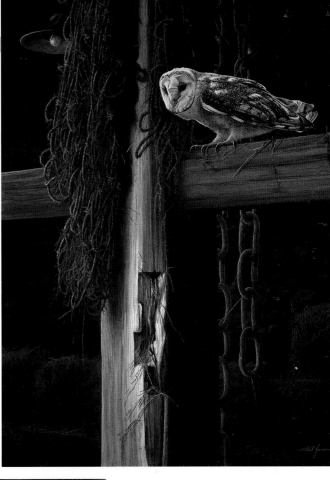

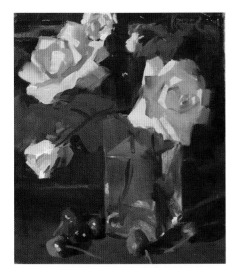

White Roses **Donna Krizek**
A deceptively simple but effective monochromatic sketch painting to establish the values within white rose petals and the complex nature of transparency and shine in glass. This study also shows the values in the cast shadows behind the vase.

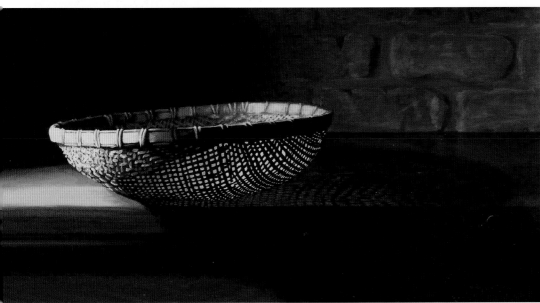

Sifting the Light
Joseph Krawczyk
This splendid example of powerfully used values places a radiant yellow against deep black shadows. The luminosity of the yellow light falling on the shelf and illuminating the basket is dramatic. On the shadow side of the basket, the shelf is painted darker than the side in the light, even where some light filters through the woven openings of the basket. Although the bricks in the background are a quiet neutral, notice how the yellowish cast to them carries the diagonal glow of light across the painting without being obtrusive.

Color temperature

Color temperature can be a baffling concept at first. Is it the temperature of the air shown in the painting, the difference between a hot day in the desert and a cool day in the snowy mountains? Is it the color temperature of the light and how it changes the color of objects in that light? Could it be the color temperature of the paints themselves?

For starters, the primary concern of the artist lies with the color temperature of the paints themselves. The color temperature of the paints chosen can be used to evoke the hot day in the desert or the cool day in the snowy mountains, but the paints themselves are what we must understand in order to accomplish this.

It is true that the light in which you paint will affect how the finished painting looks. If you have a painting created under incandescent light, take it outdoors to see the changes. Or point your automatic camera at a scene and photograph it with the cloud setting and then with indoor light bulb setting and observe the difference. This is why artists often choose natural north light for a studio, as it varies the least. The handicap of not being able to paint after dark leads other artists to choose various forms of daylight-equivalent electric lighting solutions for the studio.

But none of this speaks to the important issue of the color temperature of the paints we use. Since the 1700s, yellow and red have been regarded as warm colors, with blue and green regarded as cool colors. Popular myth has it that warm colors advance visually and cool colors recede visually. Yet modern scientific understanding of how the eye and brain perceive color does not altogether support these assumptions.

Oddly enough, research suggests that sunlight is not yellow at all but rather a pale green. We have not suspected this to be the case because of the amazingly agile way our brains process incoming visual information to create color in our minds. But if sunlight is truly a pale green, this can hardly be considered a cool color.

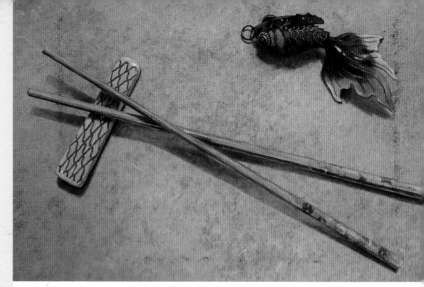

■ UNDERSTANDING COLOR TEMPERATURE

The main reason warm colors are differentiated as warm is that they are typically high in chroma and light in value. Cool colors may be high chroma but mostly are lower in value. The difference between warm and cool has nothing to do with the myth of advancing or receding colors.

Our eyes know perfectly well that the blazing red-oranges of a sunset are not nearest us in the landscape. Those "receding" blues are generally the result of using pale tints of blue, so that is a result of chroma and value rather than just the hue itself.

Contrasts between warm and cool colors are an enormously useful fundamental principle of painting, so we need to understand how to use them effectively. While the complexities of vision and color perception are staggering, the best scientific consensus we have is that red-orange holds the position as hottest of the warm colors and its complement of cyan the position of the coolest of the cool colors.

Arigato
Lorena Kloosterboer
At a glance, you can see that cool blues and cyans dominate this painting. Hints of magenta, low-chroma red, and earth colors offer a warm contrast to the higher-chroma and more saturated blues.

Variations on a Theme
Elizabeth Crabtree
A series of small, quick paintings like this one can be a great way to explore alternate warm and cool color relationships. Toward the left, cool monochromatic blues establish a definite mood, while toward the right, intense red-orange and red colors illustrate the warm extreme. Other paintings in the series produce other possible combinations of warm and cool colors.

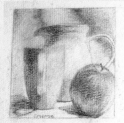
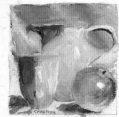
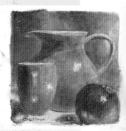
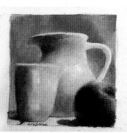
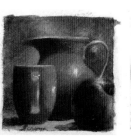
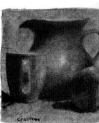

WARM AND COOL COLORS

Dividing the Sundell Color Wheel according to the warm and cool color concept, it becomes obvious that colors on or near the dividing line may not be warm or cool at all, but show qualities of both.

For the painter, it is often the relative relationships of warm and cool colors that matter the most. We can evaluate any color in relation to another color in terms of which is the warmest and which is the coolest.

For example, comparing blue-violet with magenta, it is evident that magenta is closer to red-orange, the hottest placement on the color wheel, and therefore warmer than blue-violet. But if we compare magenta with red, it is cooler than red because red is closest of those two colors on the color wheel to red-orange. So whether we regard magenta as warm or cool is determined by its relationship to our choice of a comparison color on the color wheel.

Looking at more subtle variations, French Ultramarine Blue has slightly more red in its appearance than standard Ultramarine Blue, so it is considered to be warmer than Ultramarine Blue. Consulting the Artist's Color Wheel by Bruce MacEvoy on page 16 will help show you positions of the pigments in many acrylic paints so you can quickly establish their warmth or coolness in relation to each other.

By paying attention to these relative comparisons, warm and cool contrasts in your painting can be emphasized where you want to attract the viewer's eye and minimized where you do not want a powerful focal point. These warm and cool contrasts add a wonderful vibrant look to a painting, making them an invaluable tool for the artist.

Warm colors

Cool colors

Three Crofts **Jim Woodman**

The color balance in this painting swings dramatically to the warm with the powerful mass of hot red-orange across two-thirds of the painting. The sky with its soft cool blue intensifies the warm emphasis. Notice that a deliberate imbalance between warm and cool colors has been used in this painting. Equal amounts of warm and cool are not nearly as powerful as a deliberately invoked imbalance.

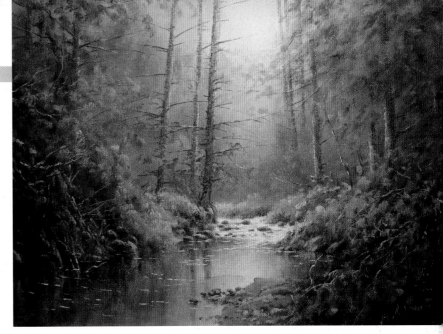

Romantic Woodland **Joe Hush**

A glowing warmth suffuses this landscape with softly blended yellows and oranges mixing into the green foliage and shadows. A partially neutralized blue-violet in the tree trunks and shadows provides a cooler note against all the warm colors.

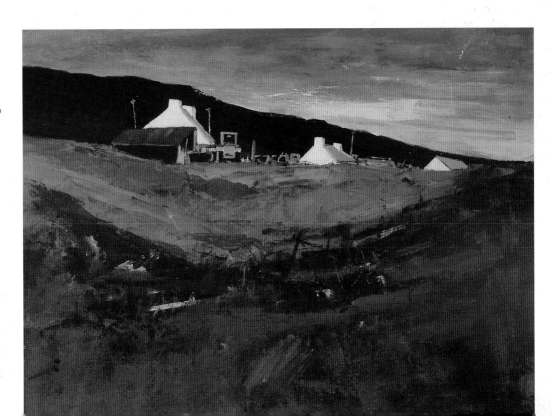

Neutrals and earth tones

Neutral grays and earth tones effectively enhance the more brilliant colors in a painting. They can also be used for either subdued or dramatic moods. The power of their subtlety in creating mood is often underused in acrylic painting. Many artists overlook them because acrylics were initially regarded as brightly colored paints that mixed harshly. Let's examine other possibilities.

Single-pigment paints that are already neutral, such as the earthy colors that include Yellow Ocher and Raw Umber, can be employed. Multi-pigment paints such as Alizarin Crimson Hue and Naples Yellow Hue are available. Mixing with their complements can neutralize high-chroma paints. Mixing three colors equidistant on the Sundell Color Wheel produces neutralized grays.

Learning to choose the most appropriate method of mixing neutrals for the specific purpose is an important skill for an artist. The manufactured multiple-pigment paints have no little flickers of unevenly mixed paint color enlivening them, and they do not shift into other colorations across an area by gradually emphasizing one color in the mix a little more. The rich diversity accessible through mixing is far more interesting than homogenous purchased neutral mixtures.

NEUTRAL PIGMENTS ON THE COLOR WHEEL

Most of the neutralized colors, including earth colors in this color wheel, are single-pigment paints substituted into the Sundell Color Wheel. Exceptions are Lapis Lazuli, a powdered natural stone, and Alizarin Crimson, a multi-pigment mixture. The illustrated paints are as follows:

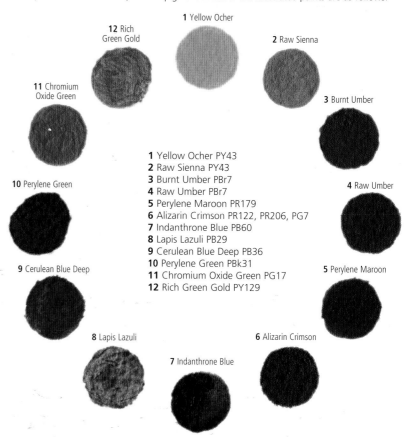

1 Yellow Ocher
12 Rich Green Gold
2 Raw Sienna
11 Chromium Oxide Green
3 Burnt Umber
10 Perylene Green
4 Raw Umber
9 Cerulean Blue Deep
5 Perylene Maroon
8 Lapis Lazuli
7 Indanthrone Blue
6 Alizarin Crimson

1 Yellow Ocher PY43
2 Raw Sienna PY43
3 Burnt Umber PBr7
4 Raw Umber PBr7
5 Perylene Maroon PR179
6 Alizarin Crimson PR122, PR206, PG7
7 Indanthrone Blue PB60
8 Lapis Lazuli PB29
9 Cerulean Blue Deep PB36
10 Perylene Green PBk31
11 Chromium Oxide Green PG17
12 Rich Green Gold PY129

USING THE NEUTRALS COLOR WHEEL

Consider the Neutrals Color Wheel above as a starting point, not a destination. Often other ways of creating neutrals will be superior for your paintings rather than simply choosing your paint from this color wheel. However, there will be times when the paints on this color wheel can work beautifully for you.

Earth colors
Single-pigment earth tones are the most useful group of paints on the Neutrals Color Wheel. These paints were originally natural clays made into paint but in modern times are manufactured pigments. The iron oxides easily dominate this category. Yellow Ocher, Raw Sienna, Burnt Umber, and Raw Umber fall into this group.

Blue colors
Indanthrone Blue is such a powerful pigment that it is excellent for dark-valued neutrals, but when tinted with Titanium White it may not be neutralized enough, depending on the purpose. Lapis Lazuli is chosen simply because of a lack of other choices. Far more earthy colors are available than blue neutrals. Cerulean Blue Deep is a reasonable choice for its category. Greater selections of neutralized blues are readily achieved by mixing the wide range of higher-chroma blues with their complements.

Greens
Greens and yellow-greens pose another set of issues. More choices are available, but not necessarily excellent choices. Cobalt Green, unlike the various cobalt blue paints, is decidedly dull and lifeless, even though it is a single-pigment paint. Chromium Oxide Green is another single-pigment neutralized green, which is more "alive" than Cobalt Green. Mixing with other colors readily alters Chromium Oxide Green to a range of desirable neutrals.

MIXING EARTH TONES TO NEUTRALIZE OTHER COLORS

Raw Umber is the star performer in this group. Raw Umber can be mixed with practically any other color to neutralize it. Yellow Ocher is another valuable earth tone, but it will turn greenish when mixed with blue pigments. Otherwise, it is as useful as Raw Umber. For greater variation, the two can be used together in many neutralizing mixtures.

The swatches shown here were mixed directly as they were painted on heavy watercolor paper. All tints are made with Titanium White.

Yellow Ocher + Chromium Oxide Green

Yellow Ocher works extremely well with Chromium Oxide Green.

Yellow Ocher + Chromium Oxide Green + Titanium White
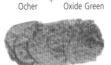
You can see the versatility of the previous mixture as a tint.

Yellow Ocher + Raw Umber + Chromium Oxide Green

Using both Yellow Ocher and Raw Umber in a mixture with Chromium Oxide Green extends the possibilities further.

Yellow Ocher + Raw Umber + Chromium Oxide Green + Titanium White

The tint of the previous mixture shows subtle and useful variations that can be used readily in foliage, landscapes, and other subjects.

Raw Umber + Hansa Yellow Medium

You can immediately see how subdued Hansa Yellow Medium appears when mixed with Raw Umber.

Raw Umber + Cadmium Red Medium

This mixture smolders with a deep glow.

Raw Umber + Ultramarine Blue
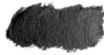
Raw Umber greatly reduces the chroma of Ultramarine Blue in this example.

Raw Umber + Ultramarine Blue + Titanium White

Tinting the previous mixture produces softly grayed blues.

Raw Umber + Cobalt Blue

Different blue pigments interact with Raw Umber to produce unique variations.

Raw Umber + Cobalt Blue + Titanium White

Those variations carry over into the tints of the mixtures.

Perylene Green
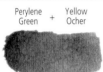
Perylene Green painted heavily on the left and thinner on the right. It is pictured unmixed, as it is not a commonly used green, although it has great potential for painting neutrals.

Perylene Green + Yellow Ocher
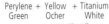
A lovely neutralized color results from this mixture.

Perylene Green + Yellow Ocher + Titanium White
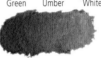
The tint of the previous mixture shows an even more subtle neutralized mixture.

Perylene Green + Raw Umber + Titanium White
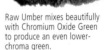
The tint of Perylene Green mixed with Raw Umber is another combination that offers wonderful potential in painting.

Raw Umber + Chromium Oxide Green

Raw Umber mixes beautifully with Chromium Oxide Green to produce an even lower-chroma green.

Raw Umber + Chromium Oxide Green + Titanium White
The tint of the previous mixture shows additional potential for foliage variations.

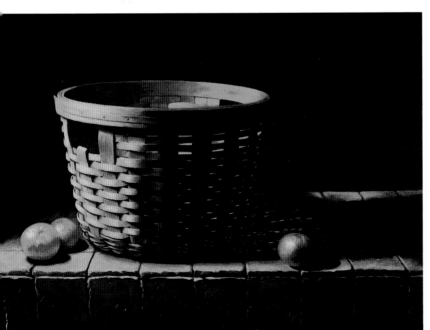

PLEASE LEAVE BURNT SIENNA AT THE STORE

Actually, the earth tone Burnt Sienna can be used successfully as long as no Titanium White is added. Since most artists use Titanium White constantly in their work, the unpleasant chalky pinkish coloration from tinted Burnt Sienna is a predictable outcome. This does not improve the painting when it happens. But if you have a passionate desire to paint with a truly ugly color, go ahead and use it that way.

If you want a similar look that lacks the chalky pink problem, use Quinacridone Burnt Orange, Quinacridone Burnt Scarlet, or even Quinacridone Sienna in the mixture instead. Your painting will sing happily.

Hearthside Joseph Krawczyk
Earth tones dominate this painting with its strong value contrasts. No bright high-chroma colors appear in the painting and it also lacks cool neutrals. This work shows how subtle neutrals can create a powerful painting.

NEUTRALS FROM COMPLEMENTS

The mixing of neutral colors from complements can be reviewed on pages 56–59. Many options exist in the Sundell Color Wheel with the list of substitutions on page 17. These examples should inspire you to test your own collection of paints on heavy watercolor paper to explore what they have to offer.

The following examples are mixed directly on heavy watercolor paper and the tints are made with Titanium White.

Phthalo Green + Quinacridone
(Yellow Shade)   Rose

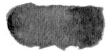

The two complements create a subtle neutral gray where they are most evenly mixed in the center.

Phthalo + Quinacridone + Titanium
Green   Rose   White
(Yellow
Shade)

This tint of the previous mixture exhibits the soft gray more clearly.

Quinacridone + Bismuth
Violet   Yellow

This mixture shows how far pigments that are complements can vary from a neutral gray.

Dioxazine + Hansa Yellow
Purple   Medium

This pair of complements also mixes to a warmer neutral that is still useful.

Pyrrole + Cobalt
Orange   Teal

Once again the two complements warmly neutralize each other.

Cobalt + Cadmium
Blue   Orange
          Medium

This particular mixture is an especially desirable combination for the yellow-orange/blue complementary axis.

Cobalt   Cadmium   Titanium
Blue + Orange + White
         Medium

The soft grays obvious in this tint show why this combination is so valuable for painting.

Phthalo   Cadmium   Titanium
Green + Red Medium + White
(Blue Shade)

This is another complementary combination that deviates from neutral gray but is useful in painting.

WATER, DISTANCE, AND NEUTRALS

Two landscapes solve the problem of establishing distance and painting water with neutralized colors. Each creates an entirely different mood.

Bedruthan Steps **Paul Geraghty**

This painting reveals a great expanse of space, in contrast to the close intimacy of the following painting. Higher-chroma colors appear at the bottom of the canvas nearest the viewer. The colors neutralize and lighten in value in a carefully controlled progression to the pale and indistinct horizon. Warm neutrals on the beach play against the cool neutrals of the water, but the overall color temperature of the painting is unquestionably cool.

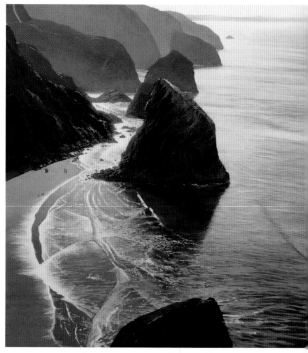

Time for Reflection **Paul James**

While many people would consider this a somber or melancholy scene, the title implies a quietly reflective mood in tune with the season. With low-chroma color, the strength of the painting lies in the control of values. We sense the quality of light on a fall evening with the sky reflected in the stream. The cooler neutrals in the far trees, which also have lightened in value, indicate distance.

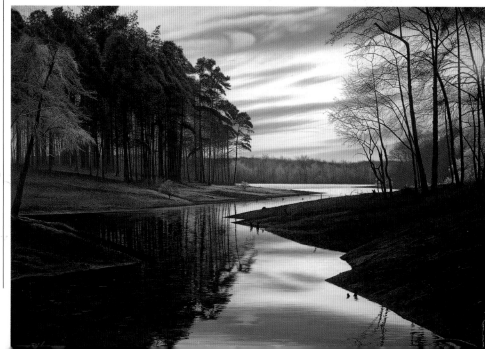

Carefully selected neutrals can make accents of bright color really pop. The artists worked with neutrals in contrasting ways to make it happen in these two paintings.

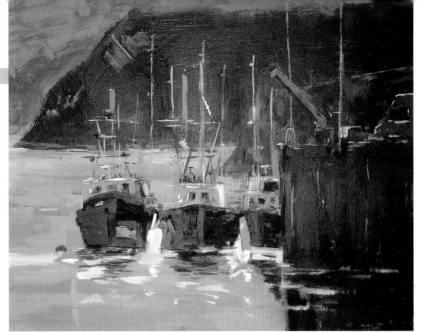

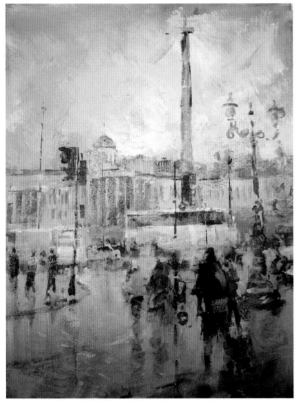

Moored at Portree **Jim Woodman**
Complementary blues and oranges provide the main palette for this painting. The blues are far more neutralized than in the painting at left and large areas are devoted to dark, somber grays. Those brooding grays were laid over a layer of orange that can be seen in bits and pieces throughout the painting. Those orange accents bring the scene to life.

With the use of neutrals, color temperature can be established in your paintings. Compare the cool emphasis in *Winter's Embrace* below, with the warm emphasis in *Hearthside* on page 73. Both paintings effectively use neutrals to altogether different ends.

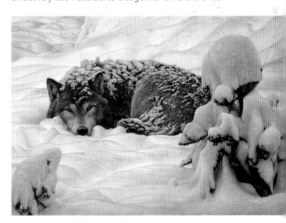

Winter's Embrace **Daniel Smith**
You nearly feel like shivering looking at the cool neutral grays in this painting. The few warm earthy neutrals in the animal fur only accentuate the overall cool temperature of this painting. No high-chroma colors have been used in this work either, but it completely contrasts with Hearthside on page 73.

Winter in Trafalgar Square **Sera M. Knight**
Painterly splashes of variegated neutrals are used for the majority of this painting. The neutrals tend toward cool blues, which make the bright red accents really catch the eye. Distance is implied with warmer neutrals in the foreground dissipating to cooler neutrals farther back in the painting.

As explained in the Primary palette on pages 50–51, the three primary colors mix to an approximate neutral gray. Since the Sundell Color Wheel is comprised of single-pigment paints, any three paints equally spaced around the wheel will also mix to an approximate neutral gray. Look at the intriguing variations in the following examples, all tinted with Titanium White.

Phthalo Green (Blue Shade) + Cadmium Orange Medium + Quinacridone Violet + Titanium White	Ultramarine Blue + Bismuth Yellow + Cadmium Red Medium + Titanium White	Phthalo Green (Yellow Shade) + Dioxazine Purple + Pyrrole Orange + Titanium White

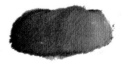

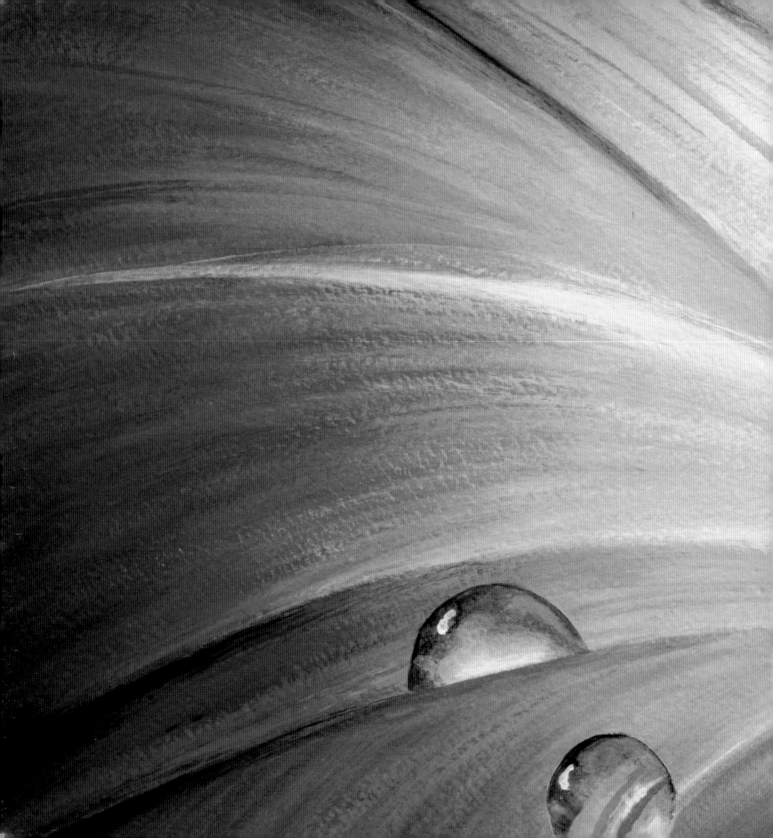

choosing pigments for painting

The value of everything you have learned about your materials and the aesthetics of using them comes alive in the application of that knowledge to a wide range of subject matter. This is when you can fully appreciate the solid foundation you have built for yourself. You are ready to create exceptional color in acrylics as your inspired visions find their way into the paintings on your easel.

Choosing and using a color scheme

Standing before the easel contemplating a pristine white canvas, the artist is faced with major decisions about how to proceed. What paints should be chosen for the palette? How should the subject be interpreted through those color choices? What selections will help create the desired appearance and mood? Choosing a color scheme is not necessarily a simple matter, although it greatly simplifies the painting decisions that follow. On the following pages, photographs of a number of painting subjects and potential color schemes are analyzed—try out the suggestions to hone your skills.

■ EXERCISES IN CHOOSING COLOR SCHEMES

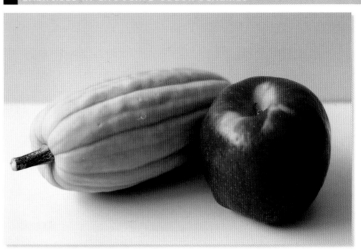

■ TEN STEPS FOR CHOOSING AND USING A COLOR SCHEME

1 Identify the main color of importance in the chosen subject.

2 Look at the other colors in the subject to see how they relate to that main color on the Sundell Color Wheel (see page 17).

3 When a pattern of color relationships begins to emerge, determine which color schemes include those particular relationships.

4 With one or more color schemes under consideration, notice any colors in the subject that do not fit those color schemes.

5 Evaluate how to alter those dissonant colors to bring them into alignment with your possible color scheme choices.

6 Decide which of those color schemes will work best for your interpretation of the subject you want to paint, keeping in mind the mood you want to create.

7 Using the chosen color scheme, select the actual paints for those placements on the Sundell Color Wheel.

8 Lay out your palette, leaving more space for the main color and any other colors that will be used extensively.

9 Mix any combinations you will need, such as neutral mixtures, in large enough quantities to ensure that your colors remain consistent where they need to be.

10 Proceed to paint your interpretation of the subject.

Analagous color scheme The color scheme in the above photo of a squash and an apple can be easily resolved. Either the yellow-orange of the squash or the red of the apple can be considered the main color. Looking at them on the color wheel, an analogous palette becomes an obvious choice if we ignore the touches of green on the apple and squash stem. A widely spaced analogous palette of New Gamboge, Naphthol Red Medium, and Quinacridone Violet could make a beautiful painting of the subject. This palette selection uses substitutes from page 17 for the yellow-orange and red placements on the Sundell Color Wheel.

New Gamboge

Naphthol Red Medium

Quinacridone Violet

Titanium White

Ultramarine Blue

Cerulean Blue

Perylene Green

Chromium Oxide Green

Bismuth Yellow

Raw Umber

Raw Sienna

Permanent Green

Titanium White

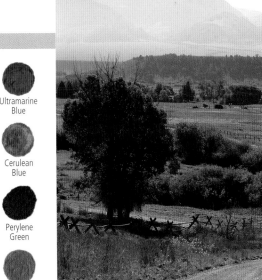

Modified analogous color scheme At a glance, the analogous color scheme looks like a perfect choice for the landscape shown in the photo above. The blues and greens harmonize and blend beautifully. Noticing the hints of yellow or yellow-green in the flowers and meadow, we realize this might have to be an extended analogous palette. Ultramarine Blue, Cerulean Blue, Perylene Green, Chromium Oxide Green, and Bismuth Yellow could work well for this purpose.

Unfortunately, those colors due not lend themselves to a naturalistic rendering of the road or jack fence. Still, the harmony of the analogous color scheme speaks to us in the landscape, while the road and fence add to the composition. One solution is to modify the analogous color scheme by adding Raw Umber and Raw Sienna to the palette in order to accommodate the road and fence. Raw Umber could be useful for tree branches and modifying greens in deep shadow as well. In that case, the dark Perylene Green would not be as necessary, and perhaps Permanent Green could be selected in its place.

Sometimes the perfect choice is not so perfect after all, but can still be used with a simple adjustment, since the look of the finished painting is more important than arbitrarily staying within rigid guidelines. After all, the use of a color scheme is meant to enhance the interpretation in paint of our chosen subject, not hinder it.

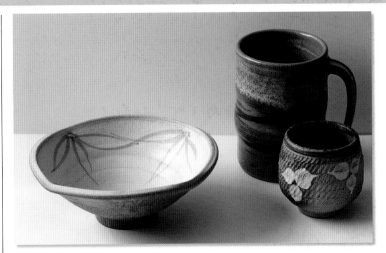

Complementary color scheme Rich, earthy orange hues greet our eyes in this photo. The pale teal blue on the tall mug speaks of a complementary relationship to the earthy orange. An interesting palette for this subject could be the choice of Quinacridone Burnt Orange for the red-orange placement on the Sundell Color Wheel and the choice of Cobalt Teal for its complement.

For a somewhat different look, the colors could shift to Quinacridone Gold for the yellow-orange placement on the color wheel and Cobalt Blue for the complement in the blue placement on the wheel.

Tetradic color scheme To paint the neutralized greens in the mug and cup shown in the photo, the palette could be extended to the tetradic color scheme, adding Quinacridone Magenta and Rich Green Gold for the magenta and yellow-green placements. This would create a tetradic color scheme when added to either of the previously mentioned complements, a rectangular one with the Quinacridone Burnt Orange and Cobalt Teal pair, and a square one with Quinacridone Gold and Cobalt Blue.

     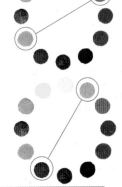 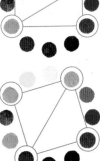

Quinacridone Burnt Orange

Cobalt Teal

Quinacridone Gold

Cobalt Blue

Quinacridone Magenta

Rich Green Gold

Titanium White

Titanium White is included in all the palettes below

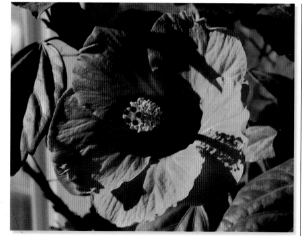

Cadmium Orange Medium

Cobalt Blue

Cadmium Red

Phthalo Green (Blue Shade)

Tetradic color scheme 1 Yellow-orange is clearly the main color in this photo of a hibiscus. The stamen shows a little red as well. The tetradic palette is the most limited one that will produce yellow-orange, red, neutralized green, and a neutral gray. Cadmium Orange Medium mixes with its complement, Cobalt Blue, to make a soft gray, while Cadmium Red combines with Phthalo Green (Blue Shade) to create a neutralized green for the leaves.

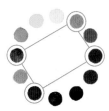

Quinacridone Rose

Chromium Oxide Green

Tetradic color scheme 2 An alternate tetradic color scheme could use Cadmium Orange Medium with the Cobalt Blue complement, but shift to Quinacridone Rose for the colors in the flower. Its complement, Chromium Oxide Green, would mix neutral greens.

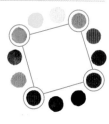

Quinacridone Violet

Bismuth Yellow

Tertiary color scheme The first tetradic color scheme could be expanded to a tertiary color scheme by adding the complementary pair of Quinacridone Violet and Bismuth Yellow. This would enhance the shadows, particularly in the flower itself.

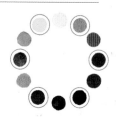

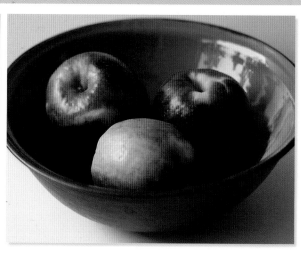

Titanium White is included in both the palettes below

Cadmium Orange Medium

Pyrrole Orange

Cadmium Red Deep

Cobalt Turquoise

Split-complement color scheme 1 The above photo poses some challenges for selecting a color scheme. Red is the main color. It relates to the yellow and yellow-orange in the apples well enough, but the turquoise-green interior of the bowl is a little jarring. Cobalt Turquoise would be the nearest paint match, and it does not complement red but does complement the red-orange placement on the color wheel. Shifting the apples to more of a red-orange and omitting the yellow and yellow-green in the apples could make a workable split-complement palette of Cadmium Orange Medium, Pyrrole Orange, Cadmium Red Deep, and Cobalt Turquoise.

Split-complement color scheme 2 Another approach could be taken. If rosier apples are painted, a different potential split-complement palette is revealed. Shifting the deep turquoise-green interior of the bowl to a green or yellow-green, a palette of Quinacridone Rose, Perylene Green, Phthalo Green (Yellow Shade), and Bismuth Yellow becomes a lively option.

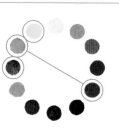

Quinacridone Rose

Perylene Green

Phthalo Green (Yellow Shade)

Bismuth Yellow

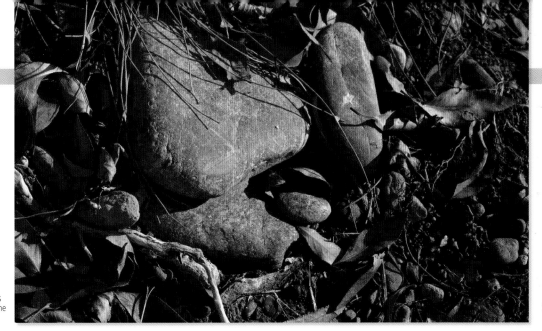

Titanium white is included in both the palettes below

Titanium white is included in both the palettes below

Two pairs of complements

Low-chroma earth colors and neutrals abound in this image. The most striking contrast arises from the muted orange leaves that are complementary to the muted blue-gray rocks. Cadmium Orange Medium complementing Ultramarine Blue would provide a great starting point for this painting. The soft neutral grays made possible by mixing those two paints would be extremely effective.

However, adding a second complementary pair of colors would create more interest. The largest rock has a faintly purplish hue, so Dioxazine Purple with a yellow complement to neutralize it makes an appealing option. Choosing Cadmium Yellow Medium for that yellow would provide a more opaque color to work against the powerful tinting strength of Dioxazine Purple. Tints of Cadmium Yellow could be used for small accents in the leaves.

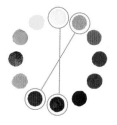

Cadmium Orange Medium

Ultramarine Blue

Dioxazine Purple

Cadmium Yellow Medium

Split-complement color scheme 1

Choosing a split-complement palette could be effective for this image. Looking at the list of substitute colors for the color positions on the Sundell Color Wheel (see page 17) is helpful in selecting such a palette.

Can you see how using Yellow Ocher, Quinacridone Gold, and Quinacridone Burnt Orange with a complement of Cobalt Blue would work? The luscious neutrals from mixing Cobalt Blue with those colors could make a lovely background of rocks and earth with lively leaves painted in the quinacridone colors.

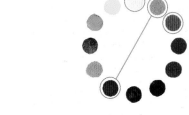

Yellow Ocher   Quinacridone Burnt Orange   Quinacridone Gold   Cobalt Blue

Split-complement color scheme 2

An earthier variation of the previous split-complement palette could be selected. Yellow Ocher, Raw Sienna, and Burnt Umber could be used with a complementary Ultramarine Blue. A quieter painting would result, as none of the vibrant and semitransparent quinacridones would be present.

   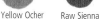

Yellow Ocher   Raw Sienna   Burnt Umber   Ultramarine Blue

Neutral color scheme

For further exploration, refer to Neutrals and earth tones on pages 72–75. You could also choose to use triadic neutrals to create the background and rocks for this painting. Another option would be to use Raw Umber to reduce chroma in Ultramarine Blue or Cobalt Blue in the painting instead of mixing with the complementary orange color. Learning to create a variety of lovely neutrals leads to more interesting interpretations of subjects like this one.

Light, shade, and shadow

Understanding light and how it works with shadows and shade is essential for painting the illusion of three-dimensional forms on a two-dimensional surface.

Look for the source and angle of the light falling across the subject; the shadow automatically falls in the opposite direction. Getting this established correctly in a painting is the first step for a beginning artist. But the interplay of light and color in shadows is more complex than this. The artist must learn to see what really happens to light in a shadow to create rich paintings that breathe with life and vitality.

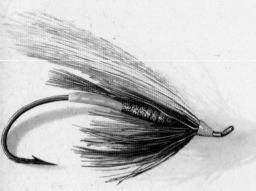

Steelhead Flies (detail) **Bern Sundell**
Here, shadow defines the form of the fly. Shadows and highlights were painted on the hook and body of the fly to indicate their shapes, but the shadow lying on the table shows us the hook arching upward, so we immediately understand the form of the fly.

CREATING A SHADOW USING A COMPLEMENTARY COLOR

A shadow, first and foremost, is an area of reduced light. Reduced light results in neutralized colors, so mixing a color with its complement creates a neutral for painting the shadow (see Complementary palette, pages 56–57).

Cadmium Red Medium

Chromium Oxide Green

Indanthrone Blue

Titanium White

Yellow Ocher

1 Paint the table with a mixture of Yellow Ocher, Indanthrone Blue, and Titanium White in a slightly uneven blend to give a livelier look to the color.

2 Paint the shadow of the pepper falling on the table with less white and more Indanthrone Blue in the mixture, establishing a cooler tone for the shadow.

3 Paint the shadows with a mixture of Chromium Oxide Green and Cadmium Red Medium, green and red being complements on the Sundell Color Wheel.

Chromium Oxide Green and Cadmium Red mix, as the pepper reflects some of its color into the shadow. This blends into the rest of the shadow, leaving the darkest area where the pepper touches the table.

Choosing a color scheme
Bowl of Eggs by Bern Sundell was painted with a modified tetradic color scheme (see Tetradic color palette, page 60). His color scheme is of blue and orange complements paired with purple and yellow complements as the dominant palette for the painting. By emphasizing the cool blues, he created a painting with a cool, breezy, moonlit feel. Compare this with the exercise on the opposite page.

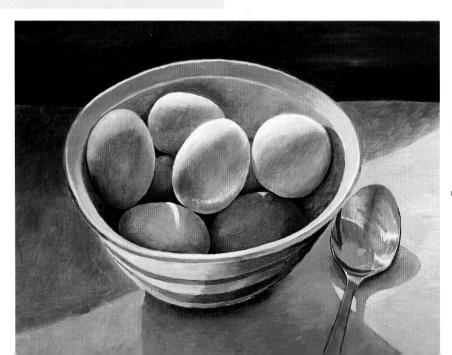

Main palette

Prism Violet

Cadmium Orange Medium

Cadmium Yellow Light

Titanium White

Ultramarine Blue

Additional palette
Cadmium Red Medium
Cobalt Teal
Raw Umber
Cerulean Blue
Yellow Ocher

EXPLORING SHADE AND SHADOW

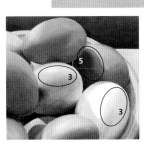

An egg is a deceptively simple ovoid shape. The painter who pays attention to the appearance of an egg can quickly learn a great deal about the many ways light behaves in shadows. Painting a bowl of naturally colored eggs from a diverse flock of mixed-breed chickens in angled light brings a whole new understanding of the interplay of light and shadow.

The angle of light falling across the eggs establishes where the shadows fall. That is only the beginning, however. Light then reflects in multiple directions from the curved surfaces of the eggs, creating myriad plays of light in the shadows. In this painting you will see six main effects of this play of light.

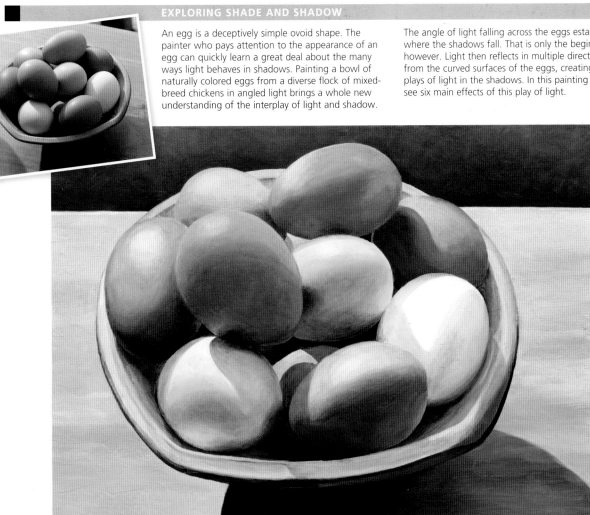

 Anthraquinone Red

 Cadmium Orange Deep

 Cadmium Orange Medium

 Quinacridone Rose

 Raw Sienna

 Raw Umber

 Titanium White

 Ultramarine Blue

 Ultramarine Violet

 Yellow Ocher

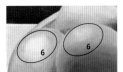

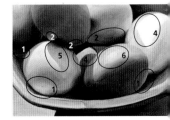

1 Light can be observed reflecting from the inside of the bowl onto the eggs, making lighter areas within the shadows. These appear as soft glows of light.

2 Similar to the reflections from the bowl, the eggs themselves reflect back onto each other. Consequently, you can see the color of the light teal egg reflected onto the pinkish magenta egg, a bright brown onto the same pinkish magenta egg, and brown onto a light teal egg.

3 The curving shape of an egg makes a soft, diffuse shadow edge where the light falls across it, gently descending into the shadow on that egg.

4 When the shadow of one egg falls across another egg, a hard edge is seen on the shadow lying on the second egg. That edge results from the abrupt cut-off of light hitting the second egg. When two eggs cast shadows on a third egg, an interesting light shape can occur between the separate shadows.

5 Where one egg touches another egg, very little light can enter, so this is the darkest shadow area. It gradually blends with the curve of the egg into parts of the shadow that receive more reflected light. These soft modulations of shade are important to notice.

6 The bright highlight where the light directly strikes the surface of the egg also has diffused edges, once again due to the curving surface of the egg.

Backgrounds

A background sounds like a simple element that can be added at the end after the important part is painted. However, the hapless artist who tries to add a background as an afterthought often makes the appalling discovery that nothing works. Such backgrounds have ruined many promising paintings. Let's explore some color strategies to help your backgrounds properly emphasize the main subject.

ANALYZING BACKGROUNDS IN PAINTINGS

Analyzing backgrounds in different paintings develops your ability to plan effective backgrounds for your own paintings. Practice identifying the strategies used in paintings that attract you. Identifying failed strategies also helps, but right now let's focus on some good examples to see what works.

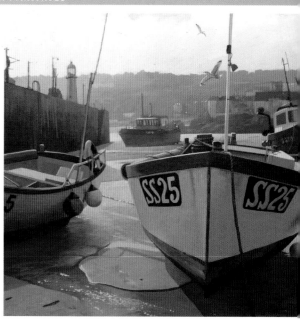

A Quiet Morning **Paul Geraghty**
Strategy number four makes the background recede into the distance. We sense a gentle morning fog in this lovely painting. Sharp contrasts in value in the foreground unobtrusively fade into those subdued wooded hills behind the harbor. The chroma of the colors decreases along with the loss of those contrasting values. This background beautifully sets the scene for the boats.

CHOOSING BACKGROUND COLORS

Here are eight strategies for choosing effective background colors.

1 Use color harmony to integrate the background with the main subject. Choose analogous colors or even the same hues used in the subject.

2 Use complementary colors to sharply contrast with the main subject. The complementary background may be partially neutralized as needed.

3 Neutral colors in the background make the main subject sparkle. Alternatively, they can make the main subject appear more substantial.

4 Adjust values to make the background recede. Neutralizing the chroma simultaneously enhances this effect.

5 Use light reversals to sharply accent a main subject. Dark values opposing light values create powerful contrasts.

6 Create a supporting background pattern for a more stylized appearance. Use colors in that pattern to accent the subject using a suitable color scheme.

7 A solid-color background puts the focus squarely on the subject. If the subject is luminous, avoid a white background because it will kill the luminosity.

8 Creatively combine these strategies to paint backgrounds uniquely suited to your subject matter. Remember, the objective is to paint a background that draws attention to the main subject.

LIGHT REVERSALS

These two paintings both use strategy number five but in totally opposite ways. Either way, these light reversals really work. This is a good example of how any strategy can be used to create altogether different looks.

▼ *Sun Struck* **Daniel Smith**
This painting is a study in values first and foremost. The low-chroma colors are quietly understated. A subtle play between warm and cool colors can be seen in the bluish sheen against the warm browns on the elk's head and antlers, while the background also has a slight bluish undertone contrasting with the warm foreground. The visual emphasis is focused on values in this painting, with deep darkness forming a backdrop for the wary bull illuminated by a stray beam of sunlight.

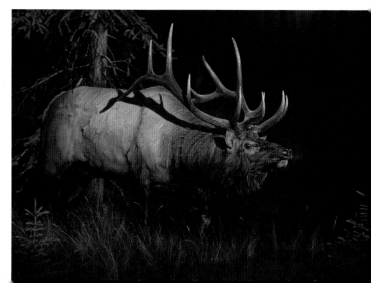

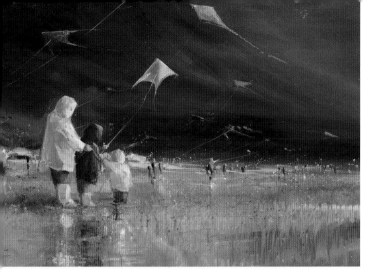

Windy Kids Jennifer Bowman
Powerful contrasts in both value and hue make this background indispensable to the main subject of the painting. The dark blue sky finds complementary orange hues in the raincoats and beach, showing the full impact of strategy number two. Furthermore, if one uses the additive color complements, the yellows in the raincoats and reflections in the wet beach serve equally well as complements to the blue sky, increasing the visual effect. This artist did not neglect value, applying strategy number five with a dark background and light main subject.

▼ **Untitled** Frederick G. Denys
The main trees are the darkest part of the painting, silhouetted against the blazing radiance of the background. Drenched in light, colors are brighter in this work, especially in the areas nearest the light source. Despite the brighter colors than used in Sun Struck (see left), contrasting values are still the backbone of this painting. It is an excellent example of how light reversal can be used with striking results.

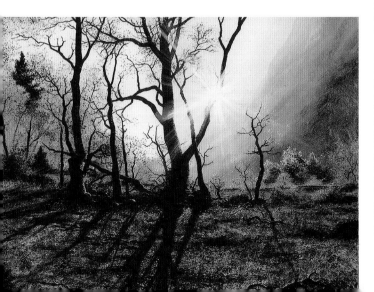

PATTERNED BACKGROUNDS

Geometric patterned backgrounds that are similar in structure establish the shared commonality of this pair of paintings in their application of strategy number six. The composition and geometric patterns themselves are almost alike, but the color choices bear no resemblance to each other.

Paint Horse Carrie Wild
Neutrals characterize the palette in this painting. Rectangular shapes dominate the background and are loosely painted. Notice the contrast between warm and cool background colors, echoing the play of warm and cool in the horse. The cool gray behind the horse pushes the subject forward. On the right, the dark rectangle introduces an element of strategy number five as well. The brighter whites in the horse make it stand out, yet it remains integrated with the background.

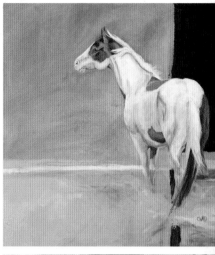

Hello Robin Pedrero
The colorful palette chosen for this painting obscures the similarity of the composition and geometric pattern to the horse painting. The loosely painted washes of color glow behind the dark bird, showing the use of strategy number five. Upon closer examination we see that the color choices follow strategy number one by using similar hues in the background and main subject. Another contrast appears in the way the background blue is lower chroma than the tiny blue foreground flowers, but the background oranges are distinctly brighter than the rusty orange in the bird.

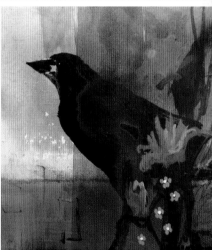

OBSERVE, APPLY, PRACTICE

Observe how backgrounds are handled in the paintings you see, noticing what strategies make them successful. Observe any flaws and think of what strategy might have solved the difficulty. Observe everything around you in daily life to find unexpected inspirations for backgrounds in your paintings.

Apply what you observe in your own paintings. Observation without action is useless. Feel free to experiment with different background treatments in your own work. Be alert to what works and what does not.

Practice your skills to improve them. Using your own failed paintings to learn what really works is part of succeeding in your art. Regard your paintings as one long creative continuum so that any failed painting is only a stepping stone to greater understanding and power in your paintings.

Skies and clouds

Skies lift our spirits with their ever-changing displays of clouds and light. Clouds dance and move across the sky, sometimes with gentle grace and other times with powerful menacing storms. Clouds catch the light, scattering beams across the waiting landscape or turning the sky molten with sunset colors. A sure way to engage your viewer is to capture the radiance of a sky in your painting.

Skies and clouds can usually be painted with a simple palette emphasizing blues, grays, and white. Complementary colors can be mixed to create a variety of grays for the sky, bringing a liveliness that is altogether missing if you settle for those dead neutral grays you can buy in tubes and jars.

For sunrise or sunset the palette expands to include reds, yellows, and oranges in particular. Night skies pose different challenges. Instead of Cerulean Blue, Ultramarine Blue, or Cobalt Blue—paints that are suited to brighter skies—deeper indigo blues are needed. Indanthrone Blue works

especially well for a night sky because the pigment is so powerful it can be painted in a range that goes nearly to black.

In most cases, painting the sky first is advantageous. This allows the blends in the sky to be smoothly painted across the entire area and any tree branches or other forms in front of the sky to be added later. Trying to paint a smooth blend in "hopscotch" patches seen through tree branches is a thankless task and frequently gives a poor result. Let your painting process be as graceful as the skies you paint and your paintings will become a source of delight.

EXAMPLE OF PAINTING A SKY

For this painting a simple palette was selected, including Cerulean Blue, Titanium White, Cobalt Blue, Cadmium Orange Medium, Quinacridone Burnt Orange, Quinacridone Gold, Raw Umber, Ultramarine Blue, and Ultramarine Violet.

 Cerulean Blue

 Titanium White

 Cobalt Blue

Cadmium Orange Medium

 Quinacridone Burnt Orange

 Quinacridone Gold

Raw Umber

 Ultramarine Blue

 Ultramarine Violet

1 Blocking in Block the painting in using Cerulean Blue in the cloudless parts of the sky and tints of a mixture of Cobalt Blue and Cadmium Orange Medium for the grays in the clouds. Paint the distant mountains in tints of Ultramarine Blue and Ultramarine Violet. Establish the foreground with tints of Raw Umber and Quinacridone Gold.

2 Build up detail Apply pale tints of Quinacridone Gold in portions of the clouds, leaving a slight yellow glow. Add tints of Ultramarine Violet to some of the gray areas of the clouds. Embellish the mountains and foreground slightly in their original colors.

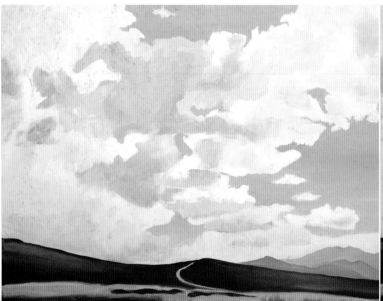

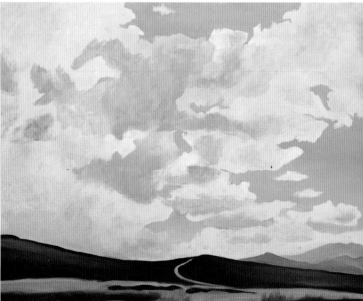

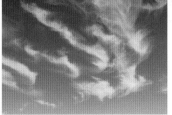
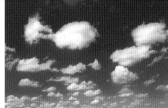
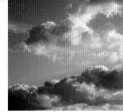

Cirrus clouds   Cumulus clouds   Stratus clouds

When pigments mix they absorb light, so they behave differently from light itself (see page 9). Pigments also vary wildly in hue, chroma, and value, so any two pigments may not mix exactly as we would predict from their placement on the Sundell Color Wheel, which organizes them by general hue categories. The prediction from a pigment mixing wheel is that opposite colors—complements—will mix to a neutral gray. In real life this varies, so testing your own collection of paints will be revealing.

Select all of the possible complementary pairs from your own palette and mix them, tinting with Titanium White, to see how they behave. You will discover a rich trove of possible grays that let you match the mood and intensity of any sky you wish to paint. This gives you great power for your sky paintings. You may find it helpful to review Neutrals and earth tones on pages 72–73 or Mixing color wet-into-wet on pages 42–43.

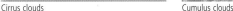

■ TYPES OF CLOUDS

While a meteorologist is concerned with the altitude of clouds and the specific types of clouds characteristic of each change in altitude, artists are more interested in the visual appearance of the clouds they wish to paint.

Clouds are grouped into three broad categories:
• Cirrus clouds are the highest in the atmosphere, thin wispy white clouds with feathery curves and swirls.
• Cumulus clouds are the puffball type of cloud, or when rising into stormy drama, those towering thunderheads. They typically have a flat bottom and are dark gray in color. The water mass in these clouds forms shadows within them.
• Stratus clouds are lower-lying flat cloud layers that include fog. They tend to be white or gray in color.

The three categories of clouds readily intermingle in the sky, since they are water droplets drifting and mixing in the air, refracting and reflecting light while moving with the wind. This adds to the delightful variety possible in your paintings. Learn to observe the shapes, colors, and play of light in the skies to improve your own cloud paintings.

3 Consider the values Work up the varying values in the sky with tinted mixtures of Cobalt Blue and Cadmium Orange Medium for the cloud grays. Controlling these values correctly is vital for the success of the painting. Notice that the forms of the cumulus clouds are becoming more recognizable and distinct. Since the clouds in the upper part of the sky are nearer to us, we are almost underneath their flat bottoms and they appear sprawled against the sky. As the clouds move to the distant horizon, those flat bottoms step away from us, becoming more obvious to our eyes.

4 The finished painting In the finished sky, some of the gray mixtures created with the Cobalt Blue and Cadmium Orange Medium complements emphasize one or the other complement. The towering cumulus cloud on the left rising from the horizon to the top of the painting has more Cadmium Orange Medium in it, while some of the clouds moving into the distance have more Cobalt Blue. Notice the refinement of values in the distant clouds, which gradually become lighter as they move away from us in the painting. Leaving subtle tints of Quinacridone Gold and Ultramarine Violet in the clouds keeps them integrated with the land in the painting because it also uses those same pigments.

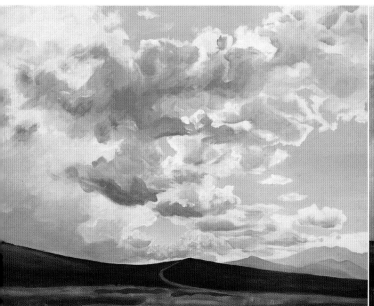

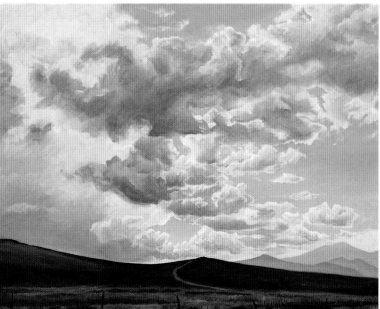

Gallery: Skies and clouds

Painting skies is exhilarating. The vastness of space in the sky above us, the dancing shapes of the clouds, and the myriad transparencies of light lure us to the paintbox. From serene washes of gentle color to turbulent choppy clouds threatening storms and lightning, skies give free range to all our emotions.

Color contrasts abound in clouds colliding with light. Sunrise and sunset express this most dramatically but in midday towering cumulus clouds provide their own share of sky drama. Watching our ever-changing skies is an endless inspiration for paintings.

Main palette
Cobalt Blue, Titanium White, Payne's Gray, and Cadmium Red

Other key colors
Cadmium Orange and Cadmium Yellow

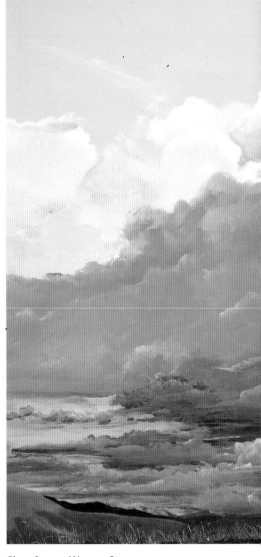

Changing Light **Paul Geraghty**
A range of blues and grays dominates this painting, but this range has a lively look because of the complementary warm yellows and oranges in the sky. Lavenders and even subtle greens crept into these clouds to add a sparkling richness. Strong value contrasts emphasize the light rays beaming through these great clouds. Skies always need something to hold them up, and this watery vista with islands and a lighthouse does the job beautifully. The quiet blue-grays of the water lead us toward the horizon and we see a startling and brightly lit cyan edge of water catching those beams of light from the radiant sky, and once again we are in the clouds…

Main palette
Ultramarine Blue, Phthalo Blue (Red Shade), Phthalo Blue (Green Shade), and Payne's Gray

Other key colors
Yellow Ocher, Naphthol Red, Mars Black, and Titanium White

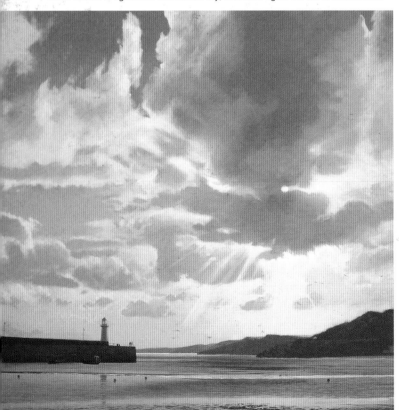

Fiery Sunset **Warren Strouse**
The tiniest sliver of land supports the artist's vision of piles of cumulus clouds. Yet this slice of land shows grasses and hills receding to the horizon with greens complementary to the sunset above it. Sometimes a little does a lot. The sky soars with color, light Cerulean Blue at the top, fluffy brightly lit clouds catching yellows, oranges, and even pale tints of red, all atop a streaming mass of shadowed clouds. Deep in these rumbling clouds of dark blues, purples, and glowing patches of orange and red, the setting sun blazes fiery red-orange into the horizon. Broad areas of peaceful color at the top change into turbulent and combative complements at the horizon. Smaller areas of both brighter and darker complementary colors add intensity to the lower part of this sky.

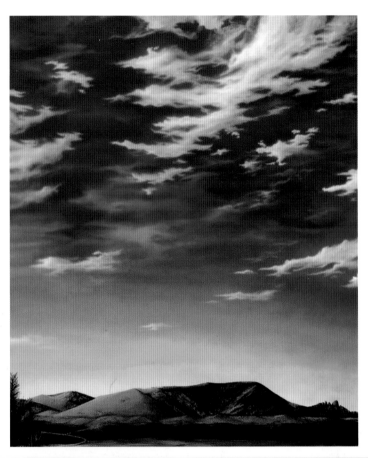

Sleeping Giant **Alan Snell**

This sky here relies on a smooth rosy golden glow at the horizon to support its turbulent cloud wisps dancing higher up. The highest cirrus clouds sing with golden and red-orange glazes of color against the intense deep blues. Values provide drama, with such a dark blue in the upper sky and shadowed deep greens in the close foreground trees. The horizon is not soft and indistinct, but sharply delineated against the sky with its own dark values. The land between the far mountain and foreground trees briefly reflects the rosy sky in a muted, neutralized way.

Main palette
Ultramarine Blue,
Phthalocyanine Blue,
Cobalt Blue, and
Titanium White

Other key colors
Cadmium Yellow, Raw Sienna,
Naphthol Red, and Ivory Black

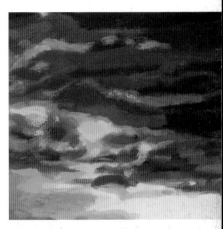

New Dawn **Jason Sacran**

This sky is not painted with soft washlike blends, but with rather choppy brushstrokes that impart a different mood to the colors on the canvas. In the detail from the middle of the painting (see right), you can see how this handling of color differs from some of the other skies shown here. Compare the approach with Sleeping Giant (see above), which uses a similar palette. The manner in which color is applied can affect emotion as much as the color itself.

Main palette
Ultramarine Blue, Cobalt Blue,
Titanium White, Cadmium
Yellow Light, Cadmium Orange,
Cadmium Red Medium, and
Alizarin Crimson Hue

Other key colors
Titanium White, Viridian Green,
and Ivory Black

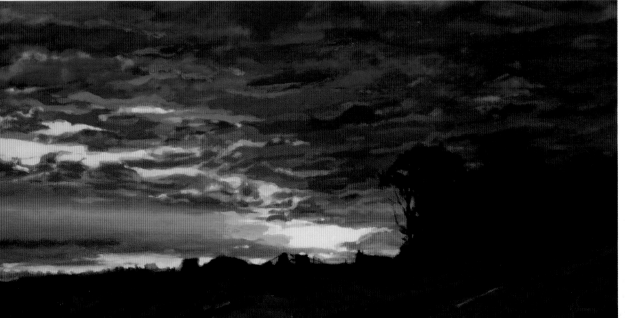

Water scenes

Painting a scene with water brings a sudden realization: We never actually paint water. Water is a clear, colorless substance, not something intrinsically paintable. What we paint instead is how light moves through water or how it reflects from water. Thinking about it in this way allows us to create the illusion of water in our paintings.

Painting water requires an understanding of how light interacts with it. If the surface of water is rippled, the reflections break up because they are reflecting at all different angles and in different directions. If the surface of the water is smooth, we see almost perfectly mirrored reflections.

Light can move through water and illuminate what lies underneath. Certain distortions characterize the underwater view, so those must be taken into account as well when painting. Light may become more diffuse when moving through water, so edges are not as sharply defined and detail may disappear.

Become alert to the changes in light, reflections, and shadows with water scenes. The more you observe, the more you will recognize what is important in painting water.

ANALYZING DIFFERENT ASPECTS OF PAINTING WATER

Examining *October Reflections* will reveal many important points about painting water. If you understand these points you can apply them to your own paintings of water scenes. Let's look at several details and see what visually interesting factors we can discover.

The water around rocks

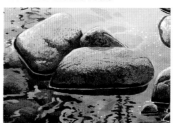

At the edge of a partially submerged rock where it emerges from the river, a silvery highlight appears. These highlights are bright white in the sun but bluish in the shadowed areas. They follow the form of the rocks and result from the slight movement of water lapping up against them. Notice the darker Raw Umber color of the rocks slightly above the water line. It is wet because of that lapping motion, and the dry rock above it is lighter in color.

Color changes

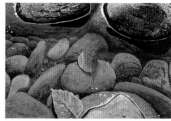

As we continue to explore the shadowy underwater world in the painting, we notice color changes below the surface of the water. The central leaf is painted with a slight bluish haze where it lies underwater. The rocks are softened with a glaze of bluish paint as well. The dark shadows next to the upper rocks in this detail are a clue to what is happening. A faint sheen of light is ever-so-slightly reflecting from the water, leaving a bluish tinge to what we see through that sheen. Nearest the larger rocks, their shadows on the water interrupt even that slight sheen and are considerably darker.

HOW LIGHT MOVES THROUGH WATER

Light rays bend when they enter water. This is called refraction and the amount of the bend is called the index of refraction. This photo shows a perfectly straight bamboo skewer in a glass of water. Notice how drastically the angle changes where it enters the water. This is because the light moves at a different angle in water than in air, so we see the illusion of a bend in the straight bamboo skewer.

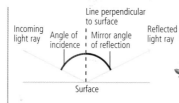

Another angle of great interest to the artist is the angle of incidence, the angle between the incoming light ray and the line perpendicular to the surface it will hit. The light reflects at the same angle away from that perpendicular line, meaning the light coming in at a certain angle will reflect at that exact same angle going away from the surface. We will only see those reflections that are angled so they come to our eyes. This is why water ripples mostly appear to be

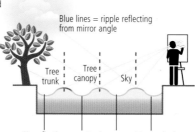

No reflection so water transparent to riverbed

horizontal, as those are the angles at which we see the reflected light.

Ripples are visible to us mostly as horizontal colored shapes, since they break the reflecting surface of water. We no longer see the sky reflected where we have a ripple. Instead, we see into the water where nothing is

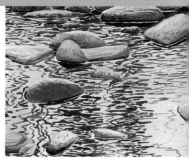

reflecting from the surface. So ripples are painted as shadows allowing us to see into the water. To accomplish this, the artist painted all the underwater rocks and allowed them to dry. Then he painted the sky reflections over the underwater rocks in rippling shapes.

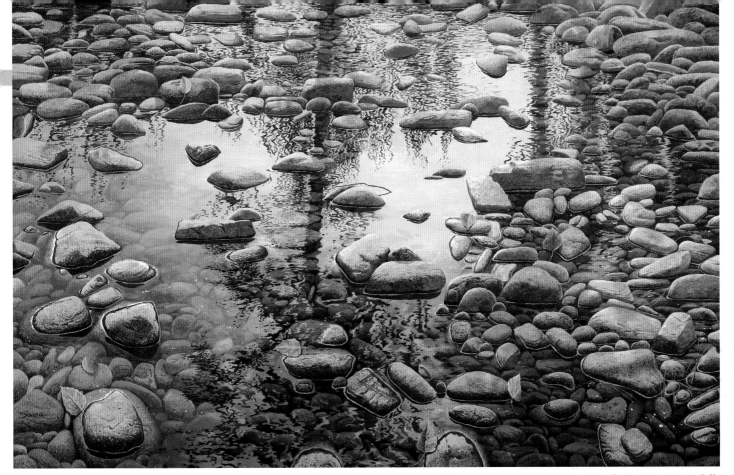

The complete illusion of water

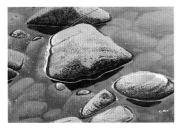

A slight bluish sheen on fairly still water gives the sense of a watery surface. The deeper shadow areas hold a darker blue. Yet the dark shadows of the rocks rising above the water have no suggestion of blue in them. The center stone appears lighter underwater on the left edge where it is not so shadowed. The shimmering highlights around the rocks enhance the visual impression of a water surface. Lapping water leaves dark, wet rings around the water line of the rocks.

The secrets of shadows

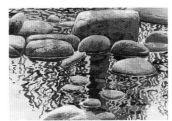

Looking further into shadows on water, in this detail we see part of the shadow of a tree trunk that falls across the middle of the painting. A shadow cannot reflect light from the surface, so we peer below the water surface to the underlying rocks. Since the rocks are shadowed, the colors are low key, dark, and rich, but the shapes are somewhat indistinct.

Broad areas of shadow

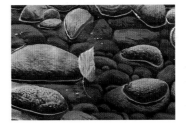

The tree shadows include broad areas of shadow in some parts of the painting because of the foliage on the trees. In this detail we see such an area. Only a few glimmers of blue haze show the sky color, a dapple of light penetrating the foliage and reflecting from the water. Mostly we see shadowed rocks lying in the water, painted in low-key earth tones.

October Reflections **Bern Sundell**
This tranquil scene of river rocks and water in the fall shows many different aspects of light and water interacting. Some areas are still and calm while others are moving with ripples. Shadows of trees interrupt the reflections of sky and partially submerged rocks rise above fully submerged rocks. The strongest value contrasts lie in the foreground. Detail diminishes as the eye moves to the top of the painting, the most distant part of the scene.

Color palette
Cerulean Blue, Ultramarine Blue, Raw Umber, Yellow Ocher, Raw Sienna, Cadmium Yellow Medium, Cadmium Orange Medium, Cadmium Red Medium, Titanium White.

Gallery: Water scenes

Sometimes water is smooth and serene, other times wild and violent, but it always brings powerful expressions of emotion. Painting water can be like painting pure color. It is really painting what surrounds water, lies under water, or lies above water, but as translated through the motion and depth of water. Illusions held in water make beautiful paintings.

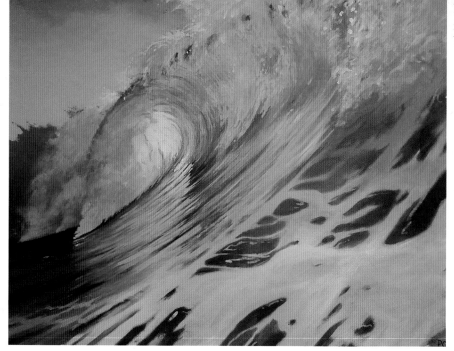

Great Wave **Paul Geraghty**

This stunning wave is an excellent example of an analogous color scheme of blues and greens. Values are somewhat muted with a little white drawing our eye to the curl of the wave rising from its dark edge. Colors blend fairly smoothly in the lower frothy areas and shift into graduated streaks of green going from dark to light. The frothy mass at the top is choppily painted in contrast to the smooth wash of the sky in the upper left. Notice how the low-chroma hues in most of the painting change to higher-chroma hues near the whitest area.

Main palette
Ultramarine Blue, Phthalo Blue (Red Shade), Phthalo Blue (Green Shade), Phthalo Green (Yellow Shade), Cobalt Green, and Light Turquoise

Other key colors
Light Violet, Anthraquinone Blue, Carbon Black, and Titanium White

Sea and Rock **Paul Geraghty**

Water is painted in this scene with low-chroma neutrals. Everything in the painting is muted, yet the painting is flushed with light. Careful handling of values creates this effect. Notice the brighter area in the middle of the distant sky, a brightness glancing off the surface of the water all the way onto the wet sand where the last wave retreats. This central radiance accented by the dark shadows of rocks and waves is what creates a strong sense of light in a painting of neutralized colors.

Main palette
Burnt Sienna, Burnt Umber, Permanent Maroon, Red Oxide, Yellow Ocher, and Ultramarine Blue

Other key colors
Violet Oxide, Naphthol Red (Medium), Mars Black, and Titanium White

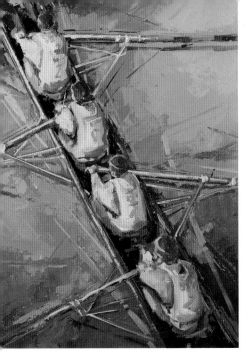

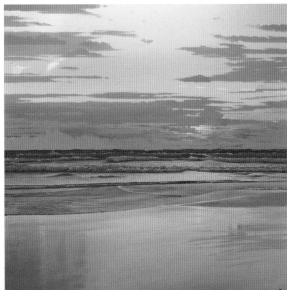

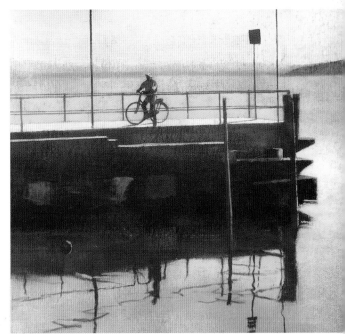

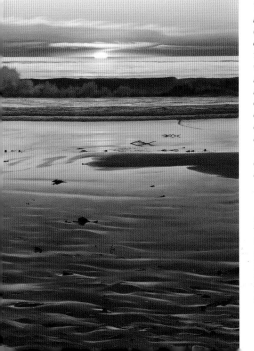

Tranquility **Paul Geraghty**

Notice the temperature of the color in this painting. Soft low-chroma blues, blue-grays, and violet-blues dominate. A small amount of yellow and red orange provide a necessary but rather muted contrast. Most of the color we see in this painting is cool in temperature. The brighter sky shows as a lower-chroma reflected watery sheen in the foreground, emphasizing that coolness. Varied horizontal bands of color provide the composition for this painting.

Main palette
Ultramarine Blue, Phthalo Blue (Red Shade), Anthraquinone Blue, Yellow Ocher, and Cadmium Orange

Other key colors
Cerulean Blue, Violet Oxide, Cadmium Yellow, Carbon Black, and Titanium White

Grand Opening Day **Jennifer Bowman**

A simple palette and an unusual point of view combine here to create a striking painting. Blues, turquoises, and cyans in highly abstracted patches of color result in water that shows the movement of this craft. Yellow greens pull the rowing figures into harmony with the water while the yellow-oranges add a zing of complementary contrast. Dark and light values create the structure of the painting.

Main palette
Phthalo Blue, Cadmium Orange, and Cadmium Red Light

Other key colors
Rich Green Gold, Cadmium Yellow, Dioxazine Purple, and Titanium White

End of the Day **Paul James**

The color temperature in this painting runs much warmer than Tranquility (see above) due to the strong yellows, oranges, and red-oranges dominating the palette. Even the dark blue crashing wave has brighter and redder (warmer) mixtures in the middle where the sun hits it. Low-chroma blues provide a complement to the dominant higher-chroma oranges and deemphasize the coolness intrinsic to blue. Values are executed with much higher contrasts in this painting and the water is powerfully enlivened with high-chroma reflections of the hues in the sky.

Main palette
Titanium White, Ivory Black, Mars Black, Burnt Umber, Burnt Sienna, Raw Umber, Cadmium Yellow, Cadmium Orange, Cobalt Turquoise, Yellow Ocher, and Lemon Yellow

Other key colors
Cadmium Red, Cadmium Red Deep, Deep Violet, Phthalo Green, Ultramarine Blue, Pale Olive Green and Hooker's Green

Untitled **Peter Nardini**

This painting is composed primarily of blues with a hint of warm browns for contrast. The strongest contrast is provided by the dark values of the pier against the lighter values of the water and sky. The water holds all the color of the sky with a few wavy dark reflections. The figure on the bicycle is painted in the same hues found in the sky and pier.

Main palette
Cadmium Orange, Phthalo Blue, Cadmium Red, Primary Yellow, Titanium White, and Black

Buildings

Buildings are our shelter from the elements, our safety, and our protection. They are our homes, the businesses we visit, places of both work and play, and they come in astonishingly diverse forms. A building can be a simple log structure or a soaring architectural display of space-age materials. Painting a building evokes the human spirit in a different way than other subject matter.

However unique buildings may be as expressions of the human spirit, they fortunately can be painted using all the principles of color in acrylics discussed in this book. Buildings can be rendered in whatever color schemes appeal to the artist. They can be integrated with color into their surroundings in the painting.

Moods can be evoked at will through changes in the color palette. So take another look at that rustic barn or gleaming neon-lit café and see what interests you about the color in the building.

Is it the way light and shadow fall across the walls? Is it the way light reflects from the ground into some of those shadows? Is it the mood created by dimly perceived interior worlds? What matters most to you when you look at the building? Can you translate that quality of mood into a color scheme that expresses it clearly?

In these ways, a building can be painted like any other subject matter. Just observe color and the play of light. Interpret the mood you wish to convey with a color scheme that inspires you, and pick up your brushes.

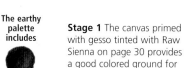

WEATHERED WOOD AND SHADOWS

In this example, a weathered barbershop from a ghost town is shown. The ramshackle structure departs from strict perspective rules due to the decay of time. It displays interesting architectural elements and long, slanting shadows along with the worn wood.

The earthy palette includes

Dioxazine Purple

Indanthrone Blue

Cobalt Blue

Chromium Oxide Green

Quinacridone Burnt Orange

Raw Umber

Yellow Ocher

Cadmium Orange Medium

Titanium White

Stage 1 The canvas primed with gesso tinted with Raw Sienna on page 30 provides a good colored ground for beginning this painting. All the areas that look rather like Yellow Ocher are the primed canvas left untouched at this stage.

The palette chosen for the painting emphasizes purple and yellow complements with a much lesser use of a neutralized red and neutralized green complementary pair. The purples will provide an atmosphere of quiet introspection.

Sketch the building onto the canvas with faint lines indicating the placement of the boards, windows, and other elements.

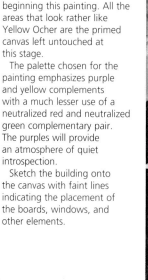

1 Apply a tint of a mixture of Cobalt Blue and Cadmium Orange Medium to start the boardwalk in front of the building. Do not attempt to indicate individual boards in this area as yet.

2 Paint the bench and step up to the door in a lighter tint of this same mixture. Use the same mixture on the inset panels in the stand for the barber pole and the left window frame.

3 At this stage, turn your attention to painting the purple shadows. Use Dioxazine Purple, Indanthrone Blue, and varying amounts of Titanium

White for tinting to establish the shadow patterns across the colored ground of the canvas.

4 In the lower left corner the shadows are the deepest, and Titanium White is not needed.

5 Paint Raw Umber in the dark recesses of the windows with tints of Indanthrone Blue where the sky reflects from the glass.

6 Paint a few weathered boards with a darker gray version of the Cobalt Blue and Cadmium Orange Medium mixture.

7 Delineate the barber pole with Indanthrone Blue, Quinacridone Burnt Orange, and pale tints of the Cobalt Blue and Cadmium Orange Medium mixture.

8 Use a little Chromium Oxide Green with Raw Umber to lay in the first leaves above the window and in the upper-right corner.

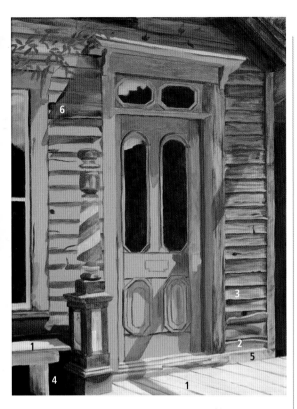

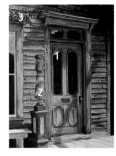

Stage 3 After a little more work establishing a solid balance of values around the door, paint the door itself. Use more tints of Yellow Ocher in the door to show that the wood is weathered differently.

The contrast of the smoother boards of the door with the rougher texture of the siding is useful as the values of the door can be brought into balance with the rest of the painting. Use darker strokes of Dioxazine Purple and Raw Umber in some of the darkest shadows to add more emphasis to the door.

1 All of the windows have been left untouched since the first layer of paint, but they need to look as though they have glass in them. Paint slightly tinted mixtures of Indanthrone Blue and Raw Umber over the Raw Umber parts of the windows. The slightly paler areas give the impression of slight reflection from glass. Adjust the sky reflections in the glass further.

2 With the door, windows, and walls completed, finish the barber pole with strong shadows and a few highlights to make it more dimensional. Scrape a little Raw Umber vertically onto the pole to show the weathering more accurately.

3 Paint the foliage with neutralized greens using Chromium Oxide Green, Raw Umber, and sometimes a little Titanium White. With the boards behind the foliage in their finished state, paint branches across them to support the leaves.

Stage 2 After the underpainting has dried, coat the entire painting with Regular Gel Medium using a flat hog-bristle brush. The brushstrokes should follow the direction of the wood grain in each board to provide a suitable wood grain texture to take the next layer of paint.

1 Once dried, complete the boardwalk in front of the building, using varying tints of the Cobalt Blue and Cadmium Orange Medium gray mixture. Refine further the step, bench, and other areas using this mixture.

2 Starting at the bottom right, unevenly apply glazes of color to each board, working with three boards at a time. You could allow the glazes to dry between coats but could also work them wet-into-wet.

3 Allow some of the colored ground of the primed canvas to remain. Lightly skim the brush across the top of the gel texture every so often to leave paint in a natural-looking wood-grain appearance.

4 Create the darkest shadows using Raw Umber mixed with Dioxazine Purple. Apply varying mixtures of Quinacridone Burnt Umber and Yellow Ocher, sometimes tinted with Titanium White, unevenly to the boards.

5 The building has grayer weathering on the boards where snow accumulated in winter, so apply the gray mixture of Cobalt Blue and Cadmium Orange Medium over some of the other glaze layers.

6 In the shadowed areas, add tints of Dioxazine Purple with a little Indanthrone Blue in uneven glazes. Notice how the previously harsh purple shadows now begin to look natural to the building.

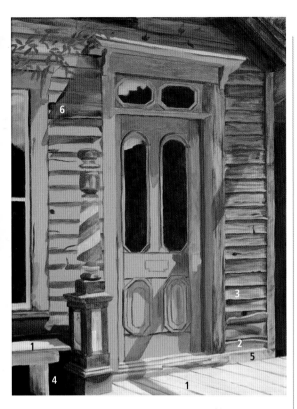

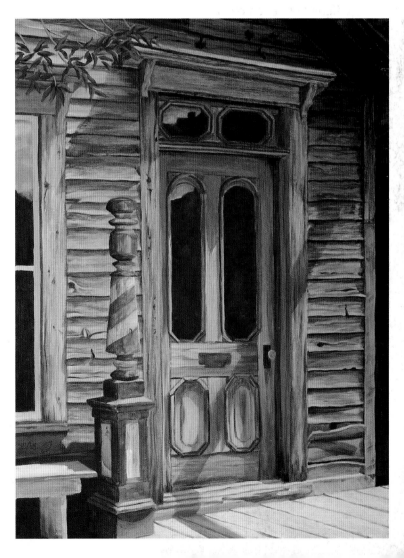

Gallery: Buildings

Buildings are such an important part of our lives it is no wonder we love to paint them. Their geometric shapes create exciting patterns of light and shade. Those hard-edged shapes contrast well with foliage. Different artists see different possibilities in painting them, so let's look at a few examples.

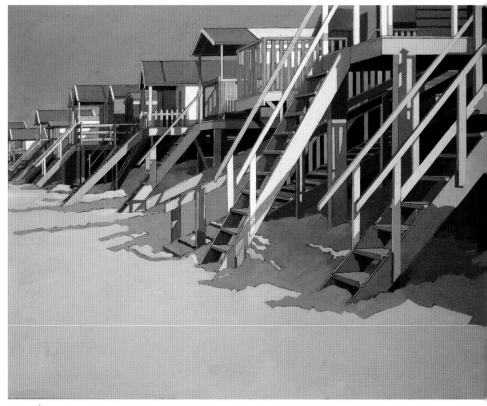

Steps John Sprakes

This painting emphasizes the geometry of the shapes in its composition, but in an altogether different manner than China Camp from Bluff (see left). The color scheme is a modified split complementary with cyans, blues, and violets opposing the low-chroma yellow-orange. A few extremely low-chroma greens and a complementary low-chroma red were added to this color scheme. The play of color in the geometric shapes provides the main interest, rather than the shapes themselves. Notice the modulations of color in the shadows and how they quietly create interest with the lighter parts of the stairs.

Main palette
Titanium White, Chrome Yellow, Cobalt Blue, Ultramarine Blue, Cadmium Red, and Alizarin Crimson

Other key colors
Aqua Green, Brilliant Purple, Blue Violet, Magenta, and Phthalocyanine Blue

China Camp from Bluff Kathleen Elsey

The abstracted geometric pattern of the group of buildings provides the main interest here. Color is actually subordinated to the composition of this painting. The red and green hues are of medium chroma but still offer a complementary contrast. A low-chroma but high-value yellow beach exists as a geometric element. The rest of the painting is executed mainly in neutrals with some dark values for contrast.

Main palette
Hansa Yellow Light, Cadmium Yellow Dark, Alizarin Crimson Hue, Cadmium Red Medium, Cerulean Blue Deep, Ultramarine Blue, Yellow Ocher, and Green Gold

Other key colors
Raw Umber, Jenkins Green, Dioxazine Purple, and Titanium White

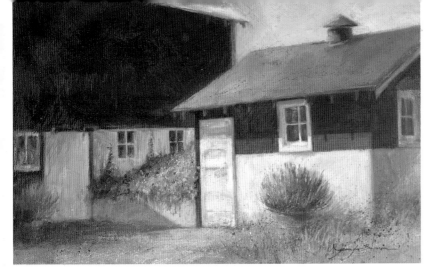

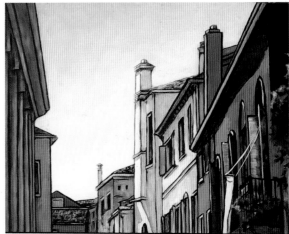

Barn **Jennifer Bowman**

High-chroma colors come into play here with an intensely bright cyan sky and vivid reds, greens, and yellows in the barn and flowers. The green is a little more subdued in chroma than the yellows and reds, so it works well with the shadows on the walls of the barn. Purples appear in the shadows on the walls, darker near the eaves of the red wall areas, and almost a bright violet on the white walls and door. We feel the effect of reflected light on the walls with this color handling.

Main palette
Napthol Crimson, Cadmium Red, Titanium White, Olive Green, and Hooker's Green

Other key colors
Phthalo Blue, Dioxazine Purple, and Cadmium Yellow

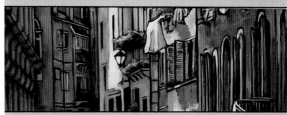

View of Spring **Barbara Louise Pence**

The play of light across the geometric shapes draws the eye to this painting. At a glance, the red and green complements make this look like a simple complementary painting. However, the wall is painted a low-chroma yellow neutralized with a purple in the light and a low-chroma purple neutralized with yellow in the shadow. This makes it a straightforward tetradic color scheme, except for the blue in the window and some of the shadows.

Main palette
Ultramarine Blue, Transparent Burnt Sienna, Dioxizine Purple, Yellow Ocher, Sap Green, and Titanium White

Other key colors
Alizarin Crimson Hue

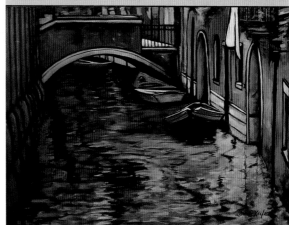

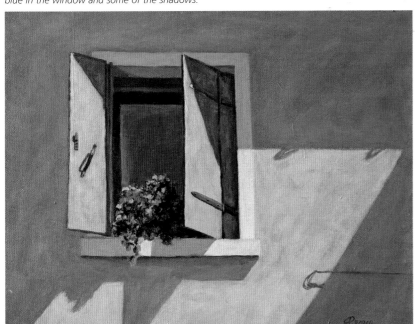

Main palette
Azo Yellow Medium, Hansa Yellow Light, Cadmium Red Light, Alizarin Crimson Hue, Ultramarine Blue, Phthalo Blue Green, Phthalo Turquoise, Dioxazine Purple, and Titanium White

Other key colors
Cadmium Orange, Cobalt Blue, Cerulean Blue, Quinacridone Violet, Opera Rose, and Quinacridone Nickel Azo Gold

Venice Glow **Lou O'Keefe**

Colors are exaggerated here with high-key blues, yellows, and violets splashing down from the top center of the painting. The lower-key blues and greens of the water change the mood of those high-key colors. Neutral shadows on the left are offset by vibrant complementary red walls and green shutters on the right. The artist achieved a glowing look with this combination of colors.

Plant life

Plants come in a bewildering variety of forms. Paintings just of the leaves could easily fill a book with all their variety of shapes and colors. Those colors also change with the seasons, the bright freshness of spring leading to deeper greens of summer and then the blazing colors of fall. Seeds and flowers add interesting elements and myriad artistic complications of their own. Painting plants can easily occupy an artist for a lifetime.

When painting plants, earth tones and bright floral colors are easier to mange than naturalistic greens. Unfortunately, many beginning painters find almost an infinite number of ways to make greens shriek in their paintings. To avoid this awful fate, learn to control chroma and value in your greens.

Vivid high-key and high-chroma greens do occur in nature, but more often as sparkling accents rather than as the dominant green of the plant. By reducing chroma, partially neutralizing the green, the color often integrates far more naturally into your painting.

Reducing value in the greens is another method to make the plants you paint look more lifelike. Shadows locate a plant in space and give it dimension, so those darker values for the shadows bring the plant into a more realistic focus.

Control the paint mixtures carefully to establish the range of color to be found in a plant. The leaves often have subtle gradations of color that blend softly. Veins may interrupt this, but they still must integrate with the smoother sections of the leaf. Really look at the plants you paint and learn to understand what you see. That will make painting the appropriate greens go from a frustrating struggle into a playful exercise.

The following two paintings explore different characteristics of green leaves and light. For leaves painted in a range of grayed blue-greens to more intense yellow-greens, see the cabbage leaves in Analogous color palette on pages 54–55.

| Chromium Oxide Green | Permanent Green Light | Hansa Yellow Medium | Raw Umber | Yellow Ocher | Carbon Black | Titanium Whi |

CHROMA, VALUE, AND NATURALISTIC GREENS: A COMPARISON

The two painting sequences on this page and opposite use the same palette to mix very different greens. This demonstrates the great difference that results from changing chroma and value in the greens: on this page the greens are intense and heavy; opposite they are lighter and fresher.

Geranium Leaves Stage 1 Begin by establishing placement of the leaves and the overall value structure in full color.

1 Paint the background with varying tints of Raw Umber mixed with a very small amount of Carbon Black. Paint the deep shadows in the leaves with Chromium Oxide Green mixed with a little Raw Umber.

2 Mix several variations of Permanent Green Light with Hansa Yellow Medium and tint them with Titanium White as needed. Use these tinted mixtures for the brightest leaf areas. Blend slightly with the shadow colors in the leaves.

3 Paint the main stalk of the geranium plant with Raw Umber and a little Chromium Oxide Green. A tint of Yellow Ocher with a little Raw Umber works well for the dried husks on the stalk.

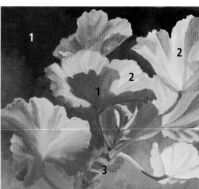

Stage 2 Paint the background, leaves, stalks, and dried husks using the same basic mixtures as before.

1 Define the leaves with more of the Permanent Green Light to blend between the shadows of Chromium Oxide Green mixed with Raw Umber and the highlighted areas of Permanent Green Light with Hansa Yellow Medium tinted with Titanium White.

2 Add more definition in the values of the stems.

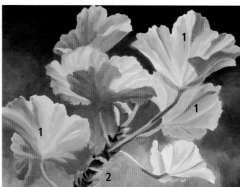

Stage 3 Continue refining the leaves, stems, and stalks with the mixtures previously used. Carefully adjust the values to make the powerful lighting evident.

1 Add Titanium White highlights in varying widths on the leaf edges.

2 Make the highlights the most brilliant on the central leaf with the large shadow to maximize the value contrast and keep the eye from wandering off the edges of the painting.

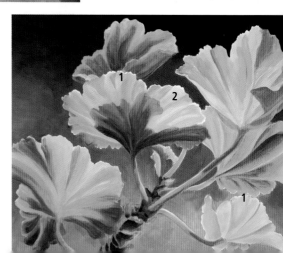

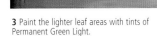

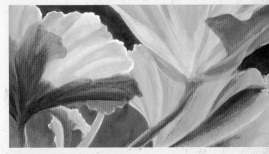

Same palette, with extra colors for the flowers

Pyrrole Orange

Cadmium Orange Medium

Nasturtium Leaves Stage 1 Paint the background in tints of Raw Umber with a small amount of Carbon Black added.

1 Most of the flowerpots can be painted with tints of Carbon Black, sometimes with a little Raw Umber added. The two earthy brown pots use a mixture of Raw Umber and Pyrrole Orange tinted with Titanium White.

2 Paint the darkest leaf areas with Chromium Oxide Green and Raw Umber.

3 Paint the lighter leaf areas with tints of Permanent Green Light.

4 Indicate the main veins with pale tints of Hansa Yellow Medium or the Chromium Oxide Green and Raw Umber mixtures.

5 Establish the flower with Pyrrole Orange in the darkest areas and tints of Cadmium Orange Medium in the lighter areas. Blend them into each other as needed.

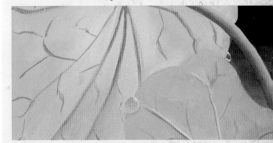

Notice how the geranium leaves show strong value and chroma contrasts. The harsh lighting makes brilliant high-key and high-chroma areas alongside dark shadows within the same leaf.

Using the same palette for mixing the greens, the nasturtium leaves display soft blends and delicate color transitions. This lighting falls softly across the leaves, showing less value and chroma contrast.

Stage 2 Continue developing the leaves and background with the previous mixtures used.

1 Carefully blend the greens in the leaves. They are not backlit so the drastic value contrasts in the individual geranium leaves opposite are not a factor. Instead we see soft gradations of color. Softly blend tints of Chromium Oxide Green and Raw Umber on the left leaf.

2 The next leaf moving right uses tints of Permanent Green Light with a little Hansa Yellow Medium and a minute amount of Raw Umber.

3 The back of the big leaf on the right shows blends of the same mixture but with some areas where either the Hansa Yellow Medium is more pronounced, or where the Permanent Green Light is more pronounced. Add more veins in the leaves, taking care with their blends as well.

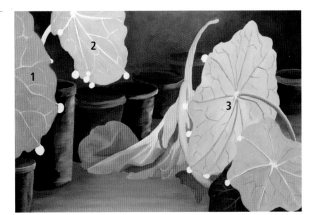

Stage 3 Make final adjustments throughout the painting and add the dewdrops.

1 Adjust the values in the flower and add a thin layer of Chromium Oxide Green and Raw Umber to the uppermost tip. Refine the veins of the leaves so they take on a delicate appearance.

The drops nearest the flower show Pyrrole Orange accents.

2 To complete the painting, add color to the dewdrops. These delightful round droplets form overnight in the greenhouse and capture myriad reflections. The dewdrops all display green mixtures, tints of Raw Umber, and Titanium White.

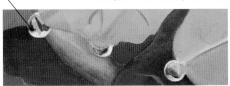

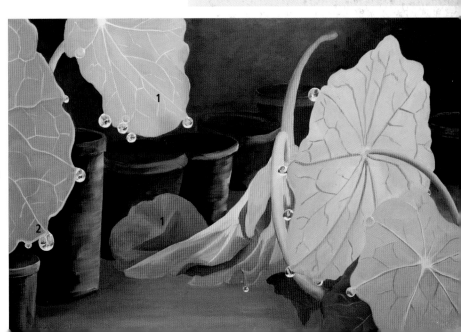

Gallery: Plant life

Plants with their leaves, seeds, fruit, and flowers bring beauty to the lands we inhabit. Rhythms of the season are revealed as they grow through their life cycles. Gardens and open spaces overflowing with plants of every description engage artists with an ongoing source of multicolored inspiration.

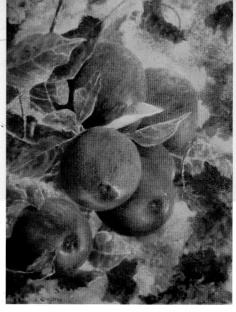

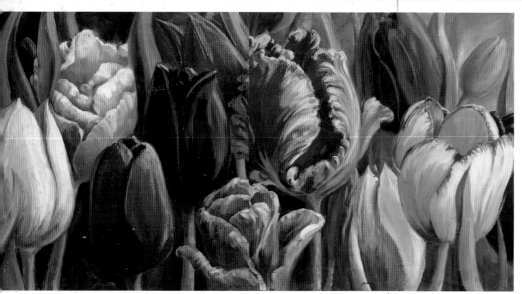

Apples Divine **Elizabeth Crabtree**
The color scheme is readily identifiable here—a straightforward example of complementary colors. The variegated reds of the apples work well with the opposing green hues of the leaves. The foliage has a good range of values and natural-looking greens, making a pleasing painting.

Main palette
Cadmium Red Medium, Cadmium Orange, Crimson Red Translucent, Payne's Gray, Olive Green Light, and Olive Green Deep

Other key colors
Burnt Sienna, Yellow Ocher, Cadmium Yellow, Titanium White, and Zinc White

Main palette
Cadmium Orange, Cadmium Red Light, Cadmium Yellow, and Titanium White

Other key colors
Phthalo Blue, Dioxazine Purple, Olive Green, Forest Green, Sap Green, and Hooker's Green

Tulips **Jennifer Bowman**
A delightful array of color greets us in these tulips. Complementary pairs of red and green along with yellow and purple accentuate the vibrant appearance of the tulips. The diverse types shown in the flowers allow some to be painted in smoother blends and others in more dramatically variegated fashion. The artist favored warm lights and cool darks in this painting to generate a three-dimensional illusion.

Dunn Ranch **Pamela Ohnemus**
This vista of flowers provides a backdrop for the daisies in the foreground, their yellow petals fluttering in the breeze. Several flowers have lost their petals completely. Aside from the cerulean blue sky with blue-violet clouds, yellows and greens dominate this painting, with a few small purple flowers to provide a complementary contrast to the yellows. The landscape is painted mainly in mid-range values, keeping a lighter feeling than deep darks would offer.

Main palette
Cadmium Yellow Medium, Dioxazine Purple, Hooker's Green, Naphthol Crimson, Titanium White, and Phthalo Blue (Red Shade)

Other key colors
Jenkins Green, Cadmium Orange, Phthalo Blue (Green Shade), Phthalo Green, and Cadmium Yellow Dark

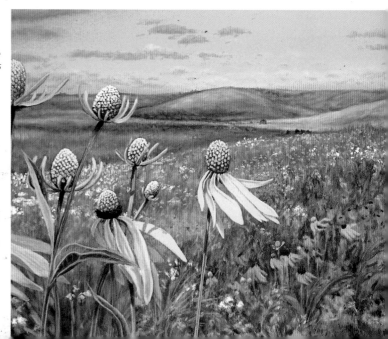

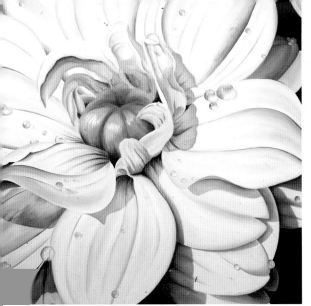

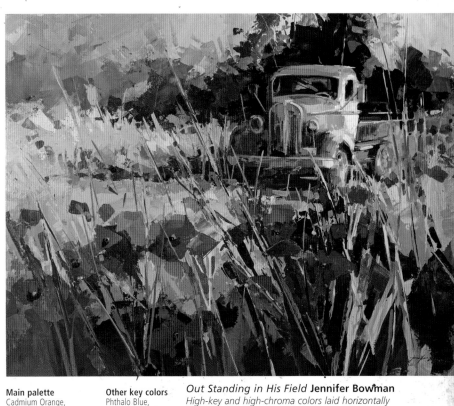

Dancing with the Dew **Lexi Sundell**
This simple color scheme uses bright cyans and purples against the yellows and yellow-oranges in the painting. A little green and blue completes the limited palette. Forty dewdrops reflect and refract light into their varied shadows on the petals. While the colors are mostly high key, strong value contrasts are present as well. This stylized interpretation of a dahlia expresses a sense of play through the unusual color combination.

Main palette
Cobalt Teal, Ultramarine Blue, Dioxazine Purple, Quinacridone Gold, and Titanium White

Other key colors
Cadmium Orange Medium, Chromium Oxide Green, and Raw Umber

Main palette
Cadmium Orange, Cadmium Red Light, Olive Green, Forest Green, Sap Green, Hooker's Green, Indian Yellow, Cadmium Yellow, and Titanium White

Other key colors
Phthalo Blue, Dioxazine Purple, and Ivory Black

Out Standing in His Field **Jennifer Bowman**
High-key and high-chroma colors laid horizontally across the middle of this painting give an open, cheery feeling to the painting. Painted with a full palette, the values are kept light but with enough strong darks to give structure and substance to the composition. The loosely painted broad strokes of color were well chosen for the application of paint in this scene.

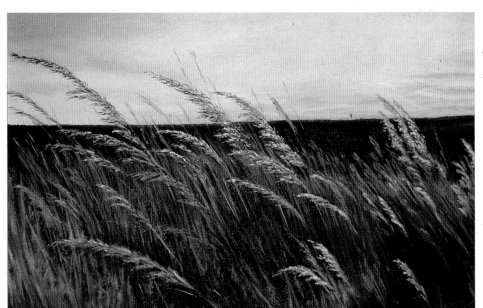

October Evening **Pamela Ohnemus**
Fall sets the stage for earth tones that are used to advantage in this painting. Strong-value contrasts accent the brightly highlighted seed heads waving in the prairie wind against the dark backdrop of the land. The main interest of this painting is the rich range of earthy colors throughout these foreground grasses.

Main palette
Cadmium Yellow Medium, Dioxazine Purple, Phthalo Green, Naphthol Crimson, Titanium White, and Phthalo Blue (Red Shade)

Other key colors
Cadmium Orange, Phthalo Blue (Green Shade), and Quinacridone Gold

Still life

Still-life painting is a beloved and long-standing tradition in art. The variety of shapes, colors, and textures possible, along with the nuances of lighting, make still-life painting a challenging and enjoyable pursuit for the artist.

Still life requires a solid understanding of painting shapes of varied textures with convincing color. Choosing suitable color schemes to convey the desired mood for the objects in the painting is vital (see pages 46–49).

Fruit and flowers are often chosen as subjects for a still life. Prior to the advent of photography, artists painting from actual displays of fruit in the studio had difficulties if they did not paint rapidly, since the fruit and flowers would often rot and decay before the painting was completed.

A whole genre of still life known as vanitas arose in the sixteenth and seventeenth centuries, featuring this type of decay in paintings. To further emphasize the concept of the brevity of life, skulls and other elements were introduced.

The fact that acrylics dry rapidly eliminates the delay of waiting for paint to dry between layers as in oil painting. A high-quality painting of fruit or flowers is made possible without having to grapple with rotting fruit or wilting flowers.

Any combination of objects can be used as subjects for still-life painting. Be open to exploring your surroundings with an eye for interesting objects that can be combined in dramatic or unusual ways. Watch for lighting angles that enliven those subjects. Above all, have fun playing with the possibilities of still life.

STILL-LIFE TEXTURES

Raw Umber

Ultramarine Blue

Manganese Blue Hue

Yellow Ocher

Carbon Black

Titanium White

An earthy, low-chroma palette suits the subject matter and mood of this painting. The subtle play of grays and browns enhances the varied textures of the feathers, mug, rock, and hard surfaces of the shelf and walls.

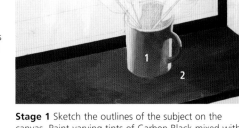

Stage 1 Sketch the outlines of the subject on the canvas. Paint varying tints of Carbon Black mixed with Ultramarine Blue in the darkest geometric forms of the wall, shelf edge, and window frame.

1 Use lighter tints of the Carbon Black and Ultramarine Blue mixture with more Ultramarine Blue for the cup, establishing the dark shadow in the middle of the cup and handle.

2 Apply tints of varying mixtures of Raw Umber and Yellow Ocher on the shelf.

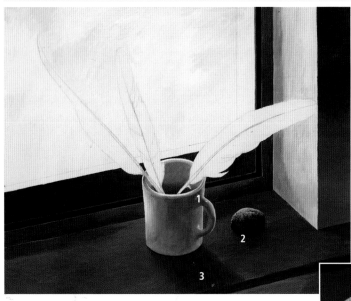

Stage 2 Paint a mixture of Carbon Black and Ultramarine Blue in the rest of the window frame. Paint a pale tint of this mixture in the window area and the lighted wall on the right side of the window.

1 Add a few small white highlights to the cup.

2 Paint the rock with a stippled texture made with tints of Carbon Black, Raw Umber, and Yellow Ocher in a variety of combinations.

3 Add another layer of the mixture previously used on the shelf. Paint shadows on the shelf with a thin layer of Carbon Black and Raw Umber.

Refine the outside of the cup and handle with another layer of paint, adding a small amount of Manganese Blue Hue in the middle of the cup.

Paint the interior of the cup with more of the mixture used on the body of the cup. Use a darker mixture of Manganese Blue Hue, Raw Umber, and Carbon Black for the shadow, blending it smoothly into the interior of the cup and keeping it darkest in the depths of the cup.

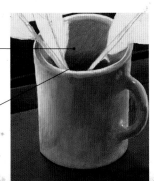

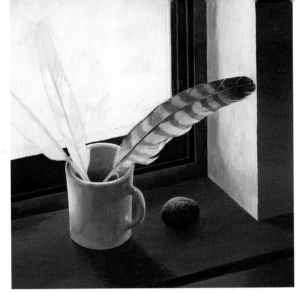

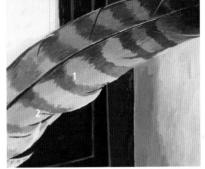

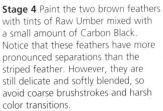

Stage 4 Paint the two brown feathers with tints of Raw Umber mixed with a small amount of Carbon Black. Notice that these feathers have more pronounced separations than the striped feather. However, they are still delicate and softly blended, so avoid coarse brushstrokes and harsh color transitions.

1 Delicately paint the striped feather with soft blends of Raw Umber, a tiny amount of Carbon Black, and Titanium White.

2 Allow a few separations in the feather to show, but do not make any coarse brushstrokes so that the soft feather contrasts with the stippled texture of the rock and the hard, smooth surfaces surrounding it.

Notice the feather on the left has a darker area near the central quill and that it blends into the lighter edge of the feather.

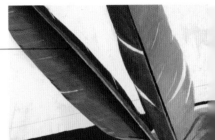

Stage 3 Continue making small refinements and adjustments on the shelf, wall, window, and cup, and start to paint the striped feather.

Stage 5 Add the missing details of the window frame with the mixtures previously used for the window frame. Use loose, painterly strokes to complete the window itself, which shows glare from the light, obscuring the scene beyond. Varying tints of Carbon Black mixed with Ultramarine Blue serve this purpose well.

Notice how the feathers in the cup appear to occupy space. The textures of the feathers contrast with the hard, reflective surface of the cup, and the roughness of the rock.

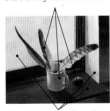

Even the smooth surface of the window contrasts with the duller smooth surface of the shelf and the slight texture of the wall. The angled light and contrasting textures make this still-life painting anything but dull despite the understated low-chroma palette used.

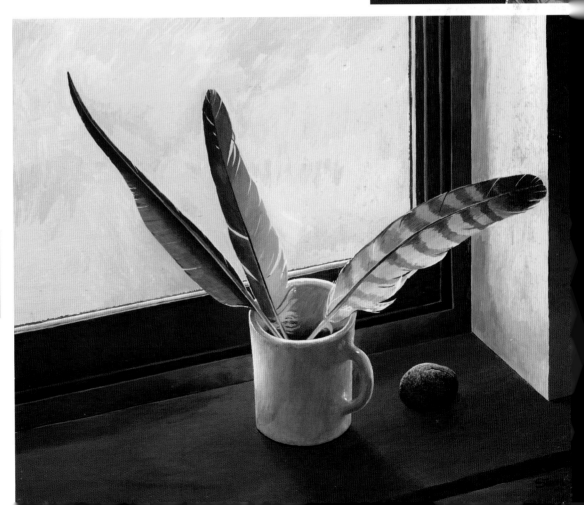

Gallery: Still life

Still-life painting opens up a tremendous variety of options beyond the traditional fruit-in-a-bowl concept. Learning to observe, to see everything with fresh eyes, can lead to unusual and interesting paintings. Still-life subjects can be so varied that they abound with opportunities to freely play with color.

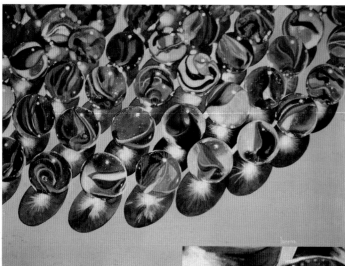

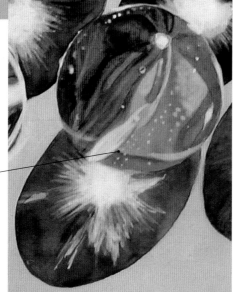

Constellation
Lorena Kloosterboer
Marbles glow with scintillating colors and the light moving through them creates lively shadows as well. A tinted ground of light gray gesso forms the background that enhances the bright colors used in these marbles.

Main palette
Payne's Gray, Titanium White, Cadmium Red Cadmium Yellow, Cobalt Blue, and Cadmium Orange

Other key colors
Burnt Umber, Brilliant Light Green (Phthalo Green variation), Burnt Sienna, and Cerulean Blue

Multiple layers of thin glazes were applied to create the glowing play of color shown in this detail from the painting. Precise control with acrylics can develop a rich and beautiful appearance.

Rainbow of Buoys **Lou O'Keefe**
Of course, opaque subjects can also be painted in lively color as these buoys demonstrate. Outlining them in black and applying the paint loosely in patches of broken color gives an almost stained-glass radiance to this painting. Softened and irregular highlights contribute to the look, which would not be nearly as radiant if most of the colors were low chroma instead of the high-chroma ones chosen here.

Main palette
Azo Yellow Medium, Hansa Yellow Light, Cadmium Red Light, Alizarin Crimson Hue, Ultramarine Blue, Phthalo Blue Green, Phthalo Turquoise, Dioxazine Purple, and Titanium White

Other key colors
Cadmium Orange, Cobalt Blue, Cerulean Blue, Quinacridone Violet, Opera Rose, and Quinacridone Nickel Azo Gold

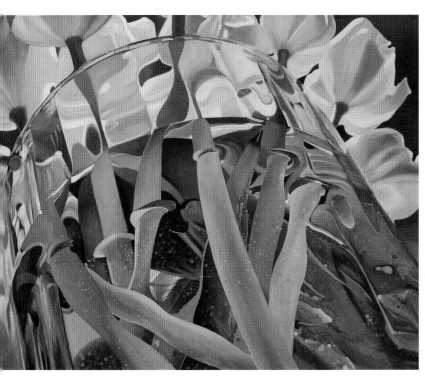

Sunshine Sonata
Lorena Kloosterboer
An unusual point of view establishes drama in this painting, accentuated by the diagonal placement of the faceted crystal vase. Both glass and water refract light, distorting the stems and flowers in arresting color patterns. The colors chosen harmonize well, with blues blending into greens that in turn blend into yellows. Everything was painted with tight control in multiple thin glaze layers. Mid-range values predominate but a few strong darks and white highlights bring additional visual impact to the subject.

Main palette
Titanium White, Cobalt Blue, Cadmium Yellow, Lemon Yellow, Brilliant Yellow Green (Phthalo Green variation), and Sap Green

Other key colors
Pale Olive, Phthalo Green, and Hooker's Green

By the Window **Rosina Flower**
An interesting approach to painting flower bouquets is shown in this loose and abstracted still life. Softly blurred edges with plenty of white added to the yellow background tints establish a look suffused with light. Light violet across the foreground is a fitting complement to the yellow. Bright splashes of blue and magenta continue the light and airy look with only the foliage adding darker values to the painting.

Sew What? **Joseph Krawczyk**
Complete understatement can be used to create a powerful image. In this painting all bright, high-chroma colors have vanished, leaving only a subdued red spool and its equally subdued complementary green spool as the focal point. Warm browns with a hint of golden light are used in the chair and basket. The suggestion of an extremely neutralized green floor disappears into intense dark shadow. This color handling establishes a softly introspective mood.

Main palette
Black, Burnt Umber, Cerulean Blue, Burnt Sienna, Raw Sienna, Naples Yellow, Yellow Oxide, Burnt Umber, Cadmium Red, and Light Green

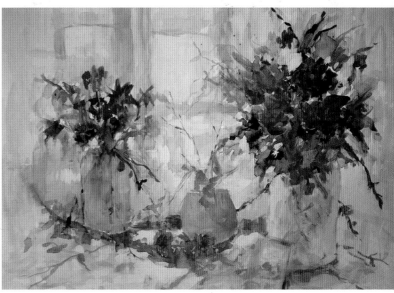

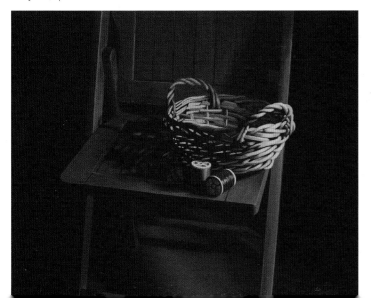

Main palette
Quinacridone Magenta, Lemon Yellow, Dioxazine Purple, Titanium White, Ultramarine Blue, and Cadmium Red

Other key colors
Cobalt Blue, Titanium White, Cadmium Yellow, and Yellow Ocher

Animals

Animals are engaging subjects for the artist, offering live personalities combined with colorful fur, feathers, scales, and other textures so delicious to paint. Eyes command attention, and the light falling across the animal can evoke any mood you want to create.

In truth, painting animals is not really different from painting any other subject. Appropriate color schemes have to be selected, the source of light has to be understood and visually communicated, and the chroma, hue, and values of the painting have to be properly rendered. Texture is a component that is helpful in creating surface contrasts, such as the difference between the smooth skin of a nose and the roughness of fur.

With any living creature, in most cases the eyes are of crucial importance in a painting. We automatically gravitate toward eyes, looking into them wherever possible. Inviting the viewer into the eyes of your animal subject is an excellent way of getting and holding their attention.

Eyes pose a particular challenge in that light falls across them, creating shadows, the surface is moist, and the colors in the eye have to be integrated into the rest of the painting to be convincing. Most of the time, eyes look lifeless until just the right highlights are added, making the animal suddenly "see" and engage the viewer.

Painting black fur effectively requires the artist to stop making assumptions and actually look at color. If a black dog is painted entirely in black, a cartoon silhouette results. As you know from the section on color temperature (see page 70), black can be either cool or warm. The dog in this example has predominantly cool black fur, so the colors are selected accordingly. Ironically, considerably more Titanium White than Carbon Black has been used to paint this black dog.

Indanthrone Blue

Raw Umber

Quinacridone Rose

Yellow Ocher

Carbon Black

Quinacridone Gold

Titanium White

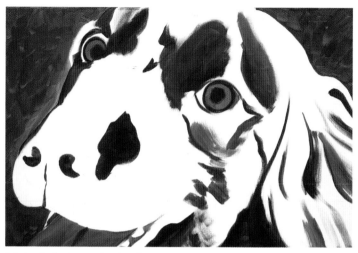

1 Paint the background with Yellow Ocher and Raw Umber. Indanthrone Blue should mark the deepest shadows, and use more of the Yellow Ocher and Raw Umber mixture in the eyes. Apply a little Quinacridone Rose with Raw Umber to the tongue.

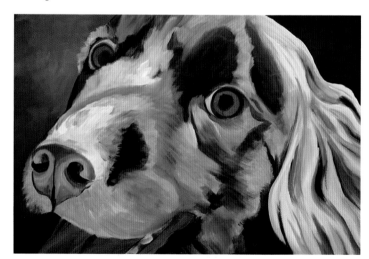

2 Paint varying mixtures of Indanthrone Blue, Raw Umber, and Titanium White over the background. Paint the rest of the fur and nose in tints of Indanthrone Blue. Paint the mouth with more Quinacridone Rose. After the paint is dry, apply a layer of Regular Gel Medium to the fur with a stiff hog-bristle brush, making texture following the direction of the hair.

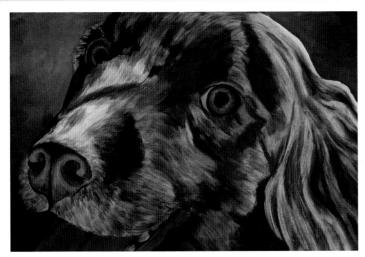

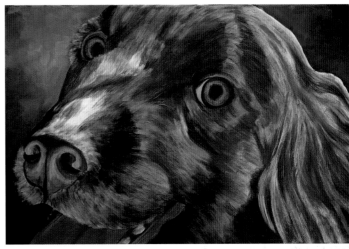

3 Once the Regular Gel Medium is dry, paint varying tints of Raw Umber and Indanthrone Blue over the fur, allowing the gel texture to help create the illusion of hair. Use the same mixture for the nose, which remains smooth. Add Quinacridone Gold to the eyes. Reduce the values in the mouth to throw it more into shadow. After drying, apply another layer of Regular Gel Medium to the fur to increase and vary the texture.

4 Work on the fur, adding more tints of Raw Umber. At this point, the fur could be completed by using Indanthrone Blue and Raw Umber only, without the use of black paint at all, but in this example, the author chose to use a little Carbon Black in step 5 to intensify the value contrasts. Add a final layer of Regular Gel Medium texture to the fur before proceeding to that next step.

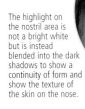

The highlight on the nostril area is not a bright white but is instead blended into the dark shadows to show a continuity of form and show the texture of the skin on the nose.

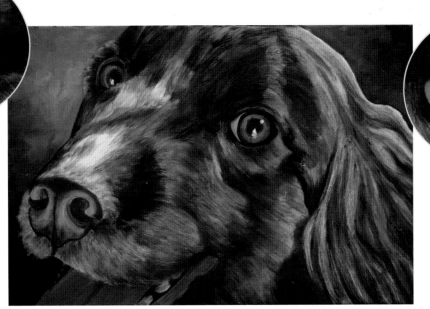

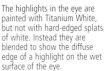

The highlights in the eye are painted with Titanium White, but not with hard-edged splats of white. Instead they are blended to show the diffuse edge of a highlight on the wet surface of the eye.

5 Add a tiny amount of Carbon Black to the deepest shadows in the dark areas of the eye, recesses in the depth of the nostrils, and the darkest shadows in the fur. Add highlights in Titanium White. Notice how the highlights in the eyes bring the happy playfulness of the dog to life.

Gallery: Animals

Animals present the artist with the challenges of painting fur and feathers in a convincing way. Even with that under control, unless the creature is seen at a distance, the eyes still have to be painted in a manner that properly conveys the spirit of the animal. Notice the many variations possible in painting fur, feathers, and eyes.

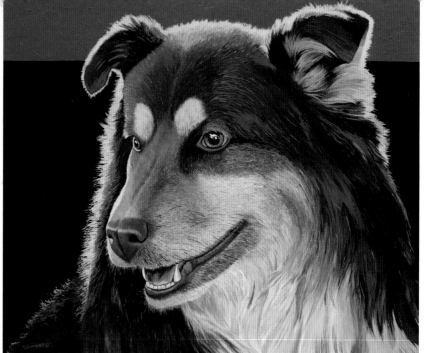

Main palette
Raw Umber, Carbon Black, Dioxazine Purple, Cobalt Turquoise, Cobalt Teal, Cadmium Yellow Medium, and Titanium White

Other key colors
Cadmium Orange Medium, Cadmium Red Medium, and Manganese Blue Hue

Colorplay **Bern Sundell**
In contrast to Ginger (see opposite) this dog is painted with realistic detail but with higher-chroma colors that startle with their unexpectedness. Turquoise greens complement the small but intense red areas and the softer yellow backlighting complements purples in the fur. Notice the eyes once again. The painting of Ginger has softly rendered eyes in keeping with the quiet colors in that painting, whereas these eyes are sharply delineated with white highlights against black pupils. These white highlights create quite a spark of life in this dog.

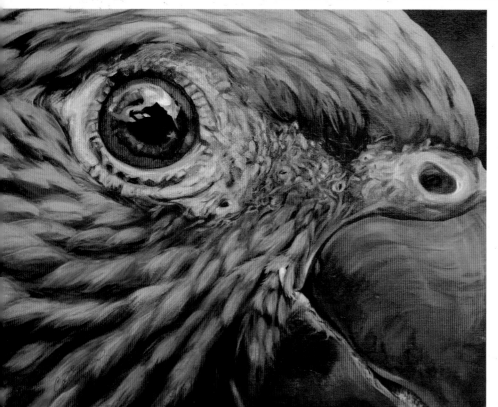

Loki **Carol Anna Fullerton-Samsel**
In order to provide strong contrast, the artist first underpainted the feathers with black before adding the other colors. Notice the lively look of the eye, in part achieved by the use of strongest value contrasts in the painting. Placing the white highlights correctly in the eye is critical in the process of making the eye radiate the spirit of the animal. Oranges in the beak and eye were chosen to complement the blues in the feathers while pale lilac highlights in the feathers complement the yellows at the nostrils. High-chroma colors are enhanced by proximity with lower-chroma colors, and high-chroma colors dominate this painting.

Main palette
Ultramarine Blue, Phthalocyanine Blue, Cobalt Blue, Yellow Oxide, Cadmium Yellow Medium, and Cadmium Red Medium

Other key colors
Quinacridone Red, Phthalocyanine Green, Burnt Umber, Raw Sienna, and Hansa Yellow Light

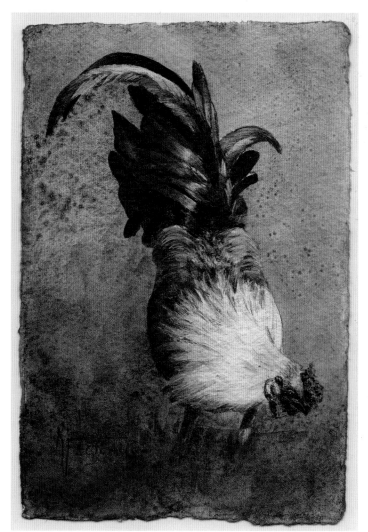

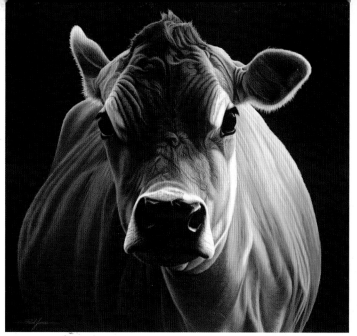

Portrait of Posh **Paul James**

An exploration of the varied textures of fur and nose skin led to this richly painted bovine. Cadmium Yellow, Orange, and Red mixtures were adjusted with siennas, umbers, and ochers. The artist deftly handled Burnt Sienna without creating an unpleasant chalky pink, a common occurrence when Burnt Sienna mixes with white. Subtle touches of violet, turquoise, and blue add life to the animal. Notice the deep black in the eyes and nose, yet the small highlights placed in the cow's eyes bring out the spirit of this animal effectively. Strong value contrasts are used in this painting.

Main palette
Titanium White, Ivory Black, Mars Black, Burnt Umber, Burnt Sienna, Raw Umber, Cadmium Orange, Yellow Ocher, Lemon Yellow, and Cadmium Yellow Deep

Other key colors
Cadmium Red, Cadmium Red Deep, Deep Violet, Cobalt Turquoise, and Ultramarine Blue

Main palette
Ultramarine Blue, Burnt Sienna, Titanium White, Hansa Yellow, and Quinacridone Red

Rooster **Kiana Fecteau**

The feathers of this bird were painted in a completely different manner than the feathers in Loki. The choice of watercolor paper as substrate allowed soft washes of color. Subdued low-chroma colors were chosen, even for the comb and wattles of the bird. Value contrasts in the tail feathers were used to effectively indicate the iridescence of those feathers. Near-whites in the neck and shoulders of the bird contrast with the blacks of the tail, adding emphasis to the rooster.

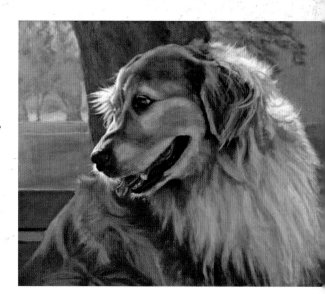

Ginger **Barbara Louise Pence**

The fur in this dog was painted altogether differently than the cow (see above right). Burnt Umber and Raw Sienna were neutralized with Dioxazine Purple. The white fur has a considerable amount of blues and purples for the shadows as well as a few greens. These complements of blue versus orange and purple versus yellow are applied in fairly low-chroma glazes made with matte medium. Matte medium is made matte by the inclusion of Titanium White particles to opacify the acrylic emulsion. This further subdues the color while adding richness by using multiple layers of semitransparent glazes.

Main palette
Transparent Burnt Umber, Raw Sienna, Dioxazine Purple, Yellow Ocher, Sap Green, and Titanium White

Other key colors
Ultramarine Blue and Alizarin Crimson Hue

Landscapes and trees

Landscapes challenge the artist to create the illusion of depth, of distance, in the painting. Since so many landscapes have green foliage, they also challenge the artist to develop skill in handling natural-looking green mixtures.

By adhering to simple principles, a complex painting that shows different layers of distance can be painted. Correct selection of the palette goes a long way to creating an effective landscape painting, so choose your color scheme with care.

A major concern is that of values. Value contrasts are more extreme in the foreground at the bottom of the painting and diminish gradually into the distance, where they lose both strong dark values and brilliant highlights.

The next principle to keep in mind is that a bluish haze can be seen in far distant areas of the landscape due to the atmosphere of the Earth. This bluish haze diminishes and colors gradually become higher chroma as they approach the foreground.

Cerulean Blue

Bismuth Yellow

Chromium Oxide Green

Permanent Green Light

Ultramarine Blue

Raw Umber

Raw Sienna

Titanium White

Precise handling of values is vital to the success of a landscape painting. Values communicate distance and establish the positional relationships between different areas and objects in the landscape.

The reference photo for this painting from page 79 in Choosing and using a color scheme is shown converted to grayscale. If the reference photo you are working with has excessively darkened shadows when converted to grayscale (as this one did originally), the loss of detail can be problematic. This photo was lightened in Photoshop to restore the detail, but it is good practice to properly observe the landscape (or take a "mental" picture) when you are taking the photo, since a camera's dynamic range is the range of values it can display in a photo and this range typically is not as extensive as our own eyes can perceive.

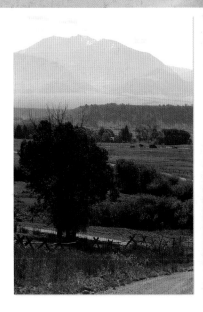

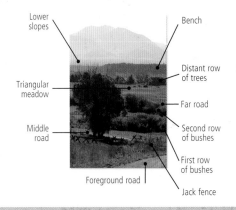

Lower slopes

Triangular meadow

Middle road

Foreground road

Bench

Distant row of trees

Far road

Second row of bushes

First row of bushes

Jack fence

Different parts of the painting are labeled for easy reference in the following painting stages.

MIXING BLUES AND YELLOWS TO MAKE GREEN

Mixing blue and yellow paints to make green can be a viable option in landscape painting. As always, you must be able to reduce chroma in the mixtures to use them effectively. Painting mixtures directly onto heavy watercolor paper can quickly reveal the potentials of different palette combinations.

Hansa Yellow Medium blends into Phthalo Blue (Green Shade). Both of these pigments are high-chroma, semitransparent colors. The blue is so powerful it takes a lot of the yellow to change it into this attractive green.

Permanent Red blends into a green made from Hansa Yellow Medium and Phthalo Blue (Green Shade). As the complement of the mixed green, Permanent Red can be used to reduce chroma in the green.

Cadmium Yellow Medium makes a more subdued green mixed into Ultramarine Blue. Cadmium Yellow Medium is an opaque paint and Ultramarine Blue is semitransparent.

Quinacridone Crimson is used to reduce chroma in the green mixed at left. Although Quinacridone Crimson is a complement to the green, the blend is reddish in appearance. It is useful to test different complements, as the pigments do not always behave in the ways suggested by color theory.

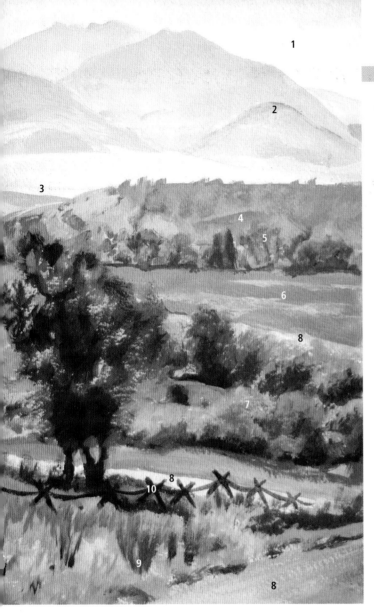

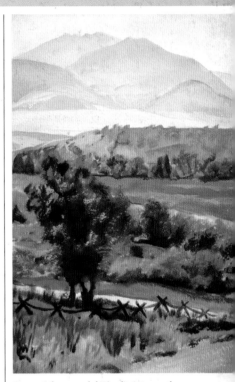

Stage 1 Paint the entire surface of the watercolor paper to roughly establish the placement and general color of the areas of the painting.

1 Start at the top with Cerulean Blue and plenty of Titanium White for the sky.

2 Paint the mountain shapes with tints of Ultramarine Blue.

3 Add small touches of tinted mixtures of Ultramarine Blue and Chromium Oxide Green, making it quite pale on the lower slopes of the mountains.

4 Darker tints of Chromium Oxide Green and Ultramarine Blue create the bench. Add a tint of a little Raw Sienna in the lighter areas of the bench.

5 With the distant row of trees introduce a little Raw Umber into the varying mixtures of Chromium Oxide Green, Ultramarine Blue, and Raw Sienna and Titanium White.

6 Paint the triangular meadow primarily with tints of Permanent Green Light, Chromium Oxide Green, and Raw Sienna with a small amount of Bismuth Yellow.

7 Use more of these mixtures for the rows of bushes and grassy areas between the middle and far roads and the tall foreground tree. Add Raw Umber with Ultramarine Blue for the shadows.

8 Paint the middle and far roads with tints of Raw Sienna. Paint the foreground road with varying mixtures of Raw Sienna, Raw Umber, and Titanium White.

9 Add the weeds and grasses in the foreground with more of the tinted mixtures of Chromium Oxide Green, Permanent Green Light, Raw Sienna, Raw Umber, and Bismuth Yellow.

10 Paint the jack fence with Raw Umber.

Stage 1 (grayscale) The first stage of the painting involves covering the entire surface with paint, roughly establishing the placement of different objects and areas of the landscape. Value relationships are incorrect but future layers of paint will correct and refine them. The main thing is to cover the glaring white of the paper or canvas so it no longer distracts the eye.

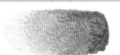

Cerulean Blue is opaque and combines with Hansa Yellow Medium to make a fairly low-chroma green mixture. This can be useful in landscape paintings.

A yellow-green mixed from Hansa Yellow Medium and Cerulean Blue is modified by Quinacridone Rose. Quinacridone Rose is the complement for yellow-green, which should create a neutral, but this is a more earthy than gray neutral.

The Hansa Yellow Medium and Cerulean Blue mixture has been blended with Raw Sienna. Notice how this pigment modifies the green in an earthy way that can settle naturally into a landscape painting.

A different earthy mixture results from blending Raw Umber into the green made from Hansa Yellow Medium and Raw Umber. This combination also could fit very well into a landscape painting.

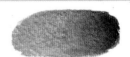

Yellow Ocher has been blended into Ultramarine Blue to make a low-chroma green differing in appearance from the other mixtures shown here. For landscape painting, modifying green mixtures with any of the earthy pigments can be useful in creating a natural look.

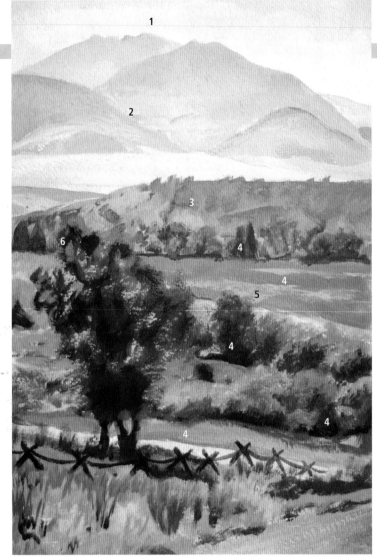

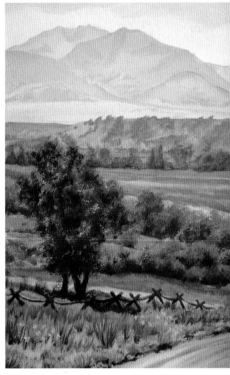

Stage 2 Now that the colors in the painting are roughly established, refining can begin.

1 Repaint the sky, making whiter clouds behind the mountains to add a little more contrast.

2 Define the shapes of the mountain shadows with tints of Ultramarine Blue and Chromium Oxide Green to create more interest in them.

3 Continue using the previous mixtures in the bench but add more tints of Raw Sienna to the exposed dirt to lighten the look of it. Be sure to either mix a little Ultramarine Blue into these tints or glaze over them to keep the atmospheric look of blue in the distance. The Raw Sienna brings it closer to the viewer than the distant mountains, but it is far enough away to still need some blue.

4 The far row of trees, both rows of bushes, and the meadow and grassy areas need serious repainting. Use Raw Umber with Ultramarine Blue for the darkest shadows and carefully decrease their darkness the farther away in the landscape they appear. Use more Raw Sienna in the far row of trees than the two rows of bushes to reduce chroma in the greens. This also adds to the illusion of distance.

5 Add more Bismuth Yellow and Raw Sienna to the green mixtures in the triangular meadow as it is too dark in value. Take care to create a progression of lower-chroma greens in the distance to more vivid greens nearer the viewer. Using more Bismuth Yellow and Permanent Green Light nearer the viewer enhances this effect. A "bad hair day" paintbrush helps stipple the foliage in the bushes and the tall foreground tree.

6 The tall tree needs repainting with more Chromium Oxide Green and a little Permanent Green Light to make the foliage more variegated and interesting.

Stage 2 (grayscale)
Creating distance in the different parts of this extensive landscape is based on the principle that the strongest value contrasts will be nearest the viewer and diminish as they recede into the distance. This means the strongest darks and lights must be created in the foreground, although this may be done in multiple stages or layers of paint. More distant parts of the painting should be lighter in value but also lack brilliant highlights. Adjustments in this step of the painting include lightening the values of the bench and graduating the values from the first row of bushes to the distant row of trees so the landscape appears to steadily recede as the shadows become paler. Define the mountains with a little more contrast than the reference photo for visual interest. The lower slopes of the mountain are more brightly sunlit and lighter in value than the shadowed, more vertical shapes of the mountains themselves.

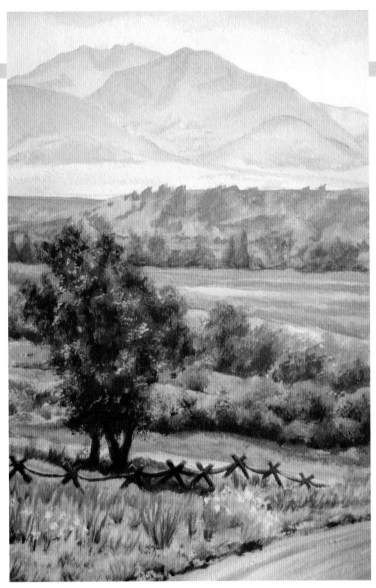

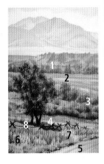

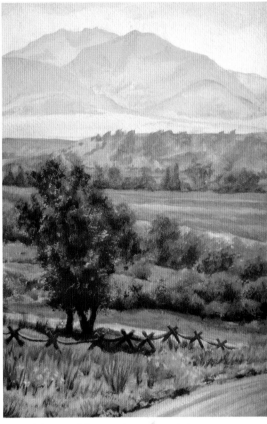

Stage 3 Continue to refine the details to complete the painting.

1 Refine the area just beyond the far row of trees before the bench rises to imply additional meadows and shrubbery. Notice that the degree of detail gradually increases from the haziness of the distant mountains to the foreground. So, keep the detail beyond the row of trees a bit vague to assist in creating the sense of distance.

2 Paint pale tints of Bismuth Yellow across the triangular meadow to create the swathes of blooming mustard.

3 Refine the two rows of bushes and the grassy areas around them.

4 Adjust the middle road with a darker tint of Raw Sienna.

5 Paint the foreground road with more distinct indications of tire tracks, using more Titanium White in the brighter areas of the road.

6 Add more detail and more contrast in the weeds and grasses in the foreground.

7 Splashes of Bismuth Yellow make good flower accents to increase the illusion that the foreground is close to the viewer.

8 Repaint the jack fence, adding a little Raw Sienna to soften the dark Raw Umber cross braces and poles in the sunlit areas. A tint of Raw Sienna can be used for the highlights on them. Leave the cross braces and poles dark in the shadow of the tree.

9 Increasing the shadows and highlights in the foreground adds more contrast, bringing it closer to the viewer. By using only two green paints modified with Raw Sienna, Raw Umber, and Ultramarine Blue, a harmonious landscape painting results. All the parts of the painting are naturally related to each other through color, and color itself is used to create an illusion of layers of distance moving backward in the painting.

Stage 3 (grayscale)
Further refinements of value include adding lighter areas in the triangular meadow and continuing to adjust foliage in the trees and bushes. The tall tree in the foreground must be darker than the other bushes and trees as they recede from the viewer, but the tree needs more detail in the foliage than the original photo reference. Define the jack fence with highlights in the sunny areas, lightening the overly dark cross braces and poles in the process.

Leave them darker without highlights in the shadow of the tree. Notice that the jack fence is slightly lighter in value where it disappears down the hillside. Darken the values in the middle road, as it remained far too bright in the previous stage. Add lighter values to the foreground road. The weeds along this road must have pronounced value contrasts with some strong shadows and brighter highlights in order to be convincing to the eye.

Gallery: Landscapes and trees

Painting landscapes poses all manner of challenges. The ever-changing skies, seasonal color changes in trees and other plants across the land, the shapes of the land itself, how it reflects in water, and the way light slants across the scene may all have to be integrated into a finished work of art. Learning how to see the way color can communicate all these factors is an art in itself.

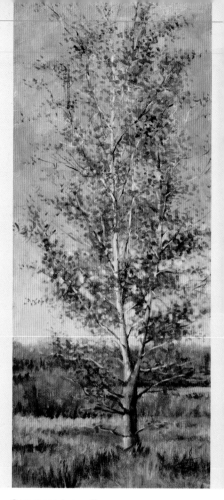

A landscape always starts with light. What are the qualities of the light? Is it early or late in the day with softly slanting rays leaving great shadows? Is it burning midday with great intensity? Is it summer, winter, or another season? Each season brings its own qualities of light.

Nothing kills a painting faster than internal contradictions in how the shadows fall, so consider the direction of the path of light. Really look at the light and know how it works with the landscape and trees you wish to paint.

The more northerly and more southerly hemispheres register strong color changes with the seasons. Yet, even as one moves nearer the equator, changes in light through the seasons can still be seen and understood.

Incorporating trees into a landscape requires an understanding of the structure of trees and how that structure catches the light. With deciduous trees, the appearance changes dramatically when the leaves change color in fall and even more when they are gone in the winter. How do the trees fit with the rest of the landscape?

Throughout this process, great attention must be given to the handling of value and chroma. Landscapes usually show distance, which is most easily communicated by value changes and chroma changes. Understanding them makes a big difference.

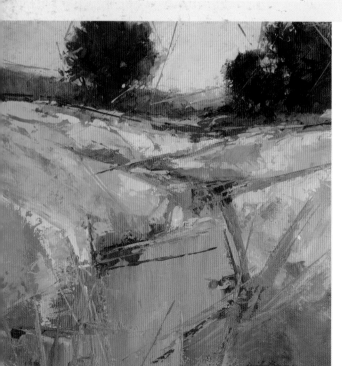

Fractured Landscape
Jennifer Bowman
This artist dispensed with almost all detail in order to explore vibrant color in the landscape. Blues are complemented with splashes of bright orange. Duller reds in the trees of the upper background complement in a quieter way the medium-chroma greens of the foreground. The greens give way to lively patches of yellow-greens and yellow-oranges. Tiny hits of purple accent those masses of yellow mixtures. This painting is simply a beautiful dance through the palette.

Main palette
Indian Yellow,
Cadmium Yellow,
Rich Green Gold,
Alizarin Crimson Hue,
and Titanium White

Other key colors
Cadmium Red Light,
Phthalo Blue, and
Cadmium Orange

Sycamore Jason Sacran
When graced with leaves the apparent form of the tree changes, with masses of foliage altering the shape. The structure of the trunk and branches is still present, complete with their expected shadow patterns. Some artists prefer to paint the entire branching structure before adding leaves. The sunlight has to highlight the leaves in a manner that fits with the shadows on the trunk and branches of the tree as well.

Main palette
Ultramarine Blue,
Viridian Green,
Hooker's Green,
Cadmium Orange
Medium, and
Titanium White

Other key colors
Cadmium Yellow Light,
Alizarin Crimson Hue,
and Ivory Black

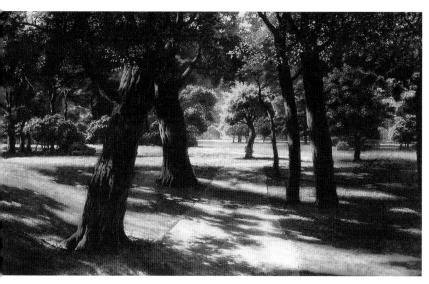

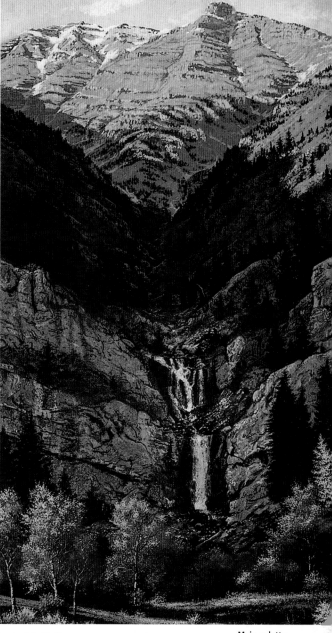

Summer Park **Frederick G. Denys**

In groupings of trees, foliage intermingles with lost and found edges so that it may not be immediately obvious which leaves belong to which tree. The trees themselves alter the light as well. Notice the dappled light falling through the leaves across the foreground trees, the grass, and the path. The brightly lit areas on the trunks of the foreground trees change in hue, chroma, and value. A naturalistic handling of the varied greens of the foliage provides much of the beauty of this painting, along with the strong value contrasts.

Main palette
Permanent Green, Chromium Oxide Green, Green Gold, Ultramarine Violet, Burnt Umber, Raw Umber, and Titanium White

Other key colors
Quinacridone Burnt Orange, Cadmium Yellow Medium, and Carbon Black

Straying Sheep **Joe Hush**

When the leaves have fallen, the branching structure of a tree is clearly revealed. The tree grows in a fractal pattern, taking the shape of the trunk with its branching arms into increasingly smaller and more delicate versions until the twigs are lace against the sky. Notice how the large tree on the right of this painting is shadowed on the right sides of the trunks and branches and illuminated on the left with lighter values.

Main palette
Cerulean Blue, Ultramarine Blue, Burnt Sienna, Raw Sienna, Chromium Oxide Green, Perylene Green, and Titanium White

Other key colors
Raw Umber, Cadmium Red Deep, and Green Gold

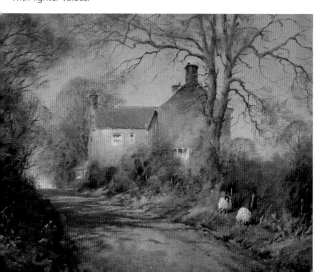

Mountain Waterfall **Frederick G. Denys**

Notice how the small sliver of sky across the top and the large shadow across the middle of this painting create the impression that we are deep in a canyon. The palette in this painting is that of fall with earthy tones and rich orange-golds. In the foreground are high-chroma aspens with strong value contrasts. Some of the individual branches and leaves are visible. As the eye moves upward through the painting, the mountain moves up and away into the distance. Shadowy silhouettes of conifers mark their presence without much detail. The colorful aspen trees become colorful masses instead of individual trees and then disappear altogether. The conifers continue into the far distance until they are mere dabs of a paintbrush.

Main palette
Cerulean Blue, Ultramarine Blue, Yellow Ocher, Cadmium Yellow Light, Burnt Umber, Quinacridone Burnt Orange, and Titanium White

Other key colors
Buff Titanium, Raw Umber, Olive Green, and Carbon Black

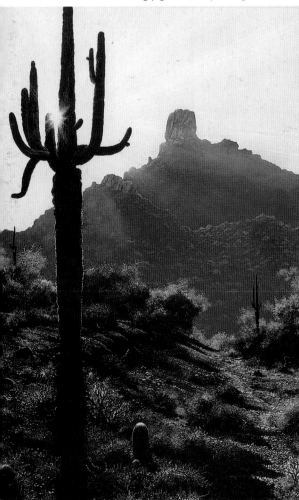

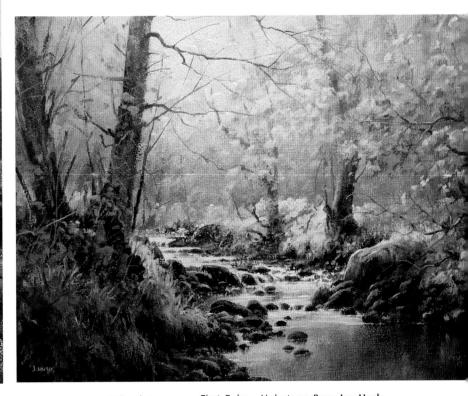

***Desert Light* Frederick G. Denys**
Landscapes do not necessarily have deciduous trees and flat meadows. This dramatic desert scene features a purple-hued mountain looming beyond a ridge covered with desert scrub. Darkest values are found in the foreground and in the silhouette of the tall cactus. This imposing saguaro is further emphasized by a sunburst of white light streaming through the pale sky. The warm earthy browns and subdued greens of the ridge are backlit with highlights around the shrubs and small cacti. Careful attention in using values that express the direction of light contribute to the impact of this painting.

Main palette
Cerulean Blue, Ultramarine Violet, Ultramarine Blue, Burnt Sienna, Carbon Black, and Titanium White

Other key colors
Cadmium Yellow Light and Cadmium Yellow Medium

Main palette
Titanium White, Ultramarine Blue, Cadmium Red, Burnt Sienna, Raw Sienna, and Cadmium Lemon

Other key colors
Red Iron Oxide, Yellow Ocher, and Cadmium Yellow

First Color—Holystone Burn **Joe Hush**
The yellow-green of emerging spring leaves sets the mood for this impressionistic painting. The palette is simple—greens and earthy browns with a little blue-gray. Darker values in the rocks and trees nearest the viewer establish distance. The soft blue-grays and less-defined tree trunks and leaves blend into that distance. A much paler blue-gray is used to paint the sparkling water of the creek, drawing us into the middle of the scene. No white highlights are used, keeping a soft glowing look to the painting.

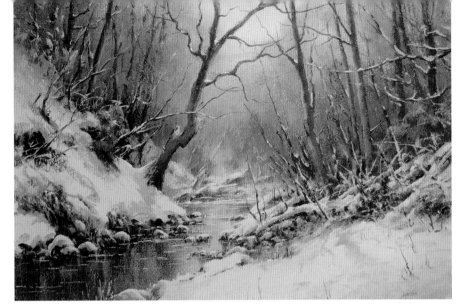

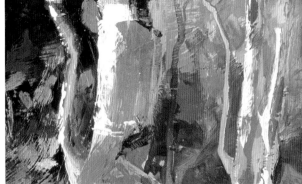

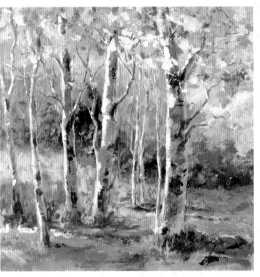

Winter Trees **Joe Hush**
The palette in this impressionistic painting is a simple one, mixing a few paints into neutralized purples and yellows, oranges, and earthy browns. The sharply outlined trees in the foreground of the painting recede into diffuse clouds of muted purple woods in the distance. The subtle reflection of the orange and yellow sky in the creek and the last orange highlights from the setting sun are not enough to warm this snowy scene. The snow itself is luminous, with pale yellow in the brighter areas and subdued purples in the shadows—complements that impart a subtle vibrancy. No pure whites are used, which creates a soft landscape.

Main palette
Titanium White, Ultramarine Blue, Cadmium Red, Red Iron Oxide, Burnt Sienna, Raw Sienna, and Cadmium Yellow

Main palette
Indian Yellow, Cadmium Yellow, Dioxazine Purple, and Titanium White

Other key colors
Alizarin Crimson Hue, Hooker's Green, Phthalo Blue, and Ivory Black

Birches **Jennifer Bowman**
This lively fall painting is lush with warm yellows, oranges, and reds. With a full palette in use, the complementary purples, blues, and greens increase the brightly vibrant effect. High-chroma hues are used with very few neutralized colors. Plenty of white adds brilliant highlights. Notice the relaxed and casual brushwork in the detail and how it adds to the overall sense of freedom with color.

Retired **Jason Sacran**
A setting summer sun illuminates the left side of the woods beyond the meadow. The golden orange glow spreads across grasses, diminishing in strength as it approaches the old tractor on the left. Neutrals visually indicate the age of the retired vehicle. Except for the glow from the setting sun, the painting is characterized by neutralized colors with only a few slightly brighter greens in the foreground.

Main palette
Cadmium Yellow Light, Cadmium Orange, Cadmium Red Medium, Alizarin Crimson Hue, Viridian Green, and Ivory Black

Other key colors
Titanium White, Yellow Ocher, and Ultramarine Blue

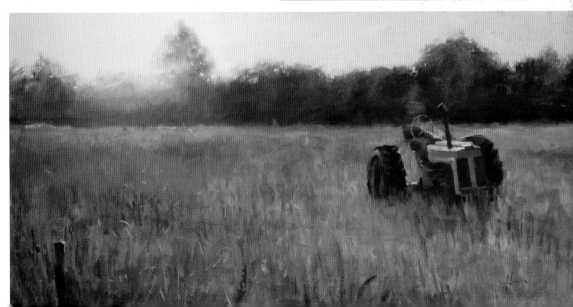

Portraits and figurative painting

The human form in movement and stillness pervades our memories, our present, and our future. Indelibly inscribed in our minds are the faces and gestures of those we know well. Painting the human figure naturally resonates deeply in our beings. Bringing this impulse into colorful expression can be a challenge, but an immensely satisfying one.

Figurative painting can initially be more difficult than painting, say, a teacup or tree. Correct proportions may elude the artist and skin color can be baffling. In order to help you work out what colors to use to paint skin tones, observe the skin of everyone you meet during the day and look for color. Start identifying as many hues as you can and you will be startled at the wide variety of colors you see.

Palette choices for skin colors should harmonize with the entire palette for the painting. One set of paints for skin colors may be chosen for a painting using cool colors and another set altogether for a painting of the same person using warm colors.

Painting sample swatches on heavy watercolor paper can help you understand how to use your paint choices effectively. Experiment with as many combinations as you can imagine for skin colors with a wide variety of paints so you become comfortable using your entire palette as needed.

EXAMPLE OF A CASUAL PORTRAIT

A relaxed portrait of a man in a battered hat is the subject of this casual portrait. A limited palette emphasizing earth tones conveys the outdoorsy nature of the man and the setting.

Stage 1 Paint the shadows of the shingles with Raw Umber. Mix Raw Umber and Chromium Oxide Green and loosely indicate the shadows in the hat and jacket.

1 Mix Raw Umber, a little Carbon Black, and a little Titanium White to indicate the beard and moustache.

2 Use Raw Umber for the glasses and mouth.

3 Mix varying tints of Raw Umber, Yellow Ocher, and Raw Sienna and block in the shirt.

Stage 2 Paint the shingles with tints of Raw Sienna. Add tints of varying combinations of Raw Sienna and Yellow Ocher with a little Raw Umber. Add a few areas of Raw Umber with Carbon Black and a little Titanium White.

1 Combine Chromium Oxide Green with Raw Umber and Yellow Ocher in varying tints for the hat and jacket.

2 Paint the hat band in tints of Raw Umber.

3 Rough in the eyebrows and beard with tints of Raw Umber mixed with a little Carbon Black.

4 Establish the skin tones with mixtures of Raw Sienna with a little Yellow Ocher and Raw Umber in varying tints.

Raw Umber

Chromium Oxide Green

Carbon Black

Yellow Ocher

Cadmium Orange Medium

Quinacridone Rose

Titanium White

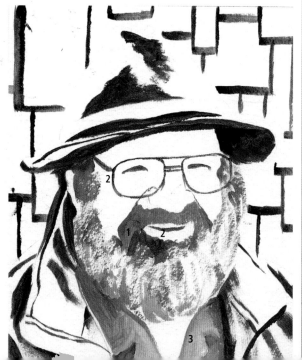

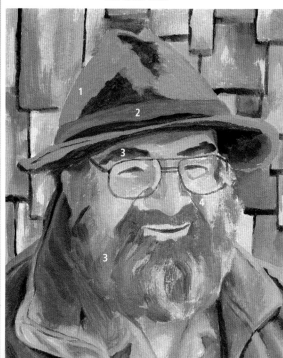

ISSUES IN PORTRAIT PAINTING

Prior to the widespread use of the camera, portraits were valued as the only way to capture and preserve the likeness of an individual. These ranged from elaborate, full-figure portraits to small, simple paintings.

Expression: Sitting for a formal portrait was a tedious business for the sitter. A relaxed, unsmiling face became standard in portraiture because a smile quickly turned into a painful grimace during a prolonged sitting.

Teeth: Current arguments against smiles that show the teeth in a portrait revolve around the problems of painting the teeth themselves. Painting white teeth in shadow without making them look stained can be challenging. Precisely defining each tooth adds too much intensity to the teeth if the shadow values are painted too dark. However, the mouth is a highly expressive part of the face. Saying the teeth should not be painted because it is hard to get the color right is about the same as saying portraits should be painted with the subject's eyes closed because it is hard to get the whites of the eyes right. Developing a delicate handling of shadowed tints is a much better solution to this problem.

Scale: The issue of scale also has to be considered. We are so responsive to the human image that scale is more important in figurative and portrait painting than other forms of painting. As a quick rule of thumb, life-size or smaller works quite well but painting someone larger than life-size provokes unexpected problems. If the image is only slightly larger than life-size, we find it makes us strangely uncomfortable because we are so accustomed to human beings around us. Once the figure is substantially larger than life-size, we can relax with the image.

Stage 3 Add a little Raw Umber to a mixture of Cadmium Orange Medium and Raw Sienna. Apply varying tints of this mixture to parts of the shingles.

1 Add more Raw Umber and Carbon Black to the shadows of the shingles.

2 Apply a mixture of Chromium Oxide Green, Raw Umber, and Carbon Black to create the deepest shadows in the hat and jacket.

3 Work with varying combinations of Chromium Oxide Green and Raw Umber to paint the hat and jacket. Tint these combinations as needed to create the lighter areas.

4 Refine the shirt with the colors previously used.

5 Add Quinacridone Rose to some of the mixtures used previously for the skin and define the features further.

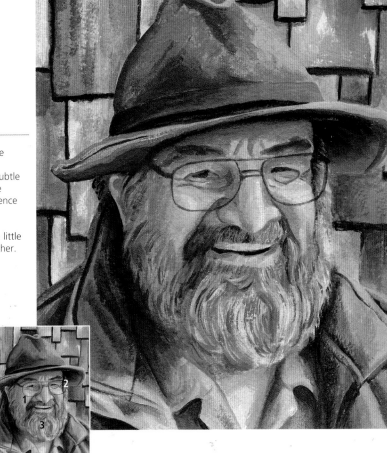

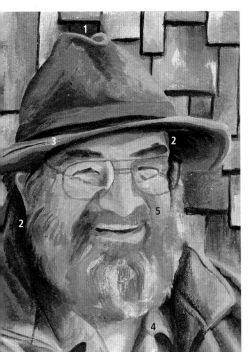

Stage 4 Continue refining the features with the mixtures previously used. Notice that subtle differences in the features are essential to capturing the essence of the person. Here, one eye squints a little more than the other and the mouth opens a little more on one side than the other.

1 Add highlights to the cheeks, nose, and lower lip.

2 Repaint the glasses with Raw Umber mixed with a little Carbon Black.

3 Paint the beard and moustache with pale tints of Raw Umber and Carbon Black mixtures for the highlighted hair and with darker mixtures for the shadows.

Gallery: Portraits and figurative painting

Everything you know about color in acrylics can be applied to painting the human form. Learning to observe nuances of light and shadow, the play of color in skin tones, and the range of values in your subject will go a long way toward creating powerful paintings of the human form. Portraits and figurative painting allow diverse palette choices and styles of painting, as we can see in the following examples.

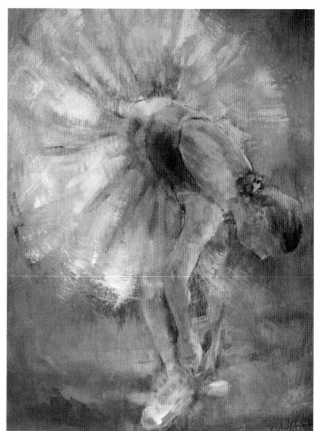

Main palette
Nickel Azo Yellow, Quinacridone Burnt Orange, Quinacridone Gold, Raw Umber, Dioxazine Purple, and Titanium White

Other key colors
Ultramarine Blue, Cadmium Red Medium, and Cadmium Orange Medium

Peruvian Woman **Lexi Sundell**
This fairly low-chroma palette was built upon two pairs of complements; purple with yellow as the main pair and blue with orange as a lesser accent pair. The skin tones were painted in tinted glazes of Nickel Azo Yellow, Quinacridone Burnt Orange, Quinacridone Gold, Cadmium Red Medium, Raw Umber, and Dioxazine Purple. A pale tint of Nickel Azo Yellow was used for highlights in the face and Dioxazine Purple was used in the darkest shadow areas. Notice how the highlights in the eyes bring them to life. Strong value contrasts characterize this painting.

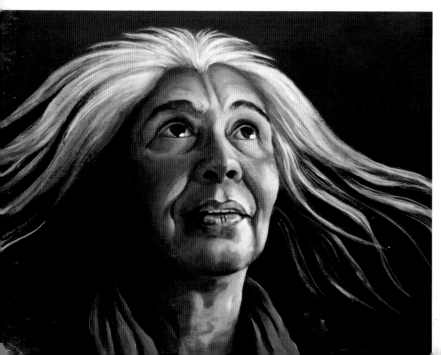

Tying the Shoelaces **Sera M. Knight**
Values in this softly impressionistic painting are kept in the mid-range. Purple and yellow are the main complements with blue and orange as a less-used pair of complements. The figure is painted with slightly more definition than the tutu. The silvery luminance in this painting arises from the combination of pastel colors and the loosely brushed radiating white areas. Layers of color are painted with the freely applied brushstrokes only partially covering previous layers. For example, the high-key Cobalt Teal in the skirt mostly covered the underlying purple and was itself partially painted over with white. A sparkling airy look results.

Main palette
Dioxazine Purple, Cerulean Blue, Cadmium Yellow Deep, Cobalt Teal, and Titanium White

Other key colors
Alizarin Crimson Hue, Cadmium Red Medium

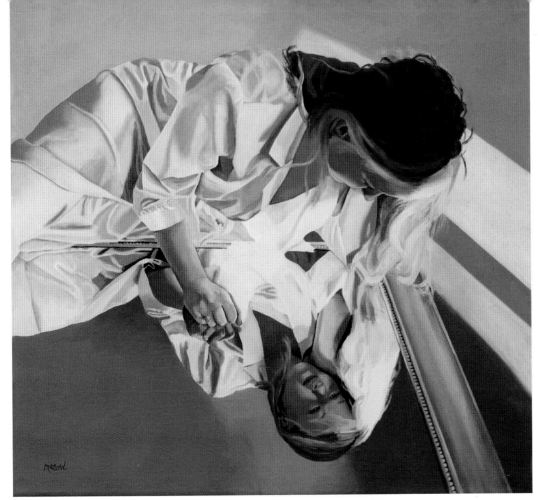

Yellow Gown **Linda McCord**

In this painting, we see precision and clearly defined edges in most areas, using a limited palette prominently featuring neutrals. The warm skin tones and pinkish gray in the background combine with the exaggerated yellow of the hair to add warmth to the painting. The neutralized green in the mirror softly frames the girl's face. Notice how the highlights on the gown are painted to give the impression of a shiny and slightly stiff fabric.

Main palette
Cadmium Yellow,
Dioxazine Purple,
Hooker's Green,
and Titanium White

Other key colors
Cerulean Blue and
Cadmium Red Light

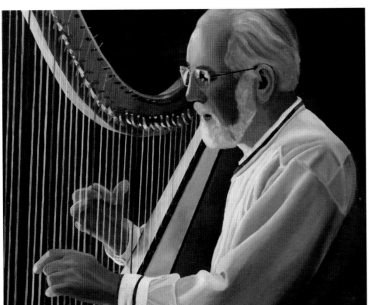

Strings **Linda McCord**

The strong red in this background blends into dark shadows, giving a rich look to this scene of a man playing a harp. The dark values in the background allow the figure to be the main interest in the painting. Lighter values in the white shirt, hair, and reflections in the glasses keep our attention focused on him. Soft blues and purple shadows in the shirt soften the look of the fabric—a fitting accompaniment to harp music.

Main palette
Quinacridone Burnt
Orange, Cadmium
Red, Cadmium
Yellow Light,
Phthalo Blue, and
Titanium White

Other key colors
Cerulean Blue and
Dioxazine Purple

Paints and brushes

Choosing the right paints and brushes is important for the acrylic painter. The most wonderful paint in the world will give poor results if applied with poor-quality, incorrectly shaped, or incorrectly sized brushes. Conversely, poor-quality paints are no help with even the best brushes carefully chosen for the painting. So how do you know what to buy?

PAINT CHOICES

Acrylics are available in fluid and heavy-body format. Before buying either, know how you want to use them. Review pages 20–23 if you are not sure. Choose paints that work well for the way you want to paint.

Remember to buy high-quality acrylic paints, because student-grade paints are usually inferior in both pigment quality and pigment density. Student-grade paints only look like a bargain until you actually try to use them.

The Sundell Color Wheel is a good painter's palette (see page 17). You could begin with those paints and a few earth colors, such as Raw Umber and Yellow Ocher, plus Titanium White and Carbon Black. It is wise to spend time getting comfortable using a basic palette to avoid overwhelming confusion with too many paints at first. Adding more paint choices later when you are ready to expand your palette is easy with the table of substitutes on page 17.

PAINT QUANTITIES

Quantity of paint becomes a question after you have decided on either fluid or heavy-body acrylics and the makeup of your palette. Paints are sold in sizes from 2-ounce (60-ml) tubes to 1-gallon (3.7-L) cans. Running out of paint in the middle of a painting is annoying, but so is finding half a jar of dried-up paint.

Unless you are starting with paintings several feet wide, buying 2-ounce (60-ml) tubes is a good starting point. A larger tube of Titanium White can be a prudent choice, as it is used almost constantly to make tints with the other paints. As you become familiar with how much paint you use, larger quantities of other colors might be useful.

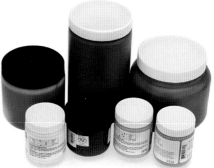

Jars of paint can be an economical choice when larger quantities of paint are needed than tubes can provide. They are not as easily portable if you want to paint en plein air, that is, outdoors on location.

THE SECRETS OF THE PAINT LABEL

Hidden away on the label of quality acrylic paint is the answer to most of your questions, thanks to the ASTM, the American Society for Testing and Materials. The best manufacturers honor ASTM standards even though the law does not force them to do so. Information listing the generic name, common name, and color index number of the pigment or pigments is placed on the label so you can make sense of your paint choices. You can also find lightfastness ratings on the paint label or manufacturer websites, allowing you to select paints highly rated for longevity.

A tube of Ultramarine Violet

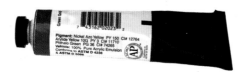

Common name

Color index number   Color index name

Sometimes the common name on the label is perfectly straightforward, such as on this tube of Ultramarine Violet.
Common name or manufacturer's name:
Ultramarine Violet
Color index generic name: Ultramarine Violet
Color index number: PV15 (P = pigment; V = violet; 15) = exact chemical composition of the pigment

A tube of Green Gold

Sometimes the common name has nothing to do with the generic name. Different manufacturers may use the same common name for different pigments altogether. The same pigment might also be used with different common names, so it pays to be observant. Looking carefully at the label, you can see that this particular tube of paint combines three different pigments.
Common name or manufacturer's name: Green Gold
Color index generic name: Nickel Azo Yellow + Arylide Yellow + Phthalo Green
Color index number: PY150 + PY3 + PG36

MEDIUMS AND VARNISHES

Along with your paints, you will need to purchase any mediums, varnishes, or other special products you wish to use in your paintings. A regular semi-gloss gel medium is a good general-purpose choice. Matte and glossy options can be used if preferred. Review the Pigment properties section if you are unsure of your needs (see page 18).

Varnish protects the surface of the dried acrylic film so that it will not suffer from embedded dust and dirt as time passes. It also gives an even reflective surface for your painting. Some paints, such as Anthraquinone Red, are naturally glossier than other paints because of the way the pigment behaves in the acrylic emulsion. Such variations disappear under matte, satin, or gloss varnishes.

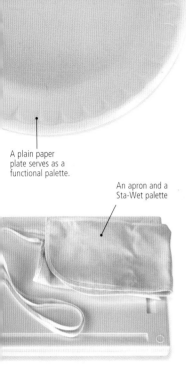

A plain paper plate serves as a functional palette.

An apron and a Sta-Wet palette

SMALL BUT ESSENTIAL EQUIPMENT

Palettes are constantly in use and deserve proper consideration when furnishing your studio. As with everything else, choices abound. Let's look at the simplest and the most luxurious solutions for palettes.

A plain paper plate serves as a functional and budget-friendly palette. Saving paint for later use on it is difficult, but a piece of plastic wrap will suffice for a short time. Styrene plates stay stiffer than plates, which absorb more moisture. Spray your paints on the plate regularly with a fine mist from a spray bottle to delay them crusting into an unmanageable mess. Once they inevitably turn into that crusty mess, throw the plate away and start with another one.

Apron and Sta-Wet palette: You may not want the apron but you will love the Sta-Wet palette. Hidden by the lid is a flat sponge and a palette paper on top of the sponge. The wet sponge holds moisture that wicks up through the paper, keeping your paint on the paper moist and ready to use. As long as the sponge is kept wet, paints can last for a couple of weeks in this palette. If you don't want to create the waste of discarded paper plates, skip all the other palette choices and buy this one. Your disposition and paintings will both improve because you won't be fighting with the paint on your palette any more.

CARE OF UNUSED PAINTS

Lids get stuck on both tubes and jars. Keeping both the lids and the threaded area on the container clean solves the problem before it happens. If a lid does get stuck, use a pair of pliers to remove the cap.

Jars are a bigger problem. They arrive in shipment with paint all over the underside of the lid. If this is not scraped away and the lid cleaned on first opening, the lid most likely will be stuck the second time you try to open the jar.

In that case, place the outside edge of the lid against a solid workbench or tabletop, without the jar itself touching anything. Give the opposite side of the lid a sharp whack with a mallet to break the dried paint bond. Do not hit the jar with the mallet. A few whacks quickly allow the lid to open easily. The lid rarely breaks in this process, but it can happen, so keeping the lid clean is the best practice.

Freezing fresh acrylic paints ruins them. They also dry out quickly if stored in the direct blast of a furnace. Spraying a light mist of water inside the jar before closing helps prevent premature drying.

BRUSHES

Brushes are available in a staggering array of shapes, sizes, and kinds of bristles. The good news is that you do not necessarily have to buy the most expensive brushes for high-quality results.

Synthetic Taklon brushes offered by many manufacturers can be both economical and enjoyable to use with acrylics. Heavy-body acrylics require a brush with a good spring to it, which Taklon provides. The bristles are also easy to clean.

Hog-bristle brushes are especially useful if the texture of a brush stroke is desired. These bristles are coarser than Taklon but also have a good springiness. If a hog-bristle brush is used to apply a layer of gel medium, it will be more difficult to clean than a Taklon brush.

Small sable or squirrel round brushes made for watercolors can be used, although they have a much weaker spring to them. After flow release is added to the paint, these little pointed brushes can be helpful for painting small details such as tiny highlights. Synthetic substitutes for sable and squirrel can also serve you well.

Flats and rounds are the most useful brushes for acrylic painting. With an assortment of sizes in these two shapes, you can paint anything you want.

BRUSH CLEANING

Acrylic paint dries quickly and can easily ruin brushes. If you are using multiple brushes for different color mixtures, leave the ones you are not immediately using in a container of water so they do not harden before you get back to them.

Soap and water works just fine for cleaning your brushes when you are finished painting. Gently work the soapy water into the bristles without bending them so hard that you wreck the brush. Continue rinsing until the water runs clear. White Taklon brushes will stain, but this is not detrimental.

Plain gel medium is the most difficult to clean because you cannot see it and you cannot really feel it during cleaning, so extra care is required.

SAFETY ISSUES

Acrylic paints are reasonably safe in studio work as long as you paint with them properly. For example, never put the brush in your mouth as a handy place to hold it for a moment. Do not allow your pets to drink the waste water in your containers. Use some common sense in handling your paints:

• If possible, let the waste water from paint brushes evaporate until the paint suspended in it becomes a thin dry crust and then dispose of it. Disposal of dried paint is much less of an environmental problem than liquid paint.

• If you need to sand a painting, keep in mind the fact that pigments such as the cadmiums are most hazardous when airborne and inhaled. Wear a respirator and sand in a well-ventilated area. Thoroughly clean the work area afterward.

• If you have cuts on your hands, wear plastic gloves until the cuts heal to prevent any problematic pigments in your paint from being absorbed.

• While acrylic paints generally have fewer toxicity problems than many other paints, they may still affect people who have extra sensitivity to chemicals. Paint manufacturer web sites offer more detailed information on specific paint pigments or other products. Some varnishes require particularly careful handling no matter what your level of chemical sensitivity. If in doubt about a product, look up the Material Safety Data Sheet (MSDS) and handle it accordingly.

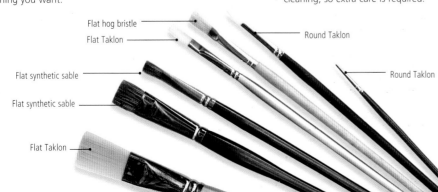

Flat hog bristle

Flat Taklon

Flat synthetic sable

Flat synthetic sable

Flat Taklon

Round Taklon

Round Taklon

Canvas and other substrates

Since it is impossible to paint with acrylics without a substrate to receive our colorfully inspired brushstrokes, let's consider the options available. As water media, acrylics can be used on watercolor paper but can also be used on canvas and boards like oils. So how do you choose the best substrate for your work?

UNDERSTANDING PAPERMAKING

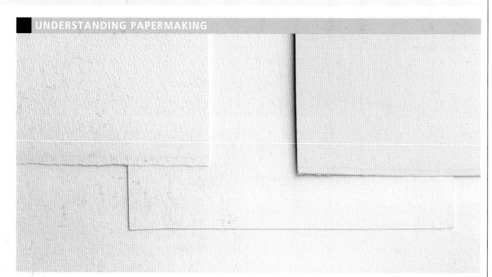

An understanding of papermaking enables you to choose an appropriate paper substrate more effectively. Paper is made by pounding pulp from various plant fibers. Wood contains cellulose that decays rapidly by yellowing and becoming brittle, as we see in newspapers. Cotton and flax do not contain cellulose and make a far more archival paper.

The pulp is beaten in a water solution and the entangled fibers are poured into a mold frame, a framework with a large screen the size of the intended sheet of paper. After the water drains away through the screen, the wet sheet is pressed to flatten it while squeezing out remaining water.

The sheet can be dried with or without heat. Heat drying makes a paper that is less likely to dry flat after rewetting because it needs the same application of heat and pressure to regain its original flatness. Sheets dried without heat can be worked with

plenty of water until they buckle. Drying them pressed flat under weights makes them readily go back to their original flatness in the studio.

Sizing refers to starches, gelatins, and other materials added to paper to alter its ability to absorb water, surface smoothness, and other characteristics. Some sizing materials acidify the paper, increasing the speed of decay.

Sizing can be added to the waterborne pulp, and this is called internal sizing as it is distributed throughout the paper. Sizing can also be added to the finished sheet, in which case it is called surface sizing.

Purchasing an acid-free paper containing no cellulose is the best choice for longevity of your artwork. Making your own paper can be an enjoyable process but is too involved and time consuming for most artists more interested in painting than papermaking.

Assorted cut pieces of watercolor paper show the difference between bright white and natural paper, the natural paper being the darker sheet on the right. A deckle edge remains along the bottom of the sheet on the left.

WATERCOLOR PAPER

Watercolor papers have attractive ragged edges called deckle edges. They are so named because the ragged edges form along the deckle frame that surrounds the screen and are a natural part of papermaking.

The worst choice you can make in buying watercolor paper is to select thin, cheaply made paper. It receives paint horribly and handles even worse.

Instead, buy 300 lb (638 gsm) paper by a quality manufacturer and you will be astounded at the difference. The heavy paper takes water media beautifully, resists buckling, and is a delight to use. You also can choose from varying amounts of surface texture depending on your painting preferences.

BOARDS

Boards are available in a wide range of types. Some are primed with gesso and others are covered with canvas. Board materials can be as simple as a form of cardboard with canvas glued over it to elaborately cradled hardwoods.

Cradled boards have a framework around the edge on the back. Nicely finished cradled boards do not have to be framed, although they can be.

Masonite is a common pressboard in use, but it is not considered archival. **Particle board** is similarly short on longevity. **Wood** tends to acid decay over time, with birch being the least susceptible. Birch is chosen for most archival works and still needs to be sealed with a varnish on the sides not primed with gesso.

CANVAS

Canvas is a well-loved substrate, with its varied textures, thicknesses, and longstanding traditions of use. Canvas is usually made from either cotton or linen, although new synthetic fibers such as polyflax are also available. Canvas can be purchased stretched or unstretched, primed or unprimed, and in sheets and rolls.

Cotton is less costly than linen and, perhaps surprisingly, is considered to be as long lived as linen canvas when properly primed. Cotton duck is more tightly woven than plain cotton. A loosely woven canvas is cheaper and gives a coarser surface that often is not desirable. Cotton canvas thickness is rated on a scale of 1 to 10 with 1 being the thickest.

Linen is considered the gold standard of canvas due to its smooth, tight weave and stiffness. Buy linen that is primed with gesso, which makes a good ground for acrylics.

Polyflax is a synthetic material that can be used alone or blended with cotton to make canvas. Polyflax is stronger than cotton and is an excellent choice when painting large canvases that exceed 6 feet (3 m) in any direction.

Pre-stretched canvas

Pre-stretched canvases can be purchased in a multitude of sizes and qualities. Typically the canvas has the standard minimum of two coats of gesso, but you may want to add additional coats to prepare the surface to your liking. If you prefer, you can simply start painting on the canvas instead.

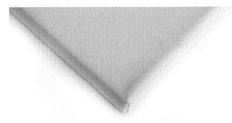

This corner of a pre-stretched canvas shows the folded corner of the canvas on the outside edge. Pre-stretched canvases come in varying quality levels. The example shown is an inexpensive canvas with coarse weave, casually rather than carefully stretched.

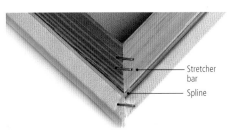

Stretcher bar

Spline

The back of the same commercially prepared canvas shows the spline that sets the canvas edge into a recessed groove to hold it in place. Staples are used only to secure the corners on this canvas.

Tools for stretching canvas

Stretching your own canvases is a simple process. Instead of a commercial spline to hold the canvas in place, staples are used along the back edge of the stretcher bars and they hold the canvas more securely than the splines do. Begin in the middle of each side and work your way out to the corners for a smooth stretch, going round and round the canvas from side to side to keep it even.

After assembling the stretcher frame, use stretching pliers to pull the canvas as you staple your canvas onto the back of the bars. They are inexpensive but effective for pulling the amount of tension you need. Remember to tension pre-primed canvases to the finished tautness you want. Raw canvases have to be left partially slack because gesso will tighten them as it dries. In large canvases this can actually crack stretcher bars if the raw canvas is stretched too tight.

Pictured right are two kinds of staplers. On the lower right is an ordinary workshop stapler that works well. For larger canvases in particular, the commercial upholstery stapler directly to the right is a good option. Connected to a hose on an air compressor with 90–100 psi (6–7 bar) pressure, it makes the process as easy as can be.

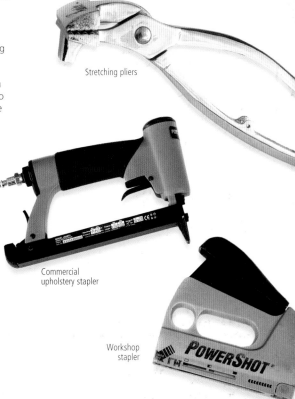

The corner joint of this stretcher frame is starting to slide together. Use a mallet to hammer it gently into place.

Stretching pliers

Commercial upholstery stapler

Workshop stapler

Paint surfaces should never touch each other because acrylic paint remains slightly absorbent and sticky when dried. You do not want your paintings sticking to each other, causing mutual ruin. Varnish does not offer enough protection to enable them to be stored touching each other.

Occasionally a canvas painting may be dented by accident or improper handling. Spraying the back of the canvas with a clean mist of water and rubbing it with an equally clean hand is usually enough to smooth the dent. After drying, the canvas will again be taut and smooth.

Shipping acrylic canvases can be done by wrapping them in 8 mil plastic sheeting, such as is used for a drop cloth in house painting. Cut 2-inch (5-cm) thick Styrofoam sheeting to size and secure it tightly on the front and back with plenty of clear packing tape to prevent rubbing. Cut additional sections of the Styrofoam to proper size for the side edges and tape that tightly in place. Repeat the process with sheets of extra-heavy cardboard for the front, back, and side edges. Use approximately an entire roll of clear packaging tape per package and this process will protect your painting, as well as avoid having to purchase costly premade painting crates.

If shipping extremely large canvases, it is more cost effective to carefully remove the canvas from the stretcher frame and ship it rolled in a tube. The best procedure is to roll the thoroughly dry canvas painted side outward (so as not to crush or crumple the paint film) with a sheet of 8 mil plastic sheeting over the face of the painting. Let the plastic film extend long enough to encircle the roll past the canvas end.

Sonotubes can be obtained at lumberyards; they are designed to use as forms for pouring concrete. One of these makes a really stout container for your painting. Roll the canvas as described around a small-diameter Sonotube and insert it inside a larger Sonotube that allows a 2-inch (5-cm) clearance all around for Styrofoam peanuts. Add wooden ends and the painting is well protected for shipping. A good-quality frame shop can restretch the canvas on new stretcher bars at the destination.

Index

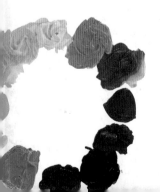

■ **Acrylic** A specific emulsion used as a binder for pigments to use them as paints.

■ **Analogous palette** Paints representing three or four adjacent hues on the color wheel.

■ **Chroma** The aspect of color referring to the saturation or intensity of the color; how bright or dull it appears.

■ **Color** The combination of hue, chroma, and value as registered by the eye and interpreted by the brain.

■ **Color index number** Pigment code referring to a specific chemical composition.

■ **Complementary color** The hue opposite another hue on the color wheel, which may be represented by various paints in that hue.

■ **Color temperature** The relative warmth or coolness of a paint in relation to another paint on the color wheel.

■ **Color wheel** A spectrum of hues joined in a circle.

■ **Duochrome** A form of luminescent acrylic paint showing two different colors, depending on viewing angle.

■ **Glaze** To apply a thin layer of lighter paint over a darker color to change the appearance, which is good for optical mixing of colors.

■ **Hue** An aspect of color that is a specific wavelength of light, such as red, orange, yellow, green, blue, or violet.

■ **Interference** A form of semitransparent luminescent acrylic paint that is opalescent and shows its own

complementary color, depending on the value of the paint layer underneath it.

■ **Iridescent** A form of luminescent acrylic paint showing pearlescent effects not dependent on the paint layer underneath it.

■ **Lightfastness** Chemical stability of a pigment under long exposure to light.

■ **Luminescent acrylic** Paints made with mica platelets, titanium dioxide, and metallic oxides in an acrylic emulsion.

■ **Neutral color** A low-chroma color that can be created by mixing complements.

■ **Opaque** Completely obscures the view of anything underneath it.

■ **Optical mixing** A method of applying paint over other dried paint layers so the colors combine visually.

■ **Palette mixing** Combining paints directly while wet before applying them to the painting in a combined color.

■ **Permanence** Longevity or durability.

■ **Physical mixing** Combining paints directly while wet, either on the palette or the painting surface.

■ **Pigment** A chemical powder that is the component in paint producing the color.

■ **Primary palette** Paints representing the hues of magenta, cyan, and yellow.

■ **Saturation** Refers to the intensity of a color, ranging from bright, full-strength chroma to a dull and diluted chroma.

■ **Scumble** To apply a thin opaque coat of paint over a darker color to soften or alter the darker color.

■ **Secondary colors** The hues of red-orange, blue-violet, and yellow-green,

which can be mixed from the primary palette.

■ **Substrate** The painting surface, such as canvas, board, or watercolor paper.

■ **Tertiary colors** The hues of yellow-orange, red, red-violet, blue, green, and yellow-green, which can be mixed from the primary palette and secondary colors.

■ **Tint** White added to a color. In this book, for convenience, tint means a mixture with Titanium White unless otherwise specified.

■ **Tinting strength** The intensity of the pigment itself in a mixture.

■ **Tone** A specific darkness or lightness that can be matched to a grayscale step in a range from white to black.

■ **Transparent** Does not completely obscure the view of anything underneath it.

■ **Tuck** A technique of darkening a corner or juncture where two adjacent shapes appear to touch.

■ **Value** Relative lightness or darkness of a color, its tone within a range from white to black, often a numbered scale.

■ **Value scale** Most commonly an even, nine-step graduation from white at number one to black at number nine.

■ **Wash** Paint diluted with water and applied to an absorbent substrate.

LIFT FLAP
for handy reference to the
Sundell Color Wheel
(see also on page 17)

The author's color wheel is designed to provide a reliable tool for the artist seeking exceptional color in acrylics. A chart is included below showing suitable substitutes for each of the 12 color positions on the wheel. This makes exploring alternate paints less daunting, since you know where they fit into an established framework.

The pigment numbers are also given with the paint name in the wheel and the chart.

Paints that are convenience mixtures of multiple pigments are included in some color categories. They are placed at the end of the list after the single-pigment choices. You can readily identify them by the multiple pigment numbers following a paint name.

The Sundell Color Wheel and substitute paint listing can also be found on page 17.

1. Yellow

12. Green-yellow

2. Yellow-orange

11. Yellow-green

Hansa
Yellow
Medium
PY73

Bismuth
Yellow
PY184

Cadmium
Orange
Medium
PO20

3. Red-orange

Phthalo Green
(Yellow Shade)
PG36

Pyrrole
Orange
PO70

10. Green

4. Red

Phthalo Green
(Blue Shade)
PG7

In each color-position pairing
(e.g., green-yellow), the main
color is named second.

Cadmium
Red
Medium
PR108

9. Cyan

Cobalt Teal
PG50

Quinacridone
Rose
PV19

5. Magenta

Ultramarine
Blue PB29

Quinacridone
Violet PV19

Ultramarine
Violet PV15

8. Blue

6. Red-violet

7. Blue-violet

---

1. Yellow
Cadmium Yellow Medium PY35
Hansa Yellow Deep PY65
Yellow Iron Oxide PY42
Nickel Azo Yellow PY150
Cadmium Yellow Medium Hue PY74
  PY65
Primary Yellow PY3 PY73 PW6
Naples Yellow Hue PW6 PY42 PY83

2. Yellow-orange
Cadmium Yellow Deep PY35
New Gamboge PY153
Azo Yellow Deep PY65
Quinacridone Gold PO49
Cadmium Yellow Deep Hue PY184
  PY74 PY65
Cadmium Orange Hue PO73 PY65
  PY74

3. Red-orange
Cadmium Orange Deep PY35
Perinone Orange PO43
Quinacridone Coral PR209
Quinacridone Burnt Orange PR206
Quinacridone Burnt Scarlet PR206
Quinacridone Nickel Azo Gold PO48
  PY150
Quinacridone Sienna PO49 PR209

4. Red
Cadmium Red Dark PR108
Cadmium Red Deep PR108
Naphthol Red Light PR112
Naphthol Red Medium PR5
Permanent Red PR170
Pyrrole Red PR254
Pyrrole Red Dark PR264
Quinacridone Red PV19
Perylene Maroon PR179

5. Magenta
Primary Magenta PV19
Permanent Rose PV19
Anthraquinone Red PR177
Quinacridone Crimson PR206 PR202
Quinacridone Magenta PR122

6. Red-violet
Cobalt Violet Hue PV19 PR122 PW4
  PV23
Alizarin Crimson Hue PR122 PR206
  PG7

7. Blue-violet
Dioxazine Purple PV23
Carbazole Violet PV23
Indanthrone Blue PB60
Permanent Violet Dark PB60 PR122
Prism Violet PV23 PW6 PR122

8. Blue
French Ultramarine Blue PB29
Phthalo Blue (Green Shade) PB15
Cobalt Blue PB28
Cobalt Blue Deep PB73
Anthraquinone Blue PB60
Cobalt Blue Hue PB29 PB15 PW6

9. Cyan
Cerulean Blue P36
Cerulean Blue Deep PB36
Cerulean Blue Chromium PB36
Cobalt Turquoise PB36
Primary Cyan PB15 PW6
Manganese Blue Hue PG15 PG7 PW6

10. Green
Cobalt Green PG26
Cobalt Green Deep PG26
Permanent Green Light PY3 PG7
Permanent Green PY3 PG7
Cascade Green PBr7 PB15

11. Yellow-green
Chromium Oxide Green PG17
Chromium Oxide Green Dark PG17
Green Gold PY150 PG36 PY3
Rich Green Gold PY129

12. Green-yellow
Lemon Yellow PY175
Cadmium Yellow Light PY35
Hansa Yellow Light PY3
Cadmium Lemon PY35
Cadmium Yellow Light Hue PY184
  PY3

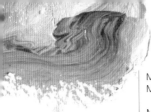

Acknowledgments

Quarto would like to thank the following artists, who are acknowledged beside their work:

Bowman, Jennifer, www.jenniferbowman.com, pp.4, 23, 61t, 85t, 93tl, 97tl, 100cl, 101tr, 114b, 117cr
© Bridget Riley 2012. All rights reserved, courtesy Karsten Schubert, London, p.9
Briggs, Shaugn, www.nz-art-work.com, p.28b
Carter, Carol, www.carol-carter.com, pp.35tr, 61bl
Crabtree, Elizabeth, www.elizabethcrabtree.co.uk, pp.70, 100tr
Denys, Frederick G, www.frederickdenys.com, pp.65tr, 66cl, 85b, 114t, 115tl/tr, 116l
Elsey, Kathleen, www.elsey.com, p.96b
Facteau, Klana, www.kianafecteau.com, p.109tl
Flower, Rosina, www.rosinaflower.co.uk, p.105
Fullerton-Samsel, Carol Anna, p.108tr
Geraghty, Paul, www.paulgeraghty.net, pp.67cr, p.74t, 84t, 88bl, 92t/b, 93tr
Hush, Joe, www.joehush.co.uk, pp.66t, 71t, 115bl, 116r, 117t
James, Paul, www.pauljamesart.com, pp.69tr, 74b, 93bl, 109tr
Kloosterboer, Lorena, www.art-lorena.com , pp.70t, 104cl, 105t
Knight, Sera M, www.seraknight.co.uk, pp.57tl, 67tl, 75cl, 120r
Kovich, Loren, AWS, www.lorenkovich.com, pp.35tl
Krawcyzk, Joseph, http://krawczykstudio.com, pp.65cl, 69b, 73b, 105bl
Krizek, Donna, p.69cl
McCord, Linda, www.lindamccord.com, pp.35b, 121t/b
Nardini, Peter, www.peternardini.com, p.93b
O'Keefe, Lou, http://louokeefe.com, pp.22, 67tr, 97r, 104tr
Ohnemus, Pamela, www.pamohnemus.com, pp.100b, 101b
Pedrero, Robin Maria, www.gallery523.com, p.85cr
Pence, Barbara Louise, www.bpenceart.com, pp.97b, 109b
Sacran, Jason, www.jasonsacran.com, pp.89, 115br, 117b
Smith, Daniel, www.danielsmithwildlife.com, pp75cl, p.84b
Snell, Alan, Helena, Montana, www.alansnell.com, p89
Sprakes, John, ROI RBA MAFA DA (Edin)—www.johnsprakes.com, pp.56br, 96t
Strouse, Warren, www.strouseandstrouse.com, p.88
Sundell, Bern, http://bernsundell.com, pp.18–19, 25, 28t, 38–39, 52, 56bl, 61br, 65br, 82t/b, 91, 108t
Sundell, Lexi, http://LexiSundell.com; http://PaintYourJoy.com
Wild, Carrie, www.carriewildart.com, p85tr
Woodman, Jim, www.jimwoodman.co.uk, pp.60b, 71b, 75tr

Quarto would like to thank Golden Artist Colors Inc. (www.goldenpaints.com), Daniel Smith Inc. (www.danielsmith.com), and Winsor & Newton (www.winsornewton.com) for supplying paint samples.

Quarto would also like to acknowledge the following: p.16 Bruce MacEvoy Artist's Color Wheel, www.handprint com/HP/WCL/cwheel06.pdf